THE BUSINESS APPRAISER
AND LITIGATION
SUPPORT

THE BUSINESS APPRAISER AND LITIGATION SUPPORT

Michele G. Miles

John Wiley & Sons, Inc.

New York • Chichester • Weinheim • Brisbane • Singapore • Toronto

Library of Congress Cataloging-in-Publication Data:
Miles, Michele G.
    The business appraiser and litigation support / Michele G. Miles
      p. cm.
    Includes index.
    ISBN 0-471-39410-6 (cloth : alk. paper)
    1. Evidence, Expert—United States. 2. Business enterprises—Valuation—United States. 3. Appraisers—Legal status, laws, etc.—United States.   I. Title.
KF8968.19 .M55 2001
346.73'065—dc21   2001017675

TO MY PARENTS, RAYMOND AND GENEVIEVE
Whose love outlasted Earth's time

AND TO MY HUSBAND, JACK PELZER
Who loves me more than anyone can deserve

Authors and Contributors

Michele G. Miles, Esquire is the Executive Director of the Institute of Business Appraisers (IBA). Founded in 1978, IBA is a membership organization providing support services to the business appraisal profession including mentoring, technical support, professional certification, database access, and education. Ms. Miles received her Juris Doctor from Tulane University School of Law. She was awarded the Order of the Coif, served as an Administrative Justice of the Moot Court Board and as a clerk in the Federal District court system. She received a Bachelor of Arts Degree in Speech Communication from Stetson University.

Ms. Miles's legal career spans three decades. From 1984 to 1998, she was a trial attorney with the Florida-based firm of Becker & Poliakoff, PA; she was elected a Shareholder of the firm in 1990. With a practice focusing on complex commercial litigation, her caseload concentrated on business damage claims, construction defects and delays, professional negligence, eminent domain, contract disputes, and equitable relief. Her administrative load with the firm included the design of one of the first database document managing systems for the integration of large amounts of data in large commercial lawsuits and conflicts control software. During her tenure with Becker & Poliakoff, she wrote and lectured on business appraisal issues and edited a reference book for lawyers on the admissibility of evidence. She has completed Florida's rigorous mediation certification program. Ms. Miles has served on the Florida Bar's Coordinating Committee on Technology.

Ms. Miles first lectured on business appraisal issues in 1990. A member of IBA's Board since 1984, she joined IBA full time in 1998. She is the author of IBA Course 7001, *Litigation Support Workshop*, and two-day seminars on *Litigation Support* and *Business Appraisal for*

Divorce. Since 1997 she has led workshops for business appraisers on testimony and litigation support skills. In small group settings and working with the actual work product of each appraiser she had conducted deposition testimony, trial direct testimony, and cross-examination. She is a course instructor for the IBA and the National Judicial College, for which she has also authored course materials. Ms. Miles has authored articles on business appraisal that have been published in a variety of technical journals.

Ms. Miles has presented at conferences held by the American Institute of Certified Public Accountants (AICPA), the American Society of Appraisers, the Practice Valuation Study Group, the National Society of Certified Valuation Analysts, and a number of state societies. Her presentation topics include business appraisal, case law interpretation, family limited partnerships, use of comparative transaction data, risk management and malpractice, and litigation issues. She is a member of the American Society of Appraisers Business Valuation Committee and the Clarence Group, which facilitates cooperation among the organizations within the appraisal community.

Steven Fred Schroder has been awarded the designation Master Certified Business Appraiser from the IBA and Accredited Senior Appraiser from the American Society of Appraisers. He is a widely recognized expert in the valuation of closely held businesses, lost business revenues, and lost wages. He has extensive experience in expert testimony and the preparation of settlement portfolios. His valuation practice is based in Sacramento Valley.

Mr. Schroeder received his Bachelor of Business Administration from the University of Nebraska. In 1975, he was awarded a Master of Business Administration degree from the University of British Columbia. He received his Juris Doctor in 1993 from Monterey College of Law. He is the former Director of the San Francisco Valuation Roundtable.

In May of 1992, Mr. Schroeder was elected Governor-at-Large of the IBA. He has over a decade of teaching experience and is the author of some of the widely-attended courses on business appraisal in the United States. He currently teaches courses in business appraisal report writing, professional accreditation, the Uniform Standards of Professional Appraisal Practice, and expert witness testimony.

He has participated in the writing of course and exam materials for the IBA and the American Society of Appraisers.

Mr. Schroeder serves as Chairman of IBA's Qualifications Review Committee, and in that capacity he has reviewed more than a thousand appraisal reports. He has served on the IBA Disciplinary and Valuation Standards Committees and contributes to professional journals and publications. He has given presentations on business appraisal for attorneys, accountants, and appraisers around the country. He is the Head of the IBA College of Fellows, which recognizes extraordinary commitment to the business appraisal profession.

Rand M. Curtiss is the head of American Business Appraisers—Cleveland, a division of Loveman-Curtiss, Inc., a nationally recognized professional organization specializing in business valuations. An honors graduate of Princeton University and the Harvard Business School, Mr. Curtiss has been awarded the designation Master Certified Business Appraiser from the IBA, and Accredited Senior Appraiser in both Business Valuation and Appraiser Review and Management from the American Society of Appraisers.

Mr. Curtiss is the author of courses on development of capitalization rates and premia, report writing and marketing for business appraisers. He has been elected Governor of the IBA and is a member of the College of Fellows. He serves on the Certification Committee of the American Society of Appraisers and the Qualifications Review Committee of the IBA. He is the author of a number of articles for leading professional journals and publications, and he has lectured extensively on trends in business appraisal. His monthly newsletter on business appraisal issues is read by law firms and business leaders across the country.

Nancy J. Fannon has been awarded the designations Certified Public Accountant and Accredited in Business Valuation from the AICPA, and Master Certified Business Appraiser and Business Valuation Accredited in Litigation from the IBA. She is a principal of Baker Newman & Noyes in Portland, Maine, specializing in business valuation and litigation support work.

Ms. Fannon received her Bachelor of Business Administration

from the University of Massachusetts, and has been awarded the Tribute to Women in Industry and AICPA's Volunteer of the Year Award. She serves on the AICPA Business Valuation Committee and has served as chair of AICPA's Business Valuation Conference.

Ms. Fannon is a frequent speaker on business valuation topics. She is on the course development and instruction team for the Accredited in Business Valuation Courses for the AICPA and has presented for both the AICPA and the IBA.

Leonard J. Sliwoski has been a professor of accounting at Minnesota State University Moorhead since 1982. He has been awarded the professional designations Certified Public Accountant and Accredited in Business Valuation from the AICPA, Master Certified Business Appraiser from the IBA, and Accredited Senior Appraiser from the American Society of Appraisers. He has been elected to the College of Fellows of the IBA and honored as IBA's Instructor of the Year.

Dr. Sliwoski operates a private consulting practice in Fargo, North Dakota, which provides business valuation and expert witness services. He is the Director of the Small Development Center at Minnesota State University Moorhead. A frequent instructor for courses sponsored by the IBA and the AICPA, Dr. Sliwoski has authored courses on discount and capitalization rates, analyzing financial statements, case studies, and advanced taxation issues.

Acknowledgments

This book is a collaboration of dozens of appraisers, lawyers, and friends.

First, thanks go to Steven F. Schroeder, MCBA, ASA, FIBA, JD. Since 1999, teaching the Institute of Business Appraiser's Litigation Support Workshop with Steve has been the best part of my professional life. Steve's teaching method bares his soul in the hope of helping other appraisers to reach ethical and professional excellence. Anyone who has the opportunity to learn from him gains immense benefits. Steve's reverence for the legal process and belief in ethical advocacy are the heart of this book. Like his professionalism, his friendship is unfailing.

A special thanks goes to my good friend Shannon Pratt, MCBA, ASA. Shannon has led the effort to educate attorneys and judges on business appraisal issues, and to expose appraisers to the development of a body of case law on business appraisal. His *Business Valuation Update, Judges and Lawyers Business Valuation Update*, and *The Lawyer's Business Valuation Handbook* have provided lists of the essentials to cover in a book of this nature. Shannon Pratt is the reason business appraisal has moved from an "industry" to a "profession."

For his numerous technical writings, and for the excellent analysis of cases on his web site (which I have been given permission to use), thanks to Z. Christopher Mercer, ASA, CFA. Reading his materials has guided my approach in demonstrating the relevancy (and the often fleeting applicability!) of case law to appraisers. His e-law newsletter is a valuable resource linking the legal and appraisal worlds (it is available at www.bizval.com). Thanks also to Barbara Walters Price of Mercer Capital for her many courtesies.

I am grateful to Gary Trugman, CPA/ABV, MCBA, ASA, for his insights on expert testimony, sharing with me his abilities on case analysis, and most especially for his book *Understanding Business Valuation*, which manages to make a technical subject an entertaining read.

I thank Jay Fishman, ASA, MBA, for his support, technical advice, and my ability to constantly reference the excellent work *Guide to Business Valuations,* of which he is one of the principal authors.

The business appraisers who have attended IBA's Litigation Support Workshop have shaped this book by sharing their experiences and wish lists for a technical work, and critiquing the prior versions of the course materials on which the book's outline was based. Their ability to examine their own shortcomings and their desire for continued improvement make each alumnus of the Workshop a valued colleague and friend.

Thanks to the IBA staff, especially Bob, John, Ave, Tara, Stu, and Manny, for shouldering much of my workload during weeks of travel and writing—and thanks for looking glad to see me when I return.

And most importantly, a lifetime of gratitude to my father, Raymond C. Miles, MCBA, ASA, FIBA. His book *Basic Business Appraisal* started the technical revolution; the IBA transaction database which he founded literally changed the way privately owned businesses were appraised. In the 1980s he wrote a course entitled *Business Valuation for Attorneys,* and brought the need for attorney education on these subjects to the attention of the profession. Now in his early 80s, my father's mind and heart are still dedicated to the improvement of the business appraisal profession, and he talks to appraisers on technical matters on a daily basis. Thanks to him, I have met all of the generous people who have contributed to this book. His personal and professional life continues to be the standard against which my own are measured.

Contents

Preface

Experience has shown that opposite opinions of persons professing to be experts may be obtained to any amount . . . it often occurs that not only many days, but even weeks, are consumed in cross-examinations, to test the skill or knowledge of such witnesses and the correctness of their opinions, wasting the time and wearying the patience of both court and jury, and perplexing, instead of elucidating, the questions involved in the issue.

—Supreme Court, 1858

As the reader can see, negative stereotypes about expert witnesses are nothing new. Every lawyer has a story about an expert whose opinions were best accessorized by a lamp post and a public defender. If you are a business appraiser planning to expand litigation support services or add them to your practice, the right attitude, training, and tools are essential.

PURPOSE OF THIS BOOK

After 15 years of trial practice, I retired from a large South Florida law firm in 1997. Focusing on complex commercial cases, I encountered a variety of expert witnesses and litigants, and spoke with other counsel and with jurists about their perceptions of the experts and their ethics. In the three years I have been serving as the executive director of the Institute of Business Appraisers, I have taught a seven-day workshop on litigation support and have spoken with many appraisers. They all wanted to do a better job in serving clients when they are retained in litigation support settings, and many were dismayed at the performance of the appraisers testifying for other parties.

What these appraisers wanted was a guidebook that would assist their understanding of the legal process and their appropriate role. Their input and the contributions of the co-authors have resulted in this book. We hope it can fill the need for a practical technical resource for business appraisers who offer litigation support services. On behalf of all the authors and contributors, thank you for lending an ear to our advice.

From the perspective of the appraiser, litigation support is a growth opportunity; it is a way to expand the practice and increase revenues. However, from the perspective of the client, it is much more. Before you read the technical portion of this book, we ask that you have your head on straight and your heart in the right place. Only then will you be able to do a good job as a litigation support professional.

The appraiser is urged to bear in mind three essentials:

1. This is not your lawsuit.
2. This might be the only litigation your client will ever have.
3. You cannot buy a reputation—but you sure can sell one.

We will look at each of these points in greater detail.

First Essential: Remember that It Is Not Your Lawsuit

You are not a real party in interest; don't act like one. Unless you are retained as a consultant who will not be testifying, you are not part of the lawyers' *team*; rather, you are an appraiser who answers to professional standards in the performance of your work.

Lawyers are renowned for a certain amount of gamesmanship in the courtroom and during the discovery process. Within the limits of the rules and professional ethics, gamesmanship is their job. The duty of the lawyer is to represent the client, not to establish objective truths.

Your job is different—it is to take a dispassionate look at the valuation question and to present an opinion of value. The party who retained you should be irrelevant to the numbers you derive. This is what is meant by *objective advocacy*—you are an advocate only for your value, not for any other issues involving the parties. Distinguish your position of advocacy for your appraisal product from the attorney's position of advocacy for the client. Too many appraisers get caught up in the thrust and parry of litigation—they label their meeting spaces "war rooms," draft the direct examination for counsel, and refer to their win and loss records. If you plan on a career that will involve courtroom testimony, avoid a level of involvement that makes the outcome personal.

Do the best work you can, present your result, and defend your opinion of value on the stand. Do not adopt your client's opinion of the opposing party—it will keep you from being objective. With the exception of the experts, everyone else surrounding the business owner is a partisan. Your job is to give them an objective opinion so they can realistically assess their posture in the litigation. This objectivity is the best service you can provide.

Second Essential: Honor the Client's Limited Opportunity to Secure Rights

Although you must approach the appraisal as an assignment, for clients this lawsuit might represent the biggest financial deal in their lifetime. The outcome may affect the future of a business that has been passed through generations, damages necessary for a defrauded party to start again, money for a departing shareholder to continue to make a living in a new enterprise, or the right to a share of a jointly built business expanded through daily sacrifices so great that they helped to sink a marriage. It can determine whether an established business gives in to the threat of protracted litigation on a baseless claim, or result in compensation for a business destroyed by state action or overregulation. The outcome can be economic life or death for every owner and employee. With this in mind, never knowingly cut corners when performing a valuation to be used in litigation—the litigants rarely get a second chance to secure their rights. This work is worth losing sleep over.

Third Essential: You Can't Buy a Reputation—But You Sure Can Sell One

Perhaps your valuation may not be the one the parties wanted to see—but it cannot be a number that will change because your client hopes for a different value. As an appraiser, your job is to search for truth, not to make wishes come true. Experts who mold their opinions around the desires of the clients are considered whores. They may get business, but they don't get much respect—and their clients don't often win as a result of their work. Don't put yourself in the position to be the butt of a lawyer's barroom humor. Chances are, you won't hear about it until your reputation has been compromised.

DEFINITIONS OF TERMS

Throughout this book the authors refer to the person or entity who retains the appraiser, also called the expert. Sometimes this will be counsel, sometimes an individual, sometimes a business. This person or entity to whom the appraiser's duty runs is referred to as *owner*; we recognize that this can encompass a spouse, a displaced shareholder, or a company. The word *client* would seem the better fit here, but that word needs to refer to the person or entity who has the relationship with the attorney.

The words *attorney*, *lawyer*, and *counsel* are used interchangeably throughout the book (although *counsel* can also be a team of attorneys). Generally, where discussing the lawyer who represents the owner/client for whom the appraiser is performing a valuation, we use the term *retaining counsel*, whether or not the engagement letter has been signed by the attorney. The term *opposing counsel* will refer to the lawyer for other parties in the case.

Every effort has been made to have this book serve as a practical resource. To this end, we have added "Reality Checks" throughout the book. These are real-life situations that have been reported to the authors or members of the litigation support workshop, or that come from our personal experiences. We hope the Reality Checks will put the technical material in context.

Michele G. Miles, Esquire

PART ONE

The Role of the Appraiser

CHAPTER 1

Anatomy of a Lawsuit

Purpose of This Chapter Few things are more embarrassing to the business appraiser than sitting through a meeting with counsel and not understanding a single word. Experts need to learn the language of litigation and the steps involved in getting a suit to court. This is the first step to finding the work. Once you understand the flow of litigation, you will be prepared to be a better service provider because you will know what can be contributed to each phase of the process. Knowing the obstacles faced by counsel in getting the suit to court (or delaying the day of trial), you as an expert will have a sense of the total picture, the effort, and the costs involved. When you understand each step of the process, you will be in a position to offer appropriate assistance where the input of an expert on appraisal issues can affect outcome.

The most challenging aspect of litigation support services is getting hired early in the process. Not only does this assist the appraiser in finding the work in the assignment that can give the appraisal the most impact, it prevents wasted time in trying to correct events that could have benefited from the appraiser's input. As you go through these materials, note the role of the appraiser in each step of the process.

WHERE TO FILE THE ACTION

Lawyers often have a choice of forums in which to bring an action, depending on the nature of the claim, the activities of the parties, and the location of the business or of the parties. The decision to file in a particular court can determine which Rules of Evidence and Procedure apply, the length of time to trial, and the handling of pretrial matters. It is an important strategic decision made by the plaintiff's counsel. Unless the state court is located in a major metropolitan area or in an area with a strong tax base, the general perception is that federal courts are more sophisticated in handling business disputes. Often, these courtrooms will have access to state-of-the-art technology. Federal courts may accept electronic filings, and preliminary matters will be handled by special masters, who can assist the case in moving more rapidly to trial.

Role of the Appraiser The appraiser should review with retaining counsel the nature of the evidence on value that the expert will present, and the potential need to bring pretrial motions for items such as site visits and document access. The expert should also discuss whether his or her testimony has been previously admitted in evidence in state or federal court (and therefore would have established credibility), and whether the expert's communication skills would lend themselves toward a more sophisticated presentation, or whether he or she is more comfortable communicating with "just plain folks." As with all decisions beyond the opinion of value, the final call remains with counsel, who is evaluating these points as they will affect other aspects of the case.

Suits can be brought in federal court if there is *federal question jurisdiction*—if federal law creates the cause of action or if the plaintiff's right to relief depends on the interpretation of a substantial question of federal law. Antitrust cases, cases dealing with regulations on interstate commerce, or securities fraud cases would be common lawsuits where appraisers would perform services, and these cases would have federal question jurisdiction.

The suit can also be filed in federal court if there is *diversity jurisdiction*—a dispute between entities from different states, or involving a foreign corporation[1] or individual (assuming the relief to be pled is above the jurisdictional limit—another area where the appraiser's advice should be sought by counsel). The rules for diversity jurisdiction require a determination of the *domicile* of each party, and diversity must be complete—that is, no one plaintiff can be a citizen of the same state as any one defendant. In the case of a class action, the named plaintiff's domicile is determinative of the diversity of the parties.[2]

Once Federal jurisdiction has been established, claims brought by defendants may be included in the federal suit, even though they might not have qualified for federal jurisdiction if the claim had been brought separately. Judicial economy and the desire to avoid inconsistent results prompt this *ancillary jurisdiction*. There are exceptions to this rule, and these generally pertain to the filing of optional claims, or claims far removed from the issues pled in the complaint.

To exploit the perceived benefits of a home-town advantage, the plaintiff's counsel may choose to bring a claim in state court even when federal jurisdiction is available. In that case, the defendant's counsel may request removal to federal court. Again, the appraiser can have input to counsel on the nature of the evidence and whether it would be better presented in a home-town court or in federal court. If removal is granted, the case will be heard in the federal district court for the district and division that includes the locale where the state action was pending.

If the action is destined for state court, jurisdiction still comes into play in determining *which* state should have jurisdiction. There is a divergence among the states on standards of proof, the way claims are defined, and the remedies that are available, as well as with interpretation of evidence and procedural rules. From the perspective of the parties, there can be an advantage to a defendant in defending the case where the company is a significant part of a local economy, and an advantage to a plaintiff in keeping a suit in a state where the defendant is an out-of-area competitor with few community ties.

A judgment rendered in one state is enforceable in other states—entitled to *full faith and credit*—but enforceability of U.S. judgments in other nations is governed by treaty, letters of agreement, and other instruments of diplomacy.

Under the modern tests, to be sued in a particular state, the defendant must be determined to have *minimum contacts* with that state. In the business context, this will generally mean that the defendant conducts systematic and continuous business in the state or solicits business through an organized plan—such as advertising by mail or through the media. The possibility of litigation or claims arising from the contact with the state must also be *reasonably foreseeable*, and a business is subject to jurisdiction in its state of incorporation whether or not the business conducts any other business activity there.

Role of the Appraiser In these matters, the appraiser should perform economic and industry analysis that would argue for or against minimum contacts with the jurisdiction and the foreseeability of suit. The appraiser's knowledge of the particular type of business and the national economy can provide information to counsel that can be used to argue for or against jurisdiction in a particular state. The most difficult calls are where the business puts a product into the marketplace that is then resold or incorporated into other products—in such instances, industry knowledge can help decide the question.

Once the issue of jurisdiction is decided, the question moves to one of venue. *Venue* is the locality within the jurisdiction where the case may be tried—it is usually of more significance in the state court suit, where the obvious distinction will be the demographics of a potential jury. Again, the communication skills of the expert witness and the type of audience to which the expert can best relate should be discussed with counsel when venue is being considered, as well as whether the expert has been accepted as a qualified witness in any courts. Motions for change of venue can be brought by the defendant on the grounds that substantial events giving rise to the issues in the complaint occurred in other venues, or that another venue might be more convenient to the parties and witnesses. Particularly where an inspection of the business would assist the court in determining the issues, a defendant could argue to change venue to the location of its main facility.

THE PARTIES AND THE CLAIMS

The *complaint* is the first document in what can become an extensive pleadings file.[3] An appraiser who is hired sufficiently in advance of its filing can affect the manner in which the valuation issues are described and the types of relief that are claimed. This improves the chances that the complaint will match later offers of proof by the expert at trial.

You may have seen complaints that have been published in connection with infamous lawsuits, or read some pleadings available on Web sites such as Court TV, which has filings on high-profile cases. The typical complaint won't bear much resemblance to these—the filings on a high-profile case are written more for the press than the clerk's office. A typical complaint is a short and unembellished statement of the ultimate facts that give rise to a claim for relief. It will include the following:

- The identity of all plaintiffs and defendants
- The grounds for jurisdiction and venue[4]
- A summary of the facts giving rise to the claim[5]
- A demand for the relief that the plaintiff seeks—which may be pled in the alternative

Special matters such as fraud, mistake, the occurrence or frustration of conditions precedent or gross negligence are pled *with particularity*—that is, in detail. If punitive damages are sought, many jurisdictions require that a hearing be held, and that a preliminary finding of their appropriate inclusion in the pleadings precede including those allegations in the complaint.

Role of the Appraiser The appraiser can have input with counsel on whether the acts of the defendant are, in a business context, sufficiently outrageous as to give rise to a claim for punitive damages.[6] In doing so, the appraiser will focus on the effect on the business of the conduct and whether it was a reasonably anticipated result.

In advising on issues such as what claims to bring and the parties who might have liability, appraisers are cautioned against advising throwing everything against the wall and taking to trial anything that sticks. All courts have penalties for frivolous lawsuits,[7] and costs imposed for bringing a baseless claim can sometimes be divided between the plaintiff and plaintiff's counsel. Judges and juries do not enjoy having their time wasted by claims that cannot be proven.

The complaint is filed, and then served upon the defendants in accordance with the rules of the jurisdiction. Should a defendant fail to respond within the time limit set forth in the Rules of Procedure, a default is entered. Unless the defendant succeeds in having it set aside upon a showing of good cause, the defendant can present no evidence. A defendant will generally respond to a complaint by filing either an *answer* or a *motion to dismiss* (the motion may also be incorporated into the answer, depending on the rules of pleading in the jurisdiction).

A motion to dismiss will focus on nonfactual issues of the claim, and is usually argued without the presentation of evidence. It therefore offers little occasion for input by the appraiser. Such a motion typically focuses on one or more of these aspects:

- Lack of subject matter or personal jurisdiction
- An argument that venue is improper
- Defects in the service of process
- Failure to state the elements of a claim
- Failure to join necessary parties
- Insufficient recitation of facts to allow defendant to respond

The court will rule on the motion, and the plaintiff may need to amend the complaint before the action can proceed. The defendant may also file a *motion for more definite statement.* This is directed to the facts alleged in the complaint and it requests additional information before a response is filed. Defendant may reiterate the arguments from the motion to dismiss or the motion for more definite statement in the answer and affirmative defenses.

Role of the Appraiser Whether retained by plaintiff or defense counsel, the appraiser should be familiar with the answer and affirmative defenses, as the parties may try to establish their existence or nonexistence through the appraiser's testimony.

Persons not originally part of the suit may be brought in on some occasions. Intervention may occur when a person not a party to the suit seeks to become a party in order to protect an interest that may be impaired as a result of the suit. In a dissenting shareholder action, for example, other shareholders may attempt to intervene and have their rights adjudicated. Through *interpleader*, a party who may be in the middle of a situation may force other parties into court to decide an issue—often who holds an asset or which of several parties rightfully claim ownership of interest. Intellectual property rights and domestic disputes are cases where the appraiser might see interpleader. Third-party claims are another level of pleading that can allow a defendant to assert claims, including those for indemnity, contribution, and subrogation.

Role of the Appraiser If the appraiser is retained by defense counsel, the nature of the issues may prompt the appraiser to suggest other parties who belong in the suit. For example, in an action for negligent performance of appraisal services, the appraiser could determine whether other consultants contributing to the report would be appropriate third-party defendants. In an action for breach of a construction contract, the appraiser could review company financials on the project to determine if the performance of subcontractors or design professionals contributed to the losses claimed by the plaintiff.

Third-party practice involves a defendant's bringing claims against a third party—putting the defendant also in the status of a plaintiff as regards the third party. The labeling of third-party pleadings can approach the incomprehensible: A defendant who asserts a third-party claim, a claim against plaintiff, and a claim against another defendant might be referred to in pleadings as defendant/third party plaintiff/counter claimant/cross claimant.

The parties may also counterclaim (defendant suing plaintiff for relief, or a third party suing defendant or plaintiff), or cross claim (defendants or third parties suing one another). The appraiser is wise to chart out the claims so that the relief sought by each party against each party can be clearly understood. This is definitely one of those situations when you can't tell the players without a program!

In the answer, the defendant will respond to the allegations of the complaint, often by referring to the complaint's numbered paragraphs. As with the complaint, the answer will be terse as the defendant admits or denies each statement, sometimes giving defenses to the allegations.

Several motions can be brought that ask the court to rule on the claims and resolve issues prior to trial. A motion judgment on the pleadings can be filed by any party after the case is *at issue*—after the final responsive pleading has been filed. It asks the court to look at the issues raised in the pleadings and decide the case without further proof.

A *motion for summary judgment* can also be filed by any party. It asks the court to look at the pleadings to the discovery and determine if there is a genuine issue of fact to be tried. The parties can also move for partial summary judgment, deciding selected issues in the case. Summary judgment motions are accompanied by the proofs in support of the argument—affidavits of the parties, deposition transcripts, and responses to discovery. The moving party has the burden of proof to demonstrate that there is "no material issue of law or fact" precluding the court's entry of judgment on the issue. The opposing party has the opportunity to respond and present proofs that refute the motion. There is a substantial time period between the filing of the motion and the filing of a response, which may allow the opposing party to take additional depositions to gather information in opposition to the motion. If the local rules provide for argument of the motion, the proofs of the opposing party will be filed in advance of the hearing.

Role of the Appraiser If appraisal issues or entitlement to damages are involved, the appraiser can consult with counsel on the valuation and business realities. Even if the motion does not deal directly with those issues, it can preview the movant's theory of the case, and what the movant (and sometimes the opponent) perceives as the strongest arguments. And the court's ruling on the motion can preview the judge's opinions on the case. For these reasons, sometimes these motions are brought even when counsel knows they cannot be won.

TAKING THE CASE THROUGH TRIAL

The right to jury trial is not an absolute. Some types of cases—most notably dissolutions of marriage—are nearly always decided via the bench trial; demands for equitable relief (such as specific performance, injunctions and declaratory relief) are also decided in bench trials. A demand for jury trial can be made in the complaint, or by any defendant at the time the answer is filed. Some states allow for a later demand to be filed. Federal practice requires that a demand for jury trial be filed within ten days of the last pleading directed to a legal issue.

Judges control the parties' progress to trial through discovery schedules and case management orders. In most cases, a pretrial order will be issued. This order will set the final deadlines for production of documents, supplementation of responses, and declaration and deposition of witnesses. It will also specify the dates for the declaration of experts and for providing expert reports. For too many lawyers, it is the issuance of the pretrial order that prompts their retention of an expert in business appraisal.

Role of the Appraiser You must comply without exception to any requirements that pertain to you in the pretrial order. If you are retained after the deadlines are fixed, review them before taking the assignment. If you cannot meet the deadlines, decline the assignment. Confer with counsel regarding any exhibits you will need to illustrate your testimony, as they will have to be produced in advance of trial. Particularly if these exhibits are summaries, maintain a file with all the supporting documents for each exhibit.

The pretrial order will also require the parties to meet and discuss settlement. Advise retaining counsel that your appraisal should, if at all possible, be completed before a settlement conference so that it can be included in an analysis of the "best day" and "worst day" at trial.[8] If the reports of appraisers testifying for other parties are available, review and comment to retaining counsel on these prior to the mediation.

Prior to the trial period, the counsel will attend the docket call. This is a cattle call for all cases that are scheduled for the weeks or months of the trial period.[9] The oldest cases on the court's docket are given priority, as are cases that are entitled to priority as a matter of law or due process—including criminal cases and eminent domain proceedings. At the docket call counsel will confirm that the team is ready for trial, and counsel is given its ranking on the docket. Sometimes counsel is given a standby date when trial will begin.

Role of the Appraiser Contact retaining counsel the day of the docket call and arrange your schedule to be available during the trial period.

In most cases, the counsel will prepare and fill pretrial briefs or a pretrial stipulation. Both of these filings will contain a recitation of the facts of the case; the pretrial stipulation will separate the facts into those that are undisputed and those for which a decision is requested from the trier of fact. The pretrial stipulation will also list the witnesses and exhibits, as well as issues of law to be decided during the trial.

Role of the Appraiser Consult with counsel on the description of the business and the nature of the damages, to make sure your testimony will be consistent with the representations in the pretrial brief or the stipulation. Read the brief or stipulation to determine that there is no new information presented that will affect your opinion—particularly in exhibits that you might not have seen. Discuss with counsel the anticipated testimony of any listed witnesses that might be relevant to your opinion. Do what you can to avoid surprise.

AT TRIAL

Unless the case is a bench trial, the jury selection process begins the first day of the trial with the interview of the venire. The *venire* is a pool of potential jurors, who are interviewed by the attorneys or the judge; sometimes questionnaires or juror profile forms are completed by the members of the venire for background information. This is *voir dire.*

Each party can exercise a predetermined number of *peremptory challenges*[10]—challenges without cause that allow counsel to act on individual perceptions of bias of the potential juror. Potential jurors can also be excluded for *cause*—being related to parties in the case or participating in a similar lawsuit that might impair their ability to consider only the facts presented. All members of the venire are present for this questioning; it is their first impression of the case and of counsel.

The questioning is intended to screen the beliefs and attitudes of the potential jurors, such as these:

- Age
- Education
- Employment history
- Marital and family history
- Hobbies and interests
- Organization membership and volunteer activities
- Prior jury duty
- Life experiences related to the case on trial[11]

Counsel notes the profile of each juror as well as the reactions of the jurors during questioning, and whether the attorney is able to establish a rapport (since the lawyer is able to question each prospective juror for fewer than five minutes, this is an imprecise gauge even in the hands of a skilled trial attorney).

At the conclusion of voir dire, each party exercises its peremp-

tory challenges. Often there are more jurors that counsel would prefer to see off the jury than can be removed through the use of the
challenges.

Role of the Appraiser Prior to your testimony, discuss with counsel
the backgrounds of the jurors and any impressions counsel gained
from the jurors while watching the proceedings.

In large or high-profile cases, the parties may hire jury consultants or even a *shadow jury* to assist with the presentation of the case.
A shadow jury will listen to the presentations (sometimes even sitting in the back of the courtroom) and discuss their impressions with
counsel. Although there is a wide range of opinions on whether these
are effective aids for trial lawyers, a testifying expert should practice
presenting her opinions and underlying facts to people who typify
members of the venire. Most courts no longer automatically excuse
any citizen called for jury duty unless they have a physical or mental
disability, are self-employed, or are a stay-at-home parent of young
children. Therefore, there is no typical juror. Your goal as an expert
witness is to be able to communicate the essential concepts to people
with little formal business training, and to develop a natural, credible style that will allow people with significant education to focus on
your position rather than substituting their own experience. In a
bench trial, knowing the background of the judge prior to taking
the bench and the types of cases that the division has been hearing
will allow the appraiser to determine how much background information may be needed in valuation terms and methodology.

Once the jury has been seated, there will be a preliminary instruction given to the jurors and counsel will present opening argument. In a bench trial, opening argument may be dispensed with
and the court may rely on the pretrial briefs.

Role of the Appraiser Opening arguments allude to the proof that
each party will present and describe the nature of the damages sought.
Be familiar with the content of the opening arguments, particularly

if you will be responsible for presenting some of the evidence that they have previewed.

The party with the burden of proof (the plaintiff or petitioner) presents first and last. The opening statement of the plaintiff will be followed by the opening statements of the defendants. Presentation of plaintiff's *direct evidence* will follow. Each witness will give direct testimony; there may also be cross-examination, redirect, and recross. At some point, the expert witnesses will testify—in most cases, this will be after one or more fact witnesses have set the stage with details of the incidents that form the basis for the claim.

The presentation of the defendant's direct evidence will follow, including the presentation of testimony by defendant's expert witnesses. Plaintiff then begins the rebuttal case. The purpose of rebuttal is to respond to the evidence presented by the defendant—not to present additional information for the plaintiff's case in chief. The court may also allow *surrebuttal* by defendants. Resist any suggestion from retaining counsel that your testimony be "saved" for rebuttal or surrebuttal—if the damages or appraisal information is new evidence on rebuttal, chances are that the court won't admit it into evidence. Counsel may sometimes attempt to add an expert on rebuttal or surrebuttal to bolster weak expert testimony during presentation of the case in chief. Opposing parties usually respond that this testimony would be duplicative, and the attempt to present such testimony often underscores the fact that the first expert witness did an inadequate job. Learn when to let well enough alone.

Role of the Appraiser This is where the appraiser's main impact will be felt—by giving competent and credible courtroom testimony. Be well prepared on your report and on any issues of other reports on which you may be questioned. In addition, know the testimony of other witnesses who may have given evidence on issues that could affect your opinions.[12]

The testifying expert has two functions—to present evidence for the trier of fact and to make a complete record in case of appeal. Pay particular attention to the standard of value for the case and make sure it is clearly recited. Make sure the essentials of your appraisal process and your qualifications go on the record. Be precise with the "magic words" that will appear in the jury instructions, and recite them confidently during your testimony.

Closing arguments follow when both parties have rested their case. The plaintiff will close first, and, after defendant's closing, will be permitted a final short address to the jury.

Role of the Appraiser This is the last opportunity for your numbers to reach the jury's ear. Review with counsel how the appraisal conclusion will be described and any terms that should be repeated to the jury to emphasize the reliability of your conclusion.

At this point, the jury is champing at the bit to get back to the jury room. Jurors have been admonished not to discuss the case during the presentation of the testimony, and at last their stored-up opinions can have vent. Unfortunately, before the jurors are sent to deliberate, they must listen to a long set of directives—the jury instructions. These are paragraphs read by the court that address the matters of law in the case and include directives on these topics:

- Credibility of witnesses
- The elements of the claims
- Causation
- Burdens of proof
- Measure of damages
- Standards of value
- Contributory or comparative negligence

The proposed content of instructions is organized and prepared in advance of trial. In most jurisdictions, jury instructions are refined immediately following the close of evidence during a *charging conference.* This is a proceeding out of the presence of the jury during which counsel reviews its proposed instructions with the court, and the instructions are accepted, modified, or substituted with other language.

The result is a complete set of instructions read aloud to the jury, and sometimes given to the jury to take into the jury room as a reference during deliberations.

Role of the Appraiser Be aware of jury instruction content prior to testimony and take care to match your use of technical terms with those used in the instructions. Although some consultants would take the position that the expert could assist in drafting the instructions, it is the opinion of this author that doing so is a bad idea in most cases. The source of most instructions is case law, which the appraiser is in a poor position to interpret. If counsel proposes to use appraisal texts to define a standard of value, the appraiser can assist in selecting the correct portions of those texts. Otherwise, the appraiser should read both the proposed instructions and the set ultimately approved by the court, and stay out of the way for the rest of the process.

Once the jury has been instructed, it will retire to consider its verdict. Although jurors might request that some testimony be read to them from depositions or the trial transcript (if available), no new testimony or evidence can be presented even if the jury has questions. Therefore, there is little the appraiser can do at this point.

In a bench trial, closing arguments and the deliberation process can occur days or weeks after the conclusion of the evidence. Often, closings are presented in written form after the trial transcript has been produced, and the court's ruling will be issued in writing (sometimes drafted by the winning party with instruction from the court).

Role of the Appraiser As with a spoken closing, this is the final opportunity to present the damage testimony to the trier of fact. In a closing brief the appraiser should assist counsel in describing both the appraisal conclusion and the underlying process with technical precision and in a concise format.

MOTIONS BEFORE AND DURING TRIAL

The pretrial order will often set deadlines for pretrial motions. These are a range of motions directed toward the evidence already in the court file, or evidence that counsel anticipates will be presented.

The most common pretrial motion that will affect the appraiser is the *motion in limine*. This motion is used to exclude possibly inadmissible evidence. From the appraiser's standpoint, this might be one of the places where a qualifications or a methodology challenge would be presented to the court. These motions are argued by counsel without the presentation of any evidence at the hearing other than that which has already been taken—often, excerpts of deposition testimony will accompany the motion or be read during the argument.

Role of the Appraiser If you are the subject of a motion in limine, there's nothing you can do except review the status of your receivable. If retaining counsel brings such a motion directed at another expert, you can identify the portions of the deposition testimony that would demonstrate the unreliability or irrelevance of the testimony.

During trial, counsel may bring a variety of motions that attempt to shortcut proceedings. Since these motions generally involve legal argument and standards of proof, we recommend that the appraiser just stay out of the way. Your main job as appraiser is to have done complete and competent work so that your testimony will not negatively affect the outcome of these motions, and to avoid conduct that might result in mistrial.

Some of these motions are briefly discussed here:

- *Motion for judgment as a matter of law,* also known as *a motion for directed verdict.* This motion is made by a party after the opposing party's evidence has had full hearing. A defendant can bring the motion after the close of plaintiff's case but before the defendant has presented any evidence; a plaintiff will bring the motion at the close of defendant's case. In a jury trial, the court will look to whether the jury could reasonably find for the non-moving party. In a bench trial, the court will consider entering judgment as a matter of law—

determining that the party has failed to meet a burden of proof.

- *Nonsuit.* In jury trials, this motion is brought by the defendant at the close of the plaintiff's proof. It is analogous to the motion to dismiss sometimes brought at the start of the case and asks the court to rule that the plaintiff's case is legally insufficient.
- *Mistrial.* The judge is asked to end the trial prior to the rendering of a verdict because of a major defect in procedure or an occurrence during the trial. If the motion is granted, the case will be retried with all proofs re-presented to a different jury. For example, if a juror dies or becomes unable to continue and there are no alternates available, the court may declare mistrial. A mistrial may also be granted if there is serious prejudice to a party through the presentation of prejudicial testimony, juror misconduct, or inappropriate tactics by counsel. If a juror performs independent investigation and reports findings to the other jurors, this type of prejudice can be argued. Another cause of mistrial can be witnesses communicating with jurors—including expert witnesses. Limit your out-of-court contact with jurors to a nod and "good morning." Never discuss the case, the parties, the issues, or the judge in the hallway, bathroom, or public area where a juror may be present.

After the verdict from the trier of fact (whether the case is tried before a jury or proceeds as a bench trial), motions are brought requesting that the court alter the outcome. Some of these motions are discussed next:

- *Motion for new trial.* This is a request that a new trial be held on some or all of the contested factual issues. A new trial can be granted where counsel's argument to the jury was improper, or where there is newly discovered evidence.
- *Motion to alter or amend judgment.* This motion is brought in an attempt to correct errors of law.
- *Motion for judgment notwithstanding the verdict.* The court is asked to rule that a reasonable jury could not have reached the announced verdict.
- *Motion for remittitur.* The court is asked to order a new trial

because the damages are excessive when related to the evidence. If the plaintiff consents to the remittitur, there is no new trial and the damages award is reduced as stated in the motion.

- *Motion for adittitur.* The companion to a remittur, a motion for addittitur requests the court to order a new trial for the purpose of increasing the amount of the verdict.

POSTVERDICT: COLLECTION OF JUDGMENTS AND AWARD OF COSTS

When the dust has settled, cost issues are next considered. Attorney's fees are not awarded unless specified by contract, or unless the cause of action entitles the parties to recover fees (generally set forth in a statute). If fees are recoverable, the parties will either agree on the amount of the fees or the court will decide the attorney's fee award after an evidentiary proceeding.

In most cases, the prevailing party will be entitled to a recovery of costs.[13] Recoverable costs will be listed in the Rules of Procedure or otherwise codified in the jurisdiction. Recoverable costs will include some portion of the expert witness fees—most notably those fees related to trial testimony and, if the deposition was used in court, some portion of the deposition fees.

Role of the Appraiser Keep detailed records of time that you have billed hourly so that counsel can have this information ready for presentation at a cost hearing. If you were retained by the nonprevailing party, you can review the charges of the appraiser to determine if the fees are reasonable, both for the amount of the fee and the work performed for the amount charged.

Unless the defendant writes a check for the judgment, counsel will proceed to identify assets through discovery in aid of execution. This will include depositions, interrogatories and additional requests for production. Often counsel will have to attempt to recover assets whose title may have been transferred from the defendant in an attempt to avoid their being subject to the judgment.

Role of the Appraiser If your assignment has given you insight into the accounting practices of the business or the nature of the corporate assets, you can assist plaintiff's counsel in identifying assets that may be available to satisfy a judgment. However, since this work can involve forensic accounting, make certain that your skills are suitable for this work. Many appraisers prefer not to consult on collection matters because it can increase the scope of research during the appraisal process beyond what is required for the valuation. This increases both the fees and client expectations of delivery of performance beyond appraisal services.

Appellate Proceedings

When a notice of appeal is filed within the time limits established by the Rules of Appellate Procedure, the next phase of the dispute begins. In the appeal, the appellate court will be limited to a review of the record that was created during the pretrial proceedings and at trial. Counsel will prepare briefs and may present oral argument. A written decision will be rendered by the appellate court, and this will sometimes include a lengthy opinion reviewing the issues, the argument, and the rationale behind the decision of the appellate court.

An appeal bond is usually required to secure the adversary's cost if the judgment is affirmed. If the appealing party had a monetary judgment rendered against it at trial, a *supersedeas bond* is required to prevent collection of the judgment during the pendency of the appeal.

The right of appeal is a creature of statute in most states. Although there is generally an automatic right to a first-level appeal (from the trial court to the appellate court), further appellate review—from the appellate court to the court of last resort in the jurisdiction—is not automatic. Often the next level of appellate court can only be reached by a demonstration that there is a significant public issue, the interpretation of a statutory or constitutional right, or a divergence among the lower appellate courts.

Any appraiser involvement would be on the initial appeal. Since the appellate court is limited to the record, the appraiser's assistance would be in the review of expert testimony and providing summaries of the testimony for inclusion in the written briefs or the presentation of oral argument.

NOTES

1. In this context, *foreign corporation* is intended to refer to a company that is not incorporated in the United States. The reader of pleadings or case law is cautioned that the term *foreign* corporation can also refer in those documents to corporations that are not incorporated under the laws of a particular state—sometimes described as *domestic corporations.*
2. Attorneys experienced in class actions generally prefer to have them filed in federal court. The federal court system is more experienced in the handling of these complex and time-consuming cases, and in some federal district courts complex litigation and class actions are placed in the division of one judge who has developed an efficient system for dealing with the claims.
3. It is a common rookie mistake to confuse pleadings and discovery. Pleadings are directed to the court, and deal with formal written statements on the existence or denial of claims and the related legal grounds. Discovery is directed to the parties, and deals with facts that support or negate the claims or defenses. Typically, all pleadings are part of the court file; discovery in many jurisdictions becomes part of the court file only if it is in support of some motion, argument, or pleading. In many cases, providing all discovery responses to the court would create a storage and time problem for court administrators. Therefore, if you travel to the courthouse to review a file, don't assume you are seeing all that has taken place in the case.
4. A minimal jurisdictional amount will be pled in the complaint. In general, lawyers simply recite that the amount of damages exceeds this minimum; it is unusual for the actual amount of dam-

ages sought to appear in the complaint. At this stage of the pleadings, the amount of damages is generally undetermined. If the appraiser is asked for an amount, and the intent is to include this amount in the complaint, the appraiser may be dealing with inexperienced counsel or an uncontrolled client.

5. The plaintiff may have a variety of causes of action that can be brought, and each cause of action will have different elements. Some of these are discussed in the following chapter. The appraiser can review the facts given to date and discuss with retaining counsel whether the elements seem to be present for a particular cause of action.

6. A common standard is whether the conduct of a defendant is "willful, wanton, or grossly negligent" sufficient to give rise to a claim for punitive damages.

7. See, e.g., F.R.C.P. 11.

8. Appraisers are often asked to provide these "best day/worst day" numbers. This is a bad idea. Too many other aspects of the case are unknown to the appraiser, including court rulings on the legal issues, the credibility of the witnesses, and the ability of the opposing party to prove its claims or defenses. Don't be a guarantor for someone else's work.

9. Unless the case is given a *special setting*—a guaranteed time period when it will be heard—cases are overscheduled for the times when the court is to be presiding at trials. Often, cases are confirmed for a trial docket that, if they were all to be tried, will take three or four times as many days as the court has set aside for trial. This allows for cases to roll off the trial docket as a result of settlement or continuances granted by the court. Cases that are not reached during the trial period are carried over to the next docket period.

10. These are sometimes called *strikes.*

11. Mauet, *Trial Techniques,* 5th ed. (New York: Aspen Publishers, Inc., 1999), pp. 43–44.

12. Often at trial, counsel will invoke "The Rule." This refers to the court's exclusion of witnesses from the courtroom until they have been "excused"—meaning that their testimony has finished. As a general principle, the exclusion does not apply to expert witnesses, but you should confirm with counsel that it is appropri-

ate for you to discuss the evidence given by witnesses who have been presented prior to your testimony. See the discussion of Rule 615 in Chapter 8, *infra*.

13. This also applies to defendants where the plaintiff was not awarded damages. In some cases—particularly where there have been counterclaims—it can be difficult to determine which party has "prevailed." The court will consider the nature of the claims and the relative successes of the parties at the fees and cost hearings.

CHAPTER 2

Claims for Business Damages

Purpose of This Chapter Most business appraisers do not know how to identify the available work because their knowledge of causes of action is limited to breach of contract, challenges to tax returns, shareholder oppression, and divorce. There are many other types of claims for which the measure of damages might require computation of the value of a business or business interest. This chapter reviews some of the claims in which business appraisal testimony might assist the trier of fact.

Let's begin with the basics: Every lawsuit starts with a petition or complaint. Each alleges one or more "causes of action"—claims for relief. Each cause of action has distinct elements and standards of proof. The basic requirements of a cause of action are an injury or breach giving rise to a claim for relief, causation, and resulting damages. The damages are categorized as compensatory or punitive. The other form of relief available to the plaintiff is equitable in nature, and it includes a range of nonmonetary remedies.

These claims arise by operation of statute, from contracts entered into by the parties, and at common law. As you review these claims, consider that both plaintiffs and defendants will need the assistance of expert witnesses. And as you read complaints, be careful not to confuse allegations with what might actually be demonstrated by the facts.

CONTRACT CLAIMS

Most plain folks think that appraisers spend the majority of their time dealing with mergers and acquisitions; most appraisers know that buy/ sell work is a minority of an appraisal practice. In litigation, there is a significant quantity of work for appraisers who can testify on actions arising out of purchase or financing of businesses (and many of these suits could have been avoided if the parties had retained an appraiser during the negotiations!).

The buy/sell contract is only one type of action sounding in contract where business damages may be an issue. The daily deals made by every business are another source of contract claims. Suppliers of services, goods for resale, or equipment used by businesses find themselves defending against claims of lost profits or diminution of business value as a result of late delivery or provision of low-quality services or product. Contract actions can include claims for the following:

- Fraud in the inducement
- Misrepresentation
- Breach of express or implied warranty
- Breach of the covenant of good faith and fair dealing (implied in every contract)

A cause of action for breach of contract has some essential elements:

- The existence of a contract (this requires proof of offer and acceptance, consideration, and a meeting of the minds on the essential terms of the contract)
- Performance or demonstrated intent to perform by the party claiming breach
- A material breach of the contract by one party that is not excused by factors such as impossibility or failure of a condition precedent
- Damages proximately caused by the breach

Privity is also an issue in contract actions. Unlike actions sounding in tort, only the contracting parties can recover for damages under the contract. This rule recognizes that the damages under the contract (which may be limited in scope) are the product of negotiations and the benefit of the bargain—or the detriment of the bargain—should be limited to the contracting parties or identified third-party beneficiaries. In most states, therefore, these damages, which represent economic loss, are not available to parties not in privity. Parties without privity are limited under the *economic loss rule* to damages arising from personal injury or property damage—the classic tort claims.

The purpose of contract damages is to place the injured party in substantially the same position as the party would have been in had the contract be performed. For this reason, the damages often go beyond the cost of replacement goods or services and into the effect the breach had on the business as a whole.

In looking at contract claims, many appraisers get involved in the documents that form the contract and forget to focus on the business. Again, this is an opportunity for appraisers to remember their roots and leave lawyering to the lawyers.

Reality Check The appraiser is retained as an expert by the plaintiff, a public-works contractor. She is given a complaint that states that the contractor purchased equipment designed to demolish bridge spans by removing concrete and leaving reinforcing steel intact so that a new span could be added to widen the bridge. The equipment, alleges the complaint, fails to perform as represented, and the contractor has to spend additional time and labor to complete contracted work, putting the contractor behind on other work and making the contractor liable for delay damages on a number of jobs. The appraiser is asked to advise on the types of damages that might be available to "place the injured party in substantially the same position as he would have been had the contract been performed." You must devise a plan for determining the damages.

Start with an interview of the owner. Read the contracts so you are familiar with the obligations of the parties, but be an appraiser, not a contract lawyer. Knowing the measure of damages for breach of contract, follow the trail of costs and losses that resulted from the failure of the equipment. Review with the owner any cost overruns or time delays for jobs that were bid with the expectation of using the equipment. Read the contracts on each of these jobs for information on how damages for delay are calculated. Discuss with the owner whether any contracts were available for bid but could not be bid on because the need to complete these delayed jobs put the company in a position without capacity to bid on other work. Determine how many of these contracts might have been awarded to the company if the company had submitted bids (using information such as the company's success record for bids based on past submissions), and calculate the lost profits.

Examine any changes in financial position since the first job on which the company planned to use the equipment. If, for example, the company had to call on the bonding company to complete the job, the company's rating may have become unfavorable, or the company may have lost bonding capacity altogether. If the need to put workers on overtime has also resulted in higher insurance ratings, this is another loss to the company.

You will see from the Reality Check how knowing the purpose of the award of damages can assist the appraiser in defining the assignment, and that the interview with the owner will ultimately factor in more than a review of the contracts. Damages such as lost profits on jobs that were not bid due to lost capacity to perform the work and the loss of bonding capacity are consequential damages. The standard for consequential damages limits those damages to those arising naturally from the breach, or within the reasonable contemplation of the parties at the time of contract.

Also important to consider in contract actions is the rule of avoidable consequences. A party cannot recover for losses that could have been avoided by taking reasonable means, including mitigation of damages. The steps an owner took to minimize the loss—or could have taken but did not—is an important part of your analysis.

The appraiser must discuss with counsel whether a different measure of damages has been agreed upon by the parties. Liquidated, or agreed, damages are a feature of many business contracts. These clauses provide for a specified sum of damages to be calculated in the event of breach, often relating to delays in performance or other reasons to limit liability. If these clauses are upheld, the duty to mitigate does not apply.

TORT CLAIMS

A tort is a civil wrong other than a breach of contract. For an act to constitute a tort, it must have three features:

- A legal duty owned by one person to another
- A breach of the duty
- Harm done as a result of the action

The entity who commits the tort is the tortfeasor. For claims arising in tort, the purpose of the damage award is to place the injured party in substantially the same position as that which was occupied prior to the tortious activity.

Tort claims include defamation, tortious interference with contract, theft of trade secrets, breach of fiduciary duty, negligence (including professional negligence), and conversion. Often these claims are also enumerated in statutes, and the attorney will plead the tort in the alternative—this may mean that the appraiser will calculate damages using several methods.

Each cause of action sounding in tort will have its own list of required allegations. Common to all tort claims will be the need to establish a causal nexus between the injury alleged and the damages that are sustained, and appraisers can often testify to this nexus.

Damage to the business can range from a temporary dip in profits to its total destruction. Given the range of damages that may flow from tortious activity, many appraisers tend to overreach when examining damages, and conclude that any deviation from historical cash flows is attributable to the alleged injury. Careful analysis of historical performance and a sustainable economic forecast of profits absent the tortious activity are essential in any tort claim.

Often the appraiser may find that even though the activity complained of is improper, the damages are minimal, or so many market factors contributed to the change in cash flows that no causal nexus can be reasonably established. When this is the case, it is the appraiser's duty to advise counsel that the emperor has no clothes and the case should settle.

MEASURING DAMAGES[1]

Regardless of whether the claim sounds in contract or in tort, damages must be proven to a reasonable certainty. Legal texts note that lost profits cases are an especial problem for demonstrating a probability of loss. Claims for damages sustained in the future must show that there is a better than 50/50 chance that the damage will occur.

Total destruction of a business or cases involving a valuation of the entity for dissolution or oppression are the simplest assignments for a business appraiser, and are often performed outside of the litigation process. Calculating lost profits offers a natural extension for business appraisal skills, and is a common method for calculating damages in both contract and tort disputes.

Lost profit damage calculations typically require the appraiser to place the defendant in a "but-for" world. That is, what would the plaintiff have been able to realize in revenues but for the occurrence of the damaging act? The amount of lost profits, therefore, is the then-present value of the difference between the but-for profit or cash flow, and the profit or cash flow that actually existed during the damage period.

Lost profits can be measured as either lost *cash flow* or lost *income*—either measure may be appropriate, depending on the facts and circumstances of the particular case. The decision to use one measure over the other is typically a function of the length of the damage period, and the nature of the cash/non-cash expenses that would have been made throughout the period.

Lost profits may be calculated by use of a *before and after* method, a *yardstick* method, and a *market model* method. Using the before and after method, the damage expert predicts what would have happened during the damage period, based on what the business was able to achieve both before and after the occurrence of the damaging act.

The yardstick method attempts to measure the financial results that the company would have had if the business had followed the trends of comparable data for the damage period. Data can be from industry sources, comparable companies, market data, or any source that could be expected to reasonably predict what the results of the company would have been through the damage period.

Using the market model method, the expert builds a spreadsheet with assumptions about sources of revenues and expenses. These are based on data developed from the company, the industry, and the economy. The assumptions are used to build a cash-flow or income projection of what the company would have done were it not for the damaging act of the defendant.

Often the damages expert will use a combination of methods, and include out-of-pocket costs as well. As with any appraisal, available data will determine what method is selected, using logic to evaluate the case at hand.

Financial damages have a beginning and an end. The terminal point is when the company returns to the profitability or cash flows that would have existed had the damage act not taken place. This is seldom a straightforward determination, and requires an assessment of the industry, the competition in the market, the economy, and other factors. Be cautious not to carry the damage period into perpetuity, and keep the period relevant to the factors that affect the business and the product.

Reality Check The appraiser is retained to calculate lost profits resulting from a breach of contract between a beverage manufacturer and a film studio. The beverage company had contracted for product placement in a high-profile film and had planned a marketing campaign timed to the release of the firm with product tie-ins. The scenes dealing with the beverage wound up on the cutting room floor. As part of your assignment, you are required to opine on the damage period.

Focus on the nature of the product. The life of a film has a number of cycles. The appraiser should calculate not only the initial release, but a re-release if the film receives Oscar nominations, when the film will be available for rental or sale, when the film is debuted on cable, and also when the film is debuted on network television or rerun. Each of these presentations of the film would have presented an opportunity for profits to the beverage company. All such opportunities were lost when the product references were deleted.

CLAIMS FOR EQUITABLE RELIEF

Nonmonetary relief may be pled in place of or as an alternative to monetary damages. The test for equitable relief requires a showing that legal remedies are inadequate (that money alone won't make the plaintiff or petitioner whole).

In both tort and contract cases the primary equitable relief sought will be *injunctive relief*. A petition for temporary injunction asks the court to preserve the status quo until a final hearing can be held resolving the issues, at which time a permanent injunction against the objectionable activity might issue. To obtain a temporary injunction (sometimes referred to as a preliminary injunction), the moving party must demonstrate the lack of an adequate remedy at law and probable success on the merits of the claim. Unavailability of assets to satisfy a damages award does not qualify as an "inadequate remedy at law," but the fact that damages may be difficult or impossible to calculate can be a factor. Therefore, your role as an expert in an action for equitable relief would be to determine whether it is possible to calculate damages to a reasonable certainty.

In contract cases, specific performance is available as a remedy, but it is extraordinary relief granted only under exceptional circumstances. This relief orders the parties to comply with the conditions of the contract (which restores at least the anticipated status quo). In order for specific performance to be granted, the court must find that the contract terms are sufficiently specific, that the requesting party has complied with all conditions precedent, and that enforcement of the contract is both equitable and feasible.

Particular defenses are applicable to requests for specific performance, most notably laches and unclean hands. *Laches* is a doctrine that recognizes that an unreasonable delay in bringing an action in equity can allow the defendant's situation to change to such an extent that detriment could result if the suit were allowed. *Unclean hands* will bar an equitable claim where the moving party's unethical or illegal conduct (directly related to the subject of the suit) precludes relief. Although appraisers can't offer much assistance on unclean hands, they can testify on whether the delay has put the defendant in a position that would not have resulted if the claim were timely made.

Because of the extraordinary nature of equitable relief, the moving party can be required to post a bond that secures the possible damage to the enjoined party, should it be determined that the preliminary relief should not have been granted. As an appraiser, determining the amount of damages if the conduct is restrained is a lost-profits calculation. Imagine, for example, that a business is planning to take a product to market in time for a major buying season—a toy in time for Christmas, or a movie to be released during a peak attendance period. A petitioner who claims title to the invention or the idea would move for injunctive relief to prevent release of the product or film. The defendant has invested thousands or millions on advance marketing, related products, and contract tie-ins, and naturally anticipates profits. The appraiser's job is to opine on the losses if the court orders or enjoins specific activity so that the bond amount can secure the potential loss to the party against whom relief is ordered.

Determining the measure of damages is not the job of the appraiser. It is a legal conclusion that is the province of the attorney. The appraiser can discuss the types of damages that would reasonably flow from the tort or the breach of the contract, the period of time where the damaging activity should affect the business, and the impact of any mitigation undertaken to reduce the amount of loss. Beyond this role, the appraiser risks overstepping and should proceed with caution.

NOTES

1. An excellent book on calculating damages is *Measuring Commercial Damages* by Patrick A. Gaughan, Ph.D. (New York: John Wiley & Sons, 1999).

CHAPTER 3

Discovery Practice

Purpose of This Chapter This is the phase of the litigation that offers the most scope for the appraiser. It is the investigative and fact-finding process that will flesh out the issues argued in the complaint, answer, and affirmative defenses. It provides the methods by which the appraiser can assemble the data needed to perform the assignment, and the appraiser's expertise can—and should—assist counsel in getting the appropriate information about the claims and defenses. This chapter reviews the discovery process and how to get the information needed to pursue or to settle the case.

There are few limits on discoverable material; under the rules of procedure of most jurisdictions, the parties can discover anything relevant to the subject matter of the litigation that is not privileged—and relevance is often broadly defined. The limits that are placed on discovery focus on the privileged material that may have become part of counsel's thought processes and the opinions of experts who are not expected to testify at trial.

Counsel sometimes uses discovery for game playing. Burdensome discovery requests can demoralize a party, drive up costs, and divert attention from other areas. It is never appropriate for the appraiser to engage in this game or to be less than completely forthcoming in discovery. There are serious consequences to expert reputations at stake, and the expert who plays "hide the ball" also risks having his opinion excluded. It is also difficult for the expert to request information from a party and count on a timely response when the expert has delayed providing similar information.

Discovery requests are proper if they can lead to the disclosure of admissible evidence—a standard that is limited if the discovery is shown to be unreasonably cumulative, if the party has already had ample opportunity in the action to obtain discovery on the issue, or if the discovery is unduly burdensome. These limitations were developed in response to discovery abuses. Accordingly, don't participate in "shotgun" approaches to discovery, which could result in the court's imposing limits before discovery on the essential issues has taken place.

Financial information about the business will almost always be relevant to the damage issues. However, courts look with a jaundiced eye at requests for data on a defendant's financial strength. The court may assume that the covert purpose of such discovery is to explore whether an anticipated judgment will be collectible. The expert should help counsel overcome these assumptions by providing tight definitions of the information required and by citing to counsel professional literature and standards that show the necessity for the information.

In recognition that discovery can promote settlement and can reduce costs to the litigants when properly conducted, Federal Rule of Civil Procedure 26 and similar rules of some states provide for the disclosure of certain information before the commencement of formal discovery. This is core information and would undoubtedly be revealed during the formal discovery process. Under Rule 26, formal discovery cannot be commenced until there has been a meeting between counsel, and counsel is required to cooperate on the formulation of a formal discovery plan. This preliminary information will include the following:

- Names and contact information of witnesses who have already been identified
- Copies or descriptions of relevant documents
- Damage computations and their basis
- Insurance agreements that may relate to the claim

TYPES OF DISCOVERY

Discovery is generally divided into written discovery, verbal discovery, and physical discovery. Written discovery includes interrogatories, requests for admissions, and depositions by written questions. The purposes of discovery include the following:

- To obtain information necessary for the prosecution or defense of the claim
- To eliminate issues
- To reduce costs to the parties by establishing as many issues as possible
- To promote settlement

Written Discovery

Interrogatories are written questions, the answers to which are made under oath and signed by a party to the suit. Under the Federal Rules, and now under the Rules of Procedure adopted by many of the states, there are limits on the number of interrogatories that can be propounded without seeking leave of court; these rules were enacted to avoid discovery abuses by overeager counsel. For some types of cases, form interrogatories are sent out first. Interrogatories can be propounded only to parties. Nonparties can be deposed by written questions, which are similar in form to interrogatories.

Role of the Appraiser The appraiser has three main functions with regard to interrogatories. First, the appraiser can assist in drafting interrogatories to define the business issues and information on damages, and to obtain information necessary to perform the valuation. Second, the appraiser can assist in drafting answers to interrogatories that pertain to the valuation, to the operation of the business, or to other elements of damages. Many experts go overboard with this role, and attempt to draft lawyer-like sets of interrogatories or to object when they provide draft responses. Given the lack of legal training common to most appraisers, this mistake can make the appraiser look foolish. Under no circumstances should the appraiser agree to write the answers or propound interrogatories without review of counsel. Attorneys may choose to object to the wording of an interrogatory, or to offer to produce documents in lieu of a lengthy response. These are judgment calls to be made by the lawyers.

The third function of the appraiser in the written discovery process is to review the responses to interrogatories—whether propounded by the party who has retained the appraiser or by another party to the suit. These answers reveal essential information about the case and the theory of the parties in the suit. While counsel, for cost reasons, may choose to be selective in providing these responses to the appraiser, the appraiser should request to see all the information that pertains to the damage issues. If the appraiser is not familiar with this information and is thus unaware of important facts, the valuation opinion may be subject to exclusion.

Requests for admissions are written discovery phrased as yes or no questions. They attempt to lock a party into position on elements of proof or portions of a claim, eliminating issues that require no additional proof. They must be answered with caution, as the rules of procedure of many states impose costs for failure to admit requests that are later proven to be true. The requests are directed at facts or the application of law to facts, but not the ultimate issues in the case (although Federal Rules allow some inquiry into these areas). The party to whom the requests are propounded must state the reason that the request cannot be admitted, and may also object to individual requests.

Role of the Appraiser As with interrogatories, the appraiser lacks the legal training to frame the wording of these questions, which are often a series of statements leading to a legal conclusion but failing to ask for the ultimate admissions of the issue. However, the appraiser can advise on issues which are important to establish to affect the damage issues. Naturally, the appraiser should also be familiar with the responses to the requests.

Verbal Discovery

Verbal discovery consists of depositions. The importance of the expert deposition merits its own chapter. The purposes of deposition include preservation of testimony so that statements are fixed and are therefore less likely to change at trial. If the deponent testifies at trial, the deposition transcript will be used for impeachment of any inconsistent statements made on the witness stand. If the deponent is unavailable for trial (as a result of illness, death, or distance, for example), the deposition testimony can be a substitute for live testimony.

Under special circumstances depositions can be taken before an action is filed, where the party seeking the testimony is unable to cause the action to be brought—in the business context, minority shareholders might avail themselves of this proceeding. At any time, each party can be deposed only once, and the Federal Rules of Procedures and the Rules of Civil Procedure of many states limit the number of witnesses who can be deposed absent leave of court.

Issuance of a notice of deposition is used to schedule depositions. Some witnesses are subpoenaed, which makes their appearance compulsory. Corporations can be subpoenaed for deposition without the naming of an individual to appear. The notice should state the matters on which the organization needs to give evidence, and the business should then produce the individual with the most knowledge on those issues. This can sometimes create confusion where the scope of inquiry at the deposition suggests other areas about which the witness may not be knowledgeable. In that case, should the witness answer, the company will be bound by the testimony even if the deponent was not the corporate representative most knowledgeable about that matter.

To aid in the provision of complete testimony, witnesses can also be required to bring documents to the deposition. The documents subject to discovery at deposition are those that could also be the subject of a request for production of documents.

The expert should insist on reviewing the deposition transcripts of the parties to the case, as well as any depositions where the facts affecting the opinion of value were discussed. For cost reasons, counsel may choose to provide only excerpts of testimony. However, the lawyer won't have the expert training on these issues, so the materials provided may not include essential information that could affect the expert opinion. The appraiser is therefore cautioned against reading only the summaries of the transcripts prepared by counsel or legal staff. Moreover, since the transcript summaries will be part of the expert's file, and may be producible at deposition, the appraiser may be forced to divulge what would otherwise have remained privileged work product.

Role of the Appraiser The appraiser can play a vital role in preparing retaining counsel for depositions. The appraiser may have a better picture of the operation of the business than will counsel, and may (indeed, should!) have a more objective view of the issues than the owner. The appraiser can suggest areas of inquiry—and particularly where there are facts that the appraiser needs in order to prepare the opinion of value, the appraiser should have input into the areas to be covered in the deposition. Management interviews are not always possible when the expert is retained to prepare a report to be used in litigation. The deposition must sometimes substitute for such an interview. In this circumstance, the list of questions that you would customarily ask in such an interview should be provided to counsel.

There is a divergence of opinion on whether the expert should attend such depositions. Where the appraiser intends to testify at trial, it is the opinion of this author that the expert should attend as few depositions as possible. This allows the expert to maintain a nonadvocacy role and to preserve objectivity. If retaining counsel is properly prepared by the expert prior to the deposition, there should be no compelling reason for the expert to be present. The expert's constant presence at deposition can place the retaining counsel in a position of weakness, suggesting that counsel cannot handle issues of this nature without coaching.

Physical Discovery

Physical discovery includes requests for inspection of documents and the inspection of premises. A request for production of documents allows the propounding party to inspect and copy documents, including computerized information.

Role of the Appraiser The request requires that documents be described with sufficient certainty to enable a person of ordinary intelligence to identify them as responsive to the request. Since these documents will involve financial and commercial issues, formulating these descriptions is an ideal role for the appraiser.

Obviously, once the documents are produced, the expert needs access to them so that any documents that could affect opinions can be considered. As with deposition review, cost considerations may cause counsel to limit access to specific documents. Given the quantity of documents that are sometimes supplied, this is reasonable cost containment—as long as the expert provides a detailed description of all categories of documents that should be supplied. Be forewarned, however, that if you are supplied with documents after your opinion has been issued, you must consider whether these documents affect your opinion and change your opinion when new information makes it appropriate.

A request for inspection of the premises allows the expert to visit the business when another party to the litigation controls access. The purpose of a site inspection is to make *visual observations*. Inquiry of employees or other persons on site is beyond the scope of this form of discovery. The expert should take notes during the inspection and determine other areas of inquiry to be explored through written or verbal discovery.

Supplementing and Compelling Discovery

There is an obligation to provide supplemental information obtained after discovery responses have been given if the information relates to the scope of the discovery that has been propounded. When additional information comes to the attention of the expert, you should notify retaining counsel and provide the details necessary for counsel to supplement the responses. Failure of a party to provide this information may result in the additional data being inadmissible at trial.

When assisting with discovery, play close attention to time limits established by the Rules of Civil Procedure (generally the first page of the discovery will reference either the applicable time limits or the section of the Rules containing those time limits). With requests for admissions, for example, the failure to provide timely responses can result in the requests being deemed admitted.

Counsel may raise objections to requested discovery for a variety of reasons, including clarity of the request, the propriety of the scope, and whether the request will require the production of privileged information. These objections can be resolved by the court before the information is required to be provided. A party may bring a *motion for protective order*, which asks the court to preclude discovery on particular issues that might be extremely intrusive or burdensome. A party seeking discovery can bring a *motion to compel discovery*. This will place the opposing party under court order to provide the necessary information, and subject the party to court-imposed sanctions if the information is not provided.

Role of the Appraiser The expert will require a minimum quantity of information in order to produce a reliable opinion. By educating counsel on the standards and professional requirements, you can provide compelling ammunition for the court that will give valid reasons to require discovery.

Standards promulgated by the major appraisal organizations provide that the appraiser's access to necessary information cannot be restricted. For example, Institute of Business Appraisers' (IBA) Standard 1.15 provides:

> 1.15 *Access to Requisite Data.* The business appraiser *must* decide what documents and/or information are requisite to a competent appraisal.

***

> (c) Essential Data. When the business appraiser is denied access to data considered essential to a proper appraisal, the business appraiser should not proceed with the assignment.

The American Society of Appraisers Business Appraisal Standards list the essential information:

III. Information Collection and Analysis
The appraiser shall gather, analyze, and adjust relevant information to perform the valuation as appropriate to the scope of work. Such information shall include the following:
A. Characteristics of the business, business ownership or security to be valued including rights, privileges and conditions, quantity, factors affecting control and agreements restricting sale or transfer.
B. Nature, history and outlook of the business.
C. Historical financial information for the business.
D. Assets and liabilities of the business.
E. Nature and conditions of the relevant industries which have an impact on the business.
F. Economic factors affecting the business.
G. Capital markets providing relevant information, e.g., available rates of return on alternative investments, relevant public stock transactions, and relevant mergers and acquisitions.
H. Prior transactions involving subject business, interest in the subject business, or its securities.
I. Other information deemed by the appraiser to be relevant.

If retaining counsel brings a *motion to compel* based on such professional standards, a court denying the motion would, in effect, be requiring the expert to deviate from the applicable standard of care.

PRIVILEGE ISSUES IN DISCOVERY

Privileged material is excluded from disclosure through discovery except in limited circumstances. The most frequent exception to discovery in commercial damage cases is the work product privilege. Particularly as to disclosures made in anticipation of litigation, the courts will protect this information, even if the disclosure to counsel is made when no suit is pending.

The work product privilege has only limited application to experts. Materials prepared and information developed by an expert at the direction of a party or the party's counsel are subject to discovery when the requesting party can demonstrate a substantial need, and an inability to obtain equivalent material by other means. The cost of obtaining this information is generally not a sufficient hardship.

An expert who performs analysis but who is not anticipated to give testimony at trial will not be required to provide discovery. Some states take the position that even the identity of nontestifying experts is not subject to disclosure. Once the expert is designated as a witness, however, the information that forms the basis of the opinions is subject to discovery. This disclosure requirement provides the necessary information for other parties and the court to determine the credibility of the opinion. Materials provided to the expert by counsel that contain counsel's mental impressions are entitled to protection in order to protect the adversary process. You must take special care to make certain that this information is not inadvertently disclosed, which could result in a waiver of the privilege.

The work product privilege is not identical to the attorney–client privilege. This privilege, which is generally defined in the rules of civil procedure and interpreted by case law, recognizes that full and frank disclosure is necessary to counsel in order to allow counsel to represent the client. Counsel would not be subject to deposition or other discovery, and the attorney–client privilege can only be waived by the client or when the attorney must disclose information in order to defend a suit brought against counsel by the client. There is no recognized expert–client privilege, and the expert should be prepared to provide all details of conversations with all persons other than counsel. This can present tremendous problems when the party retaining the expert is not accurately reporting the business income. You, as the expert, need to remember that the decision to underreport income was made by the party in the exercise of free will and that you are under no obligation to assist in this concealment. To the contrary, you are under a serious professional obligation to avoid participation in the client's illegal or improper activities.

When it has become obvious to you that the party who has retained you is concealing information, you have an obligation to advise counsel that the information on the business is not accurate and cannot be relied upon. This will enable counsel to attempt to settle the case and advise the client of his or her risks. At this point, you should insist that you be provided with reliable information. If this information cannot be provided, you as appraiser must be prepared to admit that the financial data are not accurate. Under no circumstances should you acquiesce to an instruction from counsel to use those numbers as reliable without a disclosure that they are not entitled to credibility. Agreeing to such tactics is the fastest way to get yourself labeled as a whore.

PART TWO

Preparing for Litigation Support Practice

CHAPTER 4

Education and Qualifications for the Testifying Appraiser

Purpose of This Chapter One of the first questions you will be asked on the witness stand is whether you are an expert in the area in which you intend to render an opinion. If the court does not agree that you are an expert, it's all over. Getting the right education and credentials to do this work does more than get your testimony admitted—it teaches you how to do the work in a way that provides real value to the client and protects you against malpractice. This chapter looks at the background education and training that are needed for litigation support in business damage cases.

Business appraisers can have a range of backgrounds, including accounting, academic, brokerage, and consulting experience. However, when hiring a business appraiser, it is vital that counsel concentrates on the qualifications, training, and experience of the business appraiser in *business appraisal*. When counsel retains experts, they are taught that detailed inquiry must be made into the following:

- *The efforts made by the appraiser to gain formal training into the theory and application of business appraisal methodology.* Continuing education would be included in the evaluation.

- *The number of reports that have been prepared by the appraiser.* Although not every assignment calls for the preparation of a written report, formal work product is a palpable demonstration of competence and a forecast of the appraiser's ability to present a credible and organized conclusion.
- *The appraiser's knowledge in the subject business's industry.* Regulatory, statutory, and geographic factors can dramatically affect business values, and the appraiser must have sufficient expertise to identify these factors and apply appropriate adjustments to value. However, be cautious with the business appraiser whose background is extensive within one industry if his main qualification is as an owner or CEO of a business within the industry. The professional may perform appraisals by substituting his or her own judgment for those of the owners, and lack the needed objectivity.
- *Whether the appraiser relies on "canned" business appraisal software or software personally developed by the appraiser.*[1] Although some of the appraisal software commercially available is of high quality, some programs lack documentation that enables it to be manipulated at the discretion of the user. Appraisers who rely on canned software may substitute the programmer's judgment for their own, or might use a cookie-cutter approach to business appraisal. This costs such appraisers credibility in court. Business appraisers who have developed their own appraisal software present different problems for counsel. Unless appraisers are willing to divulge all the details of such software (and even provide a copy to the opposing appraiser), the valuation conclusions may not be sufficiently replicable to pass scrutiny under professional standards governing business appraisal.[2] The appraiser should always do more work than the computer!
- *The professional standards applied by the business appraiser.* Some appraisers apply different standards for *advocacy appraisals*—that is, appraisals intended for use in litigation. The use of such differing standards is not appropriate. The expert should employ the same methods and standards regardless of whether the opinion is intended for courtroom presentation.[3]

PROFESSIONAL CERTIFICATIONS AND THE
CASE FOR PEER REVIEW

Some experts will list membership in professional organizations on their curriculum vitae and argue that membership alone should weigh toward their being qualified to give expert testimony. Be realistic—your pet could join any organization simply by sending in a membership fee. Being on the roster of the organization cannot compare to being accredited by the organization. If you give testimony and do not have accreditation from the organizations to which you belong or are not in the accreditation process for those organizations, you'll need to come up with a good reason.

Whatever the background of the business appraiser, the appraiser should possess or be working toward the professional certifications available. Business appraisal designations are available to all appraisers, and counsel will note the substantial differences among these designations. Each organization offering professional accreditation has merit, as does each credential. However, it would be a disservice to appraisers to pretend that all these designations are equal. The marketplace will not perceive them that way. To determine which credentials are given the most weight, do not rely on the organizations to blow their own horns. Just look at your bookshelf. Who wrote the books considered authoritative in the profession, and what credentials are held by the writers? Work toward making the initials after your name the same as theirs.

Most important among these designations is the availability of peer review. It is possible that a business appraiser may possess a professional designation without authoring a single report in an actual client assignment. It is equally possible that, even though the appraiser demonstrates "significant involvement" with appraisal assignments as part of earning the appraisal designation, each one of those business appraisals has been performed using flawed methodology. For these reasons, designations that involve peer review offer some assurance that the business appraiser's work product has passed juried scrutiny, rather than that the appraiser is a good test taker with a grasp of methodology but no skill or experience in its application.[4]

It is also a mistake for the appraiser to rely on a single membership organization for services, education and credentialing. To do so risks the expert being labeled a company man whose approach can be dictated more by the policies (or the products) of a professional society rather than the techniques and standards that prevail throughout the industry. The wise appraiser will have memberships in more than one organization. Whenever possible, the appraiser should be cross-certified, and one of these designations should be a peer-reviewed designation.

Each organization will claim that their designations are "peer review" designations. However, the true peer-reviewed designations are those for which the expert produces original work product (not work that is from a developed set of facts designed with red herrings for the issue-spotting of the graders), and the applicant should receive a detailed critique of the work. Without a process that provides specifics on the applicant's shortcomings, the applicant cannot use the opportunity to improve the quality of the work product. A pass/fail peer review teaches nothing and is not entitled to the same credibility as a process that aims to teach and improve the applicants.

Several organizations now offer designations in litigation support or forensic issues. There is a divergence of opinion on the value of these designations. Some practitioners view them as marketing tools to allow them to represent themselves as having training specific to litigation assignments. To credibly make this claim, be sure the litigation designation involves the aspects of litigation in which you will be testifying. Some designations are described by their sponsoring organizations as litigation or forensic designations, when they are merely additional professional education on appraisal. Although these courses may make applicants better appraisers, they don't qualify them for any additional designations in litigation support.

Members of the legal profession should be involved in the preparation of courses for the litigation setting, and they should demonstrate how the skills should be applied. Courses that focus on communication skills on the witness stand miss the point. What needs to be learned in the litigation context is what the lawyers are doing, how the expert can help, and when the expert should stay out of the way. If you take litigation-oriented education that suggests that you should be an advocate for anything other than your opinion, shift into reverse and keep going. Shading the truth or performing results-oriented work is not the way to make your way as a litigation support professional.

If you decide to seek a litigation support designation, be aware that some people may view you as having training to be a "hired gun." Get the training, by all means, if it will fill in the gaps in your education and make you a better expert. But consider the training as valuable for its own sake and not because it will provide more initials to follow your name. If you decide to obtain and use the designation, pay careful attention to your description of the training and how these credentials compare to those of other practitioners. Your own statements may give rise to client expectations, which could increase your liability.[5]

COMPARISON OF BACKGROUNDS OF BUSINESS APPRAISERS

Part of the job of the litigation support professional is viewing the experts retained by other parties and advising counsel on the strength of their qualifications or backgrounds. Retaining counsel will use this information in deposition or in a *Daubert* challenge that may seek to exclude the expert's testimony at trial. As you read this chapter bear in mind that it is not just the opinion of these authors; this is the prevailing wisdom in the legal community.

The Accountant as Business Appraiser

Although there are peculiar advantages to hiring someone with specific training in financial statement review as an appraiser, it is important to note that not all accountants—or even all CPAs—are created equal, nor are they equally qualified. There are approximately 330,000 Certified Public Accountants in the United States. Of this number, fewer than 2,000 have earned the Accredited in Business Valuation (ABV) accreditation awarded by the American Institute of Certified Public Accountants. It defies logic to assume that the remaining 329,000 CPAs are as qualified as these CPA/ABVs, who have passed a rigorous comprehensive examination and demonstrated substantial involvement in a number of appraisal assignments.

There are several *advantages* to hiring an accountant as business appraiser:

- The accountant's typical client list generally has a number of businesses whose financial statements are reviewed on a regular basis. Where the client list contains similar businesses, the accountant may have accumulated industry expertise. For example, in *Rossi v. Mobil Oil Corp.*,[6] the appellate court upheld the trial court's admission of expert testimony on profitability figures offered by the bookkeeper for the motor gasoline retailer. The bookkeeper's client list included 200 service stations, which was a factor in the determination that he was "skilled" in the area.
- Accountants are involved full-time with numbers, balance sheets, profit and loss statements, tax laws, and financial planning.
- Resources on the topic from membership organizations such as the AICPA provide excellent practice guides and outstanding education and professional conferences.

There are also several *disadvantages* to hiring the accountant as business appraiser:

- The accountant with a general practice is likely to spend only a small percentage of time on business appraisal (a possible qualifications issue in court). An interesting contrast to the holding in *Rossi, supra,* is the opinion of the Fourth Circuit in *Maher v. Continental Casualty Co.*[7] In that case, the appellate court upheld the trial court's *exclusion* of the insured's expert on lost profits. Although he was skilled in analyzing financial statements, and submitted three years of historical sales figures,[8] the expert was not an economist or otherwise versed in economic forecasting. The testimony was found to lack credibility.
- The nature of accounting training discourages the kind of subjective, "outside the box" thinking that may be required to complete many business appraisal assignments, and that may dissuade the accountant appraiser from applying some

of the common business appraisal approaches. In cases where something beyond a discounted cash flow analysis may be called for, the accountant may have to step beyond his developed instincts. Very few business appraisals can be performed within Generally Accepted Accounting Principles.

- The accountant might be currently involved with the subject business. While economy and familiarity with the business might argue in favor of retaining the business' regular accountant to perform the appraisal, business appraisal standards could be construed to define the accountant's continued relationship with the client as "a contemplated future benefit," which might disqualify the appraisal opinion. A second reason against the use of the business's regular accountant in the role of business appraiser arises when the appraisal involves the interests of parties that, though joint when the accounting work was performed, may, for the purposes of the business appraisal, now be adverse.

Reality Check The accountant who has compiled the financial statements and prepared the tax returns for a corporation that is now the subject of a shareholder oppression action is asked to perform a business appraisal for use in the litigation. Representing the minority shareholder, the business appraiser would scrutinize the corporate financial statements, and might recast expenses charged to the business (such as travel, promotion, and entertainment expenses) as income that should be imputed to the shareholders—and in such a situation, it is likely that the majority shareholders would have more income imputed to them. In effect, the accountant (now the business appraiser) is admitting that the business was run in a fashion that has disadvantaged the minority owner, and that the accountant failed to call this out in the annual financial statements. The clear impression is that the accountant will cast the financial statements in favor of whomever is cutting the check for services.

Another troublesome scenario arises when the accountant prepares not only the tax returns for the business, but also the personal returns of one or more of the business's officers, or of both the husband and wife. When a married business officer separates and the accountant is asked to serve as business appraiser for only one spouse, the question of divided loyalties must inevitably arise. It is also likely that the accountant knows where too many skeletons are buried in both the business and personal financial profiles to be truly objective in the appraisal assignment.

Accountants should not perform litigation appraisal work for clients whose tax work has been done by the same firm. Although it is not a conflict recognized by the accounting profession, it may well be a conflict that will bar the testimony in court. Even if the testimony is admitted, the accountant will often be put in a position of defending the tax work, or explaining the difference between the adjustments made to the financials in connection with the appraisal assignment and the tax returns filed with the IRS.

Adhering to this principle may cost accountants work. That's unfortunate, but necessary. Consider a formal arrangement with another firm in your area to refer out tax work for appraisal clients or appraisal work for tax clients, and include in the agreement that the referred firm will decline other work for the client if asked. In the final analysis, it is better to let some work go than risk your professional reputation by trying to serve too many masters.

The Broker as Business Appraiser

If the business has been recently offered for sale, a broker may already be involved, and the client may be interested in using the broker as the business appraiser. Brokers in the community may offer appraisal services as an outgrowth of their practice (growing tired of being asked to "just give a number" and developing a fee for doing so). Many brokers who perform business appraisal have substantial experience and additional training. They earn professional accreditation in business appraisal; however, many have no formal training and a "shoot from the hip" approach may not match the assignment.

There are *advantages* to hiring the broker as business appraiser:

- The broker may have a "nose" for discerning the actual earnings of the business (as contrasted with the reported earnings). In many closely held businesses that depend on cash payments—including restaurants, retail stores, service businesses such as auto repair shops, and even professional practices where some patients pay in cash—the reported income can have only a tangential relation to the actual revenues of the business. By spotting those issues early, counsel can evaluate not only the real value of the business, but the ramifications of going forward with a valuation when the client may not have reported (and paid taxes) on all the income.

- Because brokers are versed in talking to potential buyers and business owners, the brokers may be able to communicate more easily with the trier of fact, or with the client who has no in-depth knowledge of business appraisal terminology.
- Brokers deal in the world of *comparables*—similar sales—and may have a ready source of information for the application of the market approach.

There are *disadvantages* to hiring the broker as business appraiser as well:

- Many business brokers have a practice that includes business brokerage as part of a larger real estate brokerage practice, and business sales may not be the majority of their traffic. Not only may their expertise in business sales be limited, but the broker who does mostly real estate sales or appraisals may not properly apply the market approach.
- Unless the broker has made a concerted effort to become educated by taking courses from the International Business Brokers Association, the American Society of Appraisers, or the Institute of Business Appraisers, the broker may have little formal training in the review and adjustment of financial statements or other issues beyond the normal experience of business brokerage. This places the opinion at risk for errors, and means the expert may not be able to credibly replicate the appraisal process for the trier of fact. Even if the broker performs a good appraisal using the market approach, without formal training the broker will not be able to determine the credibility of an appraisal that includes applications of the income approach.
- If the broker is—or has been—involved in listing the busi-

ness, or hopes to list the business in the future, there is a conflict of interest that may discredit or disqualify the valuation conclusion.

- If the broker is relying primarily on personal experience rather than objective data sources or applied theory in performing the business appraisal, the opinion of value may not have an adequate foundation. Unless the broker sells a substantial number of businesses of the type being appraised, the broker may substitute listing prices rather than selling prices as an indicator of value of the business as the only means of having sufficient data for analysis.

The Academic as Business Appraiser

Universities with schools of business, economics, or finance may have Ph.D.s or other faculty members who perform business appraisals in addition to their academic load. These academics may have backgrounds that include statistics or a focus on a particular industry that will suit the appraisal assignment. Even a small, local college may have adjunct faculty members for whom teaching is a fragment of time from a day-to-day practice that includes financial, appraisal, and consulting services.

There are *advantages* to hiring the academic as business appraiser:

- The academic may be published on business appraisal issues, or may have performed academic studies in the particular industry that includes the subject business. This enhances the credibility of the academic expert.
- The academic will typically have resources readily available for research and analysis and will use a systematic and thorough approach that can result in a more timely and even more cost-effective work product. He will be exposed to the latest writings on the topic and may have more time for following trends in the development of appraisal methodology.
- Some academics (and not only those who are adjunct faculty members) perform "real-world" business consulting assign-

ments as part of their academic role. For example, if the university has a Small Business Development Center, the academic may have daily interaction with business start-ups and acquisitions as an SBDC counselor. Many graduate schools reach out to the local business community and offer continuing education to established professionals, or targeted education to the lending industry or other professional groups. These real-life interactions can produce an expert who is simultaneously versed in the latest theory and grounded in the pragmatic world of business.

- The teaching role naturally assumed by most academics can lend itself well to an effective jury or bench presentation.

There are *disadvantages* to hiring the academic as business appraiser as well:

- The academic can be well-versed in theory but have little practical experience in its application. This may be particularly true of the career academic, who may have impressive credentials and a long list of writing credits but who may never have actually completed an appraisal assignment.
- Academic appraisers may have natural teaching abilities that *should* enable them, as expert witnesses, to effectively and credibly communicate to the trier of fact. However, academics may not possess the necessary translation ability to make needed points in simple terms. Even an undergraduate business student will have a grasp of the terms of art far above the technical vocabulary of many jurors. Unless the academic can abandon jargon to state facts and opinions in ordinary English (and without giving the impression that the testimony is "dumbed down" for the audience), little will be gained from the impressive credentials of the expert.
- If the academic appraiser goes through life steeped in academia, there may be a tendency to apply radical or cutting-edge methodology rather than tried and true business appraisal approaches with which the court has some comfort factor. Developing theories may merit close monitoring and may eventually be adopted into the conventional body of

knowledge, but those who pioneer those methods in court without considering established approaches put the client at risk.

Case law provides ample illustration of experts who have ranged beyond their true fields of expertise. Without applicable and relevant credentials, there's little guarantee that the opinion will be admitted into evidence. For example, the opinion of the Third Circuit in *In re: Unisys Savings Plan Litigation*[9] illustrates the pitfalls of unwise appraiser selection. In an action brought by Unisys employees who participated in individual account pension plans maintained by employer, the trial court excluded the testimony of plaintiff's expert witness. The appellate court held that the witness was properly excluded. In its rationale, the court cited the criteria *In re: Paoli R.R. Yard Litigation*.[10] The court must find that the witness must be qualified to opine, that testimony of the expert will be reliable, and the testimony will assist the trier of fact. The *Unisys* court applied this "fit" test to the credibility of the expert and decided that this witness's testimony did not fit for the following reasons:

1. *The "education credentials were not of the highest caliber."* The expert witness in *Unisys* received his Ph.D. from a correspondence school. Some professional designations available to business appraisers are awarded based, in whole or in part, upon take-home exams, which don't appreciably differ from a correspondence course.
2. *The witness's credential statements during voir dire were not consistent with prior deposition testimony.*
3. *The witness's expertise was in a related but not identical field.* Life insurance was the subject of the proffered testimony, but the witness's expertise was in property casualty insurance. Further, "substantial" differences between the two were admitted by the witness.

Industry specialists are particularly vulnerable on this issue. Often, the desire to continue to build an appraisal practice will tempt the industry specialist or general consultant to accept assignments beyond their expertise. Consider, for example, the dental industry specialist (whose credentials may be mainly a life career as a dentist) who appraises the practice of an orthopedic surgeon. A similar pitfall awaits the accountant with no formal business appraisal training, as any reasonable accountant would admit that not all accounting work involves appraisal. The broker who does few business appraisals is also at risk, as any reasonable broker should admit "substantial" differences between brokerage and appraisals. The academic economist, statistician or analyst may fare no better than these in the "substantial differences" arena.

These "substantial differences" can even exist within a particular industry. Much has been written, for example, on the differences between publicly traded companies of moderate size and smaller-size, privately held businesses within the same industry. For example, in *Trustees of the University of Pennsylvania v. Lexington Insurance Co.*,[11] the appellate court upheld the trial court's disqualification of a claims examiner who offered expert testimony on the reasonableness of a $7 million settlement in a medical malpractice action. The court found that the witness had several years' experience as a claims adjuster, but insufficient experience in claims of this magnitude.

The diverse backgrounds of business appraisers all have merits and demerits. Often, these qualities are not apparent until too late in the appraisal process. For these reasons, there is no real substitute for professional certification, and particularly those certifications that include peer review. Be honest with yourself about your qualifications and your core competencies. If you do not have sufficient experience and training, get the needed education before you begin marketing your services. Associate with an organization that can provide technical support and peer review. Several of the organizations provide mentoring as a cost of the accreditation process, or technical support for appraisal issues as a benefit of membership.

Be honest with retaining counsel and with clients about your background and experience. Everyone has a first time. Don't paint your designations to be what they are not—it is too easy to be unmasked. Rather, put yourself in a position to be accurately represented as someone who is continuing the necessary education and training to constantly improve your work product. If you have made professional development a priority, you will have more credibility even if you have not yet achieved all your professional goals.

NOTES

1. A distinction must be made between software written specifically for the performance of business appraisals and common spreadsheet software, such as Lotus and Excel. Spreadsheets, statistical software and graphics programs are a normal and appropriate tool for organization and evaluation of financial data, although their utility, like that of business appraisal software, depends on the skill of the user.

2. See the discussion of the Appraisal Standards Board's Advisory Opinion on the use of Automated Valuation Modules [AVM's] in Chapter 14, *Admissibility of Expert Testimony and Valuation Reports.*

3. See *Kumho Tire Co., Ltd. v. Patrick Carmichael,* 119 S.Ct. 1167, 1178 (1999).

4. While "peer review" services may be offered by organizations as part of seminars or separate consulting services, these services are not a substitute for peer reviews that are part of the accreditation process. Seminar peer reviews do not involve in-depth review of the work product of each participant. Consulting peer reviews are heavily dependent on the skill of the reviewer, and training may not be consistent. A consulting peer review will rarely offer the appraiser the opportunity to correct the noted errors and solicit additional feedback. For those reasons, tightly controlled accreditation peer reviews are better demonstrations of the professional competence of the appraiser. It is also important to define peer review as more than a pass/fail of a report. A real peer review will provide detailed feedback of the work product, pointing out differences of opinion that may result in rejecting the report, as well as any problems that would make the report fatally flawed.

5. In *Mattco Forge v. Arthur Young & Co.,* 6 Cal. Rptr. 781 (Cal. App. 2d Dist. 1992), an accounting firm offering litigation support services was the target of a malpractice suit. In defining the standard to which the firm should be held, the court emphasized that the firm's marketing materials touted the firm's expertise in litigation support. This led to client expectations that particular care would be paid to issues, such as privilege and chain of custody of documents, which were particular to litigation assignments.

6. *Rossi v. Mobil Oil Corp.*, 710 F.2d 821, 830 (Temp. Ct. App. 1983).
7. *Maher v. Continental Sualty Co.*, 76 F.3d 535 (4th Cir. 1996).
8. The court described the three-year term of profit history as unsatisfactory and "relatively brief," *Maher,* 76 F.3d 541. In many assignments involving closely held business, even less historical data may be available, given the ad hoc nature of many business records.
9. *In re: Unisys Savings Plan Litigation,* 173 F.3d 145 (3rd Cir. 1999).
10. *In re: Paoli R.R. Yard Litigation,* 35 F.3d 171 (3rd Cir. 1994); *appeal after remand,* 113 F.3d 444 (3d Cir. 1997).
11. *Trustees of the University of Pennsylvania v. Lexington Insurance Co.,* 815 F.2d 890 (3rd Cir. 1987).

CHAPTER 5

The Essential Library for the Testifying Appraiser

Purpose of This Chapter You can't do a good job without the right tools. This chapter details the books, journals, and other tools that, at a minimum, should be in your appraisal library.

BOOKS ON THE REQUIRED READING LIST

This book does not attempt to teach the expert how to be an appraiser or how to calculate economic damages. But there are many books that do attempt that task and do an outstanding job. Many of these books have risen to the status of *treatises,* authoritative works on the subject. At trial, the attorneys will attempt to discredit your testimony by impeaching with treatises. The attorney will approach you with book in hand and ask you to demonstrate how your work conforms with methodology accepted throughout the profession. Therefore, if you don't want to look like an idiot, you need to know what is in these books.

> *Basic Business Appraisal,* by Raymond C. Miles,[1] published by IBA Press.
> *Business Reference Guide,* by Thomas L. West, published by Business Brokerage Press.

Business Valuation Body of Knowledge, by Shannon P. Pratt, published by John Wiley & Sons.

Lawyer's Business Valuation Handbook, by Shannon P. Pratt,[2] published by the American Bar Association.

Guide to Business Valuations, by Jay E. Fishman, Shannon P. Pratt, J. Clifford Griffith, and D. Keith Wilson, published by Practitioner's Publishing Company.

Handbook of Advanced Business Valuation, by Robert F. Reilly and Robert P. Schweihs, published by John Wiley & Sons.

Handbook of Business Valuation, by Thomas L. West and Jeffrey D. Jones, published by John Wiley & Sons.

How to Use the IBA Market Database, by Raymond C. Miles, published by IBA Press.

Law Dictionary for Nonlawyers, by Daniel Oran, published by West Legal Studies.

Quantifying Marketability Discounts, by Z. Christopher Mercer, published by Peabody Publishing.

Understanding Business Valuation, by Gary Trugman, published by the American Institute of Certified Public Accountants.

Valuing Small Businesses and Professional Practices, by Shannon P. Pratt, Robert F. Reilly, and Robert P. Schweihs, published by John Wiley & Sons.

Valuing a Business: The Analysis and Appraisal of Closely Held Companies, by Shannon P. Pratt, Robert F. Reilly, and Robert P. Schweihs, published by John Wiley & Sons.

TECHNICAL JOURNALS AND OTHER SOURCES

Technical journals address not only the cutting edge methodologies, but also discuss tried-and-true methods, often in a new light. The distinction must be made between technical journals, which are edited with processes that can approach academic-level peer review, and periodicals that assist in keeping up with industry news or developments within the sponsoring professional organizations. Although both have value, only technical journals should be used for information on what is state of the art.

Business Appraisal Practice, technical journal of the Institute of Business Appraisers

Business Valuation Review, technical journal of the American Society of Appraisers Business Valuation Committee
Valuation Strategies, published by RIA Group

Industry publications provide more than information about organizations and case law summaries. They often feature articles on valuation of particular business types or computation of damages. These articles are authored by guest contributors, and when one of these authors is retained by another party in litigation where you are also retained, the articles may contain prior inconsistent statements that can be of use when retaining counsel is preparing for cross-examination.

Shannon Pratt's *Business Valuation Update,* published by Business Valuation Resources, LLC
The Valuation Examiner, published by the National Association of Certified Valuation Analysts

Databases provide real-world evidence of business value. Do not make the mistake of using only one database. The assignment should dictate the most appropriate data, and the expert is always better served by consulting more than one source. Likewise, do not combine data from these sources into your spreadsheets; the data points do not have identical definitions from one database to another, and there may be duplicate transactions.

Bizcomps (*www.bizcomps.com*)
Done Deals (*www.donedeals.com*)
IBA Market Database (*www.instbusapp.org*)
Pratt's Stats (*www.brmarketdata.com*)

PROFESSIONAL STANDARDS[3]

Your library should include copies of the standards of all organizations that regulate the profession, not merely the standards of the organizations to which you belong. The standards enacted represent the professional requirements of the profession. For the same reason, you should also be familiar with the Uniform Standards of Professional Appraisal Practice (USPAP), even if the organizations in which you have membership don't require that you perform assignments in compliance with USPAP.

You are also responsible for knowing the requirements for the designations that might be possessed by experts hired by other parties. Take note that the requirements for designations are revised annually, and that current information can be obtained from each organization.

NOTES

1. Several chapters of books for attorneys on trial techniques suggest that requiring the appraisal expert to correctly identify Raymond C. Miles and Shannon Pratt should be part of the challenge to the qualifications of every expert.
2. This book, published by the American Bar Association, is what attorneys are being taught about business appraisal. Some of the material in this book was contributed by Michele Miles.
3. The professional standards of the American Institute of Certified Public Accountants, the American Society of Appraisers, the Institute of Business Appraisers, and the National Association of Certified Valuation Analysts are included in Appendix B.

CHAPTER 6

Engagement Letters for Litigation Support Assignments

Purpose of This Chapter Litigation appraisal assignments often rise and fall under the terms of the engagement letter. This chapter will discuss some essentials to be considered when drawing up your contract for services, the options available, and how they may affect the performance of the assignments.

In any appraisal assignment, an engagement letter serves a number of purposes:

- Defining the relationship between the parties
- Detailing the tasks to be undertaken by appraiser and client
- Clarifying payment schedules and rates
- Fixing the interest to be valued
- Putting the attorney on notice of your understanding of the assignment

In the litigation support context, particular attention should be paid in the engagement letter to the timing of litigation, the additional work often demanded of the appraiser on short notice, and the fact that the appraiser often cannot control the production dead-lines. Each of these should be addressed by clauses in the engagement letter.

USING COUNSEL TO PREPARE ENGAGEMENT LETTERS

Although there are many good examples of engagement letters in books on business appraisal, management of accounting practices, and legal form books, I recommend having an engagement letter prepared by your own counsel. There are several reasons for this. First, the lawyer is specially trained in the nuances of contracts, whereas the appraiser's experience will be superficial, or based on limited personal experiences. You would be reluctant to let your attorney prepare a business appraisal, even if there were excellent forms available. Don't assume you know all there is to know about contracts.

Second, there is more to contracts than their drafting—contract enforcement and interpretation is developed through the court decisions of your particular state. It is counsel's job to keep abreast of these developments. Your contract should be reviewed annually with counsel to make any needed changes as a result of case law developments or changes in your practice or client base.

Third, your counsel has probably seen more engagement letters than you have. Lawyers can be a valuable source of information on how other experts are defining relationships with counsel and client, setting fees and timing of payments. And, since your attorney has probably seen some that have failed to protect the appraiser, you have a chance to learn from the mistakes of others.

Finally, your using counsel for legal work establishes a legal duty to you from counsel—should the contract work be negligently performed, you can have recourse against counsel. Better to seek damages if your contract fails adequately to protect your interests than to have only yourself to blame!

The phrase *your own counsel* means exactly that—do not use the counsel for the owner for this work—seek out and retain experienced counsel of your own. Only when you are represented by a lawyer without conflicts in the assignment can you rely on the work product.

ESSENTIAL CLAUSES FOR ENGAGEMENT LETTERS[1]

Identity of Client

Rules governing privilege in your practice area may dictate whether the client should be defined as counsel or the owner of the business interest. The retainer letter should also clearly define which individual—counsel or owner—will ultimately be responsible for paying the appraiser. Don't assume that the counsel for the owner will champion your cause for payment, particularly if the counsel is also waiting for payment!

Scope of Work

This clause should contain an unambiguous definition of the nature of the engagement, and what can—and cannot—be concluded from the work defined. At a minimum, this should include the following:

- The business interest to be appraised
- The standard of value
- The date of valuation
- Purpose of the valuation
- Any limitations in scope of the assignment
- The format and extent of the report

Business owner and counsel will often assume that tasks beyond valuation will be included for the retainer fee. It must be clearly stated that forensic accounting, discovery of employee defalcation, or advice on increasing shareholder value will not be included unless specifically set forth. Equally important is to state whether testimony or assistance with discovery are included in the retainer fee—or if (as is generally the better practice) they are to be billed at a separate hourly rate.

> **Example:** Appraiser agrees to perform an appraisal rendering an opinion of the fair market value of a 100% interest in the
>
> (*continued*)

business known as the Acme Novelty Company, as of December 1, 1997. The valuation report will be used only for presentation in the litigation known as Case No. 99-1874.

Intended Audience for the Report

If one of the purposes of an engagement letter is to establish a legal duty running from the appraiser to the client, it is vital to define those who are going to receive the report, and the reliance they are entitled to place upon it. In the litigation support context, this clause recognizes that—either for cost considerations or ignorance of counsel or the parties—an appraisal report prepared for one purpose may end up in court offered for another. Where the standard of value or date of valuation may not be appropriate to the context, the appraiser can face liability for the unanticipated use.

Ongoing developments in the law of professional negligence should be monitored by the appraiser's personal counsel. Privity of contract has become key to potential liability in this area, so identifying the intended audience for the report is an important risk management tool. The *economic loss doctrine* is one of the limitations on the liability of service providers such as accountants, attorneys, and design professionals. In its essentials, the doctrine provides that unless the party seeking relief is in direct privity of contract with the service provider, there can be no recovery for purely monetary damages. However, "intended third party beneficiaries" may be able to recover against professionals in a negligence action. Defining who is intended to benefit by reading the report can help control this liability.

Example: Owner agrees not to copy or reproduce the report or any part of it in any manner, or to disclose any information contained in the report to any person not named in this Agreement without the express, written consent of Appraiser, or to use the report for any purpose other than that which is stated in this

Agreement. If Owner reproduces or copies any portion of the report or discloses anything contained in the report to any person, or attempts to use the report for any purpose other than that which is stated in this Agreement, Owner agrees to save, defend, hold harmless, and indemnify Appraiser from any damages, costs, or legal fees for which Appraiser may become liable as a result of Owner's reproduction or disclosure of the report.

This clause can attempt to assign the duty to defend and indemnify the appraiser if the report is used for another purpose, but its limitations include limitations on the pocket of the party making the disclosure. Many appraisers have begun to include a *shrinkwrap* clause as part of their reports. Similar to the licensing agreements included with commercially available software, the clause requires the report user to accept its conditions prior to reading the report.

Appraiser's and Client's Roles

Define the responsibilities of the client to supply documentation and other data that will form part of the basis of the valuation opinion.

The appraiser may opt to include a list of documents to be provided by the client as an appendix to the agreement,[2] and should set out the time frame in which they should be provided. The agreement should make plain that any delays in providing needed information will result in a delay in issuing of the report.

Example: Owner is required to provide the financial data set forth on the financial checklist appended to this Agreement. Appraiser is entitled to rely on the accuracy and authenticity of all information provided by Owner, without independent investigation or verification. If any of this information later proves to

(continued)

be inaccurate, incomplete, negligently prepared, or misleading, Owner hereby waives all rights and defenses pertaining to the inaccurate, incomplete, negligently prepared or misleading information.

Other Consultants to Be Employed for the Assignment

Particularly where the report will be used in support of courtroom testimony, the appraiser should take a realistic look at the limits of his competence and delegate portions of the appraisal for which the appraiser has limited formal training. This may run against the grain for consultants who believe themselves to be all things to clients, but undertaking portions of the appraisal beyond valuation of the business interests may not serve the client well. Remember that your opinion has to have a sufficient foundation to qualify for admissibility under the applicable Rules of Evidence, and if your qualifications are not up to snuff on real property or equipment valuation, the entire report may be excluded from evidence.

If other consultants will be used, the engagement letter should specify whether the business appraiser will be responsible for their supervision, or whether the appraiser will accept the information at face value and rely on the client for representations of accuracy of the information supplied by other appraisers. In a complicated appraisal, this issue should be discussed with the counsel in charge of the litigation because it can change the number of witnesses at trial and the workload of each expert. Knowledge of the judge assigned to the case, the Rules of Evidence in the practice area, and case law on the subject makes counsel the better person to weigh these risks— and bear the consequences!

Example: During the performance of the work outlined above, Appraiser may deem it necessary to hire third parties to provide services on Owner's behalf. These services may include consulting or testifying experts. Owner agrees that it shall be responsible for paying all fees and expenses directly to these service providers, or for reimbursing Appraiser for these expenses.

Other Types of Anticipated Costs and Their Billing Rates

Any significant passthroughs to the owner should be listed here to avoid surprise and allow counsel to budget. This may include travel, online research time, clerical services, courier services, and duplication fees for voluminous documents. If significant out-of-pocket expenses are anticipated, a cost deposit will be in order.

Example: Appraiser's statements will include out-of-pocket expenses advanced on Owner's behalf and other charges for support activities. These items may include travel, postage, research services, long distance calls, duplication services, and courier services.

Standards of Conduct

When properly drafted, this clause can be both a shield and a sword. When used as a shield, it sets forth the professional standards to which the appraiser will adhere in performing the appraisal. These should, at a minimum, include the standards of any professional associations in which the appraiser has membership, and where appropriate and agreed to by counsel, the Uniform Standards of Professional Appraisal Practice.[3]

The more useful application of this clause is as a sword against business-owner misconduct or excessive control of the appraisal process. The desire for a results-oriented appraisal can drive the owner to provide only selective documents, to manipulate the standard of value, or do any number of things that would result in an unreliable work product. Although jaded appraisers may convince themselves that they should do what they are paid for, never lose sight of the fact that what you are paid for is an *appraisal*—an opinion of value of a business interest based on an applicable standard of value, performed in accordance with sound principles. Your work product will have a life beyond the instant litigation—as will the testimony you give in court to support it. There may be appraisers who will give the client the number they want—let them have the business.

A solid standards clause will set out the consequences of an owner's request that you depart from established standards. It should contain a provision to put the contracting parties on notice of your claim that you can't comply with the demand without compromising your professional ethics, and a time frame for the request to be withdrawn. It should also allow you a golden parachute.

Example: Appraiser will perform the engagement in compliance with the Business Appraisal Standards of the Institute Business Appraisers, Inc. and in accordance with good professional standards. If Owner attempts to interfere with the performance of the engagement with the effect of impairing Appraiser's ability to complete the engagement in compliance with these standards, Appraiser shall have the absolute option, upon 10 days' written notice, to withdraw from the assignment. Upon withdrawal, Appraiser will have no further obligation to perform work or provide work product. Upon withdrawal, Appraiser shall be entitled to immediately receive payment for all billed services.

Fees and Payment Schedules

The timing of payment is as important as the amount of payment. The cardinal rule here is "as much as possible as soon as possible." In the litigation support assignment, it is particularly important to get as much of the fee as possible up front. Imagine the difficulty in collecting fees if the lawsuit is settled and the opinion of value is no longer needed; if the owner and counsel reach a parting of the ways and a replacement lawyer brings in a new expert; if the opinion of value fails to meet owner expectations; or if the court decides the suit against the owner. Avoid these issues by setting a payment schedule that provides you with a retainer amount sufficient to cover your work until the next payment is due under the agreement.

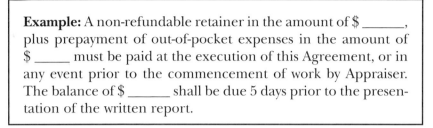

Example: A non-refundable retainer in the amount of $ _____, plus prepayment of out-of-pocket expenses in the amount of $ _____ must be paid at the execution of this Agreement, or in any event prior to the commencement of work by Appraiser. The balance of $ _____ shall be due 5 days prior to the presentation of the written report.

It's almost always best practice to provide your opinion of value only *after* full payment for production of the report has been received. Litigants (and counsel) face tremendous pressure to carry their point, and may choose to find another expert if your opinion fails to meet expectations—best to get paid before you deliver what may be received as bad news. This applies to a verbal report as well as to a written report.

The next consideration is whether to work for a fixed fee or an hourly fee. Generally, a fixed fee allows both the client and the appraiser to plan time and budget for the work. If, however, there are significant unknowns at the time the engagement letter is presented, an hourly fee may better ensure that the appraiser won't bear the burden of contributing unpaid time to the appraisal.

Often, when the engagement letter is signed, discovery is in its infant stages and the amount of time needed for the appraisal is unknown. For this reason, few appraisers agree to a fixed fee for assistance in discovery. The lengths of depositions and of trial testimony are out of the control of both the appraiser and counsel; it is almost always appropriate that this time be handled at an hourly rate.

For deposition or trial testimony, the appraiser will have the option to charge a minimum of a half day or full day, and can also choose to charge a higher hourly rate than for other work. The rationale for this is that appraisers give up the ability to set their own priorities for the time period of the testimony, and are unavailable to deal with other matters that might otherwise demand attention for the time they would be captive in deposition or in court. It's a good idea to investigate local custom for experts before settling on a hard and fast rule. Local custom—and sometimes the rules of local practice—will also dictate whether your time at deposition will be paid by the counsel for the side who retains you or by the party who schedules you for deposition. Your fee schedule should specify that your hourly rate is charged portal to portal, and whether you will appear for deposition if your fees are not paid in advance.

At the time the case is set for trial, the pace of litigation can be stepped up, and many counsel forge ahead without regard to the payment status of experts. Protect yourself against a significant unpaid receivable by providing in the engagement letter that all outstanding charges must be paid upon an event in the litigation—a notice for trial, your name being provided as an expert on the witness list, or other event.[4] The ability to enforce your right to payment at this time—or to require a significant additional deposit to cover anticipated future work—avoids your being put in the position of denying counsel if you are asked to carry your unpaid billing. Be careful to make clear in your engagement letter that these deposits are not estimates of anticipated charges.

Example: At the time this action is set for trial, Owner shall pay to Appraiser an additional retainer of $ _____ to be applied to future charges. Appraiser shall be notified of the date she is anticipated to render trial testimony. Ten days prior to the anticipated testimony date, all outstanding fees and costs due Appraiser shall be paid in full, and Owner shall pay to Appraiser an additional retainer of $ _____ to be applied to the charges for trial testimony and trial preparation. Should Owner fail to make these payments as required, Appraiser shall be under no obligation to perform additional services or to testify at trial.

Clearly define payment due dates and any interest charges you intend to impose as a carry charge.

Example: Appraiser's statements are due 30 days from the statement date. Any statement not paid within thirty days from the date of the statement will be subject to an interest charge of $1^1/2\%$ per month—18% annual percentage rate—from the 30th day after the date of the statement until it is paid in full. Any

---

> payments made on past-due statements shall be first applied to the oldest outstanding statement, including any due and unpaid interest.

"No Pay, No Play"

Such a clause provides that the appraiser may stop work at the time the payment schedule is not met or the receivable reaches a certain aging—generally 45 or 60 days. Making these responsibilities clear allows you to stand on your rights without resorting to tactics that could sour the appraiser/owner relationship prior to trial. As a courtesy, provide in the engagement letter that a reasonable notice will be provided—10 business days is reasonable—prior to expiration of the stated period.

> **Example:** If payment from Owner is more than 45 days past due, Appraiser shall have the right, after 10 days' written notice, to discontinue further provision of services and shall be entitled to collect all billed fees even if no work product has been produced.

Daubert **Clause**

Admissibility of expert testimony has become an increasingly litigated issue; in some jurisdictions bringing a challenge under *Daubert* or *Kumho Tire* is part of lawyer due diligence.[5] Provide in your engagement letter that so long as you have used your best efforts in the assignment, your fees will be paid even if the court should eventually exclude all or part of your testimony.

> **Example:** The fees due appraiser are not contingent upon any appraisal result or event occurring in the litigation. Appraiser shall use his best efforts in the performance of the assignment, and shall be entitled to full payment of all fees without regard to any ruling of the court or ultimate use of the report in evidence or the testimony of Appraiser.

Mandatory Condition Precedent to Suit

Possession is nine-tenths of the law, and even more when payment of fees is the issue. Discuss with counsel whether your jurisdiction will support payment of all billed charges as a mandatory prerequisite to the owner's filing suit for any reason, including professional negligence. Often, such suits are filed in an attempt to compromise an outstanding fee due to the appraiser. Requiring that before such a suit is filed all fees billed have been paid can be a significant dissuasion to any owner considering litigation against the appraiser—and if the suit goes forward, at least the appraiser will have received the billed fees and can use them to defray the expenses of litigation.

> **Example:** Payment of all accrued fees is a mandatory condition precedent to the filing of any action for recovery against Appraiser.

Fee Mediation

Submission of fee disputes to nonbinding negotiation gives the parties the opportunity to vent dissatisfactions at low cost. Often, the reason that the appraiser has not been paid has little to do with the quality of the work product, and more to do with disappointed expectations of the litigant or a cash shortage. A mediator who is specially trained in dispute resolution can act as both therapist and umpire to resolve the issue in a few hours, often for less than $500. As a risk management tool, information gleaned in fee mediation can allow the appraiser to determine the risks of attempting to collect the fee and whether the owner is likely to allege malpractice, making the collection attempt an expensive exercise.[6]

> **Example:** Either party shall have the option, prior to the commencement of any legal proceeding against Owner or Appraiser, to demand that the issues be submitted to nonbinding mediation. Said mediation shall take place within 30 days of the demand at the offices of _____ with a media-

> tor selected jointly by the parties. The expenses of the mediator are to be paid equally by the parties.

Limitation of Liability

Such clauses, when properly written, are not one-sided "can't touch me" provisions. Rather, good limitations clauses make a logical connection between the liability assumed by the appraiser, the appraiser's liability to control this risk, and the fees received from the engagement. The determination of these *liquidated damages* will hinge on how these clauses are treated by the courts in your practice area, and often legal "magic words" and even special type fonts are required to make them fully enforceable. Such clauses are the perfect example of drafting that should **not** be undertaken by the appraiser! Be aware, however, that such limitations of liability clauses are not always effective—they cannot shield the appraiser from gross negligence. The best malpractice prevention is good client selection and strict adherence to standards and good appraisal practices.

> **Example:** In consideration for performing the services described above for the fees agreed upon, Owner agrees that the liability of Appraiser to Owner or any assignee or successor in interest shall be limited to the greater of $25,000 or the fees actually paid to Appraiser by Owner. Owner agrees that, in order for Owner, its assignee or successor in interest to recover against Appraiser, Owner must prove that Appraiser was grossly negligent in the performance of the duties set forth in this Agreement.

Prevailing Party Costs and Legal Fees

Reality Check At the conclusion of litigation, you have a large outstanding receivable. In response to a demand for payment, the client files an action against you for professional negligence. You retain counsel, and after litigating the issue, you are the prevailing party.

Will you be entitled to recover your attorney fees and costs in defense of the litigation?

Probably Not. In most jurisdictions, legal fees are recoverable only when statute or contract specifically authorize, or where the court finds the suit to be entirely without merit beyond a reasonable doubt.

This means that most lawsuits are a losing proposition for the defendant. Provide in your engagement letter that if any collection activity is necessary, or if there is a claim regarding the performance of the services, the prevailing party will be entitled to reasonable costs and fees. True, this poses some risk that you may be responsible for the fees of an opposing party in the event of judgment against you, but it will also scare off the marginal claims.

Define *costs* to include reasonable payment for your time in defending the suit. Time involved with your defense or collection counsel is time away from other (paying!) clients. Recoup this lost income as part of prevailing party costs.

> **Example:** In any action against Owner or Appraiser arising out of this Agreement, the prevailing party shall be entitled to recover reasonable costs and attorneys' fees associated with the bringing or defense of the action. The term "costs" shall include but not be limited to Appraiser's time in assisting in the defense of the action, which shall be reimbursed to Appraiser at the rate of $ _____ per hour.

Agreement Altered Only in Writing

During the course of the litigation, both the scope and nature of the work may change, and may necessitate additional charges. Make certain that each additional service is subject to the same provisions of the engagement letter, and confirm the additional directives in a writing signed by the retaining party.

> **Example:** This Agreement sets forth the entire understanding between the parties and describes the services to be performed by the Appraiser. Any additional services that the Appraiser is requested to perform shall be authorized in writing signed by both parties and are subject to additional charges, terms, and conditions.

Appraisers who have not worked in a variety of litigation assignments may find some of these provisions intimidating and fear that no prospective client would agree to the engagement letter. However, the engagement letter signed between owner and counsel almost certainly contains many of these provisions. Carefully consider any client who is unwilling to enter into the engagement letter that you have asked your personal attorney to prepare. If the agreement is designed to protect your interests as the appraiser, if you choose to ignore those protections you will have only yourself to blame!

NOTES

1. It would be cheating the reader to include a chapter on engagement letters in a book of this nature without also including some sample clauses. The reader is cautioned not to adopt the provisions without consultation of counsel. There are too many variances in contract requirements from one practice area to another for these clauses to be anything more than examples to spur discussion between the appraiser and his retained legal advisor.
2. A number of good checklists have been published in appraisal literature, particularly in the *Practice Guides* published by the AICPA. At a bare minimum, the appraiser should require client production of all documents detailed in Revenue Ruling 59–60.
3. The reader is cautioned that USPAP and the Advisory Opinions that interpret its provisions are in a constant state of revision, and that the business appraisal profession and membership associations have been critical of the way in which the drafting pro-

cess is being conducted. Accordingly, the standards may not be relevant to the conduct of business appraisal in a contemporary setting. The time to make this decision is *before* the engagement letter is signed, and counsel should be prepped on the appraiser's reasons for departure from USPAP. Members of ASA should be cautioned that since ASA standards currently require compliance with USPAP, they should note the portions of USPAP from which departure is not permitted.

4. For suggestions on good timing for additional payments or clearing of receivables, see Chapter 1, "Anatomy of a Lawsuit," *infra.*

5. These cases and their implications for the testifying appraiser are discussed at length in Chapter 11, *infra.*

6. Many appraisers would also include an arbitration clause in their retainer agreement. It is the author's personal preference not to include arbitration as an available remedy for a variety of reasons. First, arbitration often requires significant up-front administrative charges, and if the appraiser is the initiator it can be expensive to begin the process. Second, the selection of an arbitration panel is an inexact science often out of the control of the parties. Third, most arbitrations are final, and if the panel has not followed the law there is no recourse. If the appraiser wants to include an arbitration clause, it is suggested that the arbitration be nonbinding, and that the clause specify that the results of the arbitration not be admissible in a subsequent judicial proceeding.

CHAPTER 7

How Should Appraisers Consider the Law?

Purpose of This Chapter Case law is widely discussed in periodicals and books targeted at business appraisers. Too many appraisers misinterpret or misapply case law, incorporating it into reports and assuming that it is applicable beyond appropriate circumstances. This chapter examines how attorneys analyze case law and provides a suggested context for the appraiser's use of reported decisions.

Thousands of cases are decided each day by the courts of this nation; a handful of those cases will go up on appeal and be the subject of written opinions. A small selection of those cases will make their way into published case reporters, and a few of those cases will become the subject of analytical articles aimed at the appraisal professions.

What happens from there can seem like chaos. Appraisers who lack legal training read these cases—and usually read the wrong things into them. They proceed to cite the cases in reports, interpret them to derive the standard of value, and even use them as sources of discounts. All of these applications can call the appraisal conclusion into question, and can embarrass the appraiser.

The court system on both the state and federal levels is divided into trial courts and courts of appeal. With certain notable exceptions,[1] trial court decisions are of no binding value beyond the individual parties in the pending action. Appellate decisions are often binding only within the appellate jurisdiction—and one state can have many appellate jurisdictions. Federal appellate decisions can be binding in some appellate jurisdictions when they decide questions of state law, and state appellate decisions can be binding in federal trial courts when federal courts consider the same issues. Appeals can be discretionary (that is, can be heard at the pleasure of the courts of appeal), or can be a matter of right—depending on the issues involved. Some reported appellate opinions are prohibited by the rules of the reporting jurisdiction from being cited as binding authority.

To make matters even more complicated—courts on the same level are not known by the same names in the state and federal system, or even from state to state. In Florida, for example, the trial court level for larger cases is referred to as the *circuit court*; the appellate court level is the *district court of appeal*. In the federal court system, the trial court level is referred to as the *district court* and the appellate level as the *circuit court* of *appeal*. The courts of last resort in some states are known as *superior courts*; the appellate court level below the superior court is known as the *supreme court*. In other states, the supreme court is the court of last resort. Under the federal system, the *U.S. Supreme Court* is the last resort of litigants—and some appeals from state supreme courts (and other state courts of last resort known by other names) can also reach the U.S. Supreme Court.

THE PARTS OF AN APPELLATE DECISION[2]

Even sorting out these distinctions may not prepare someone who is not an attorney to consider case law. Law students spend the majority of their time during their first year doing two things: Calculating the grade point averages of other students, and briefing cases. Briefing a case is a method of organizing the opinion so that its elements can be analyzed. A sample brief of a reported decision will include these things:

- The identity of the parties
- The causes of action brought by the plaintiff in the trial court

against other parties (and claims the other parties brought against each other or the plaintiff)
- The proceedings below—how the trial court ruled
- The issue on appeal
- The holding of the appellate court on the issues on appeal
- The rationale for each holding of the appellate court

The reason that students are taught to brief cases is that appellate opinions are not always laid out in a manner that makes this information easy to categorize. A layperson reading an appellate decision might find language that seems to support the conclusion the person hopes to hold—only to discover that the statement is contained in the findings of the trial court that the appellate court has overruled. Appellate courts uphold some decisions of the trial court and reverse others. Often, there is a majority opinion and a dissenting opinion, which are both reported. A judge who voted with the majority but does not agree with all elements of the majority opinion might write a concurring opinion, and so publish a separate rationale for the decision of the majority.

If the reader is not yet confused, we should move on to a discussion of *dicta*. Dicta is defined as views of the court that are not a central part of the judge's decision. It can include rules of law from other jurisdictions, a discussion of the development of the area of law, principles that the court considered but ultimately did not apply, and even hypotheticals. Although these are parts of the opinion, they are not the *black letter law* for which the case can be cited. Also included in the case, but not part of the holding or even the rationale, may be the arguments of the parties and excerpts of the trial or oral argument transcripts.

How, then, should appraisers consider the law? With greatest caution. Here are some general guidelines.

CONSIDERING THE SOURCE

If you want to rely on the holding of a case, make sure you have read the case and addressed your questions about the opinion to counsel. Most appraisers see only excerpts or summaries of cases—do you know who read the opinion and prepared the summary? If it was not pre-pared by attorneys, look at the summary with caution. Many publica-tions aimed at appraisers have attorneys on staff who do this work, but others do not.

Also keep in mind that opinions can be issued by the trial court. Often the cases reported in newsletters and case digests are trial court rulings on the admissibility of testimony, the discounts derived by the experts, or commentary on methods used to determine the dam-ages. These factual rulings are limited to the particular facts of the case. Reading the opinion of the court can give an expert important insight into what the court found credible. However, the trial court opinion should be used only for instruction, as it cannot be binding on the facts of any other case.[3]

CHANGE IS A CONSTANT WITH CASE LAW

Ever hear a lawyer talk about *Shepardizing*? It's not a method of wool production—it is a citation checking service that determines whether case law has been overruled, cited with approval or disapproval, or dozens of other mentions of a reported decision. With cases, the rule is often "here today, gone tomorrow." Attorneys use online research services to check the status of the law they intend to cite, and those services report on the newest opinions the day after they are issued, and long before they are published in case reporters or abstracted in technical periodicals. Know the status of the cases on which you in-tend to rely, and update any case law to which you have been referred just as you would update the report. A representation letter from counsel is a reasonable way to handle the current state of cases pro-vided to the appraiser (often, memoranda are written not to inform the reader, but to protect the writer).

CASE LAW AND CAP RATES

There's an increasing trend for appraisers hungry for data to look to cases for discount and cap rates. Software databases are available that compile the rates quoted in decisions—or that even use other ap-praisers' conclusions on different companies as indicators of value.

This is a terrible idea. Case law *cannot* provide cap rates or comparables. Database users do not know the expertise of the appraisers whose opinions are being used, whether there were appraisers for all parties so the court had a basis of the comparison, or sufficient data about the business being valued to determine comparability. The databases might not report the standard of value applicable to the assignment—even if the standard is reported, terms such as *fair value* can differ among the states. Case law is not the marketplace and should never be used in place of reported transactions.[4]

Appraisers who cite case law in their reports or to counsel risk embarrassment and worse. Cases can provide valuable insights into the way courts consider appraisal issues and evaluate the credibility of expert witnesses and appraisal testimony. Any references in your work product to case law should come only at the direction of counsel—after all, the attorney has insurance to cover misapplication of law, and the appraiser does not.

NOTES

1. Tax court practice and the applicability of tax opinions are an exception to this general rule.
2. Another complication is that opinions can be issued on all sorts of preliminary matters. When the appraiser reads a reported decision it could relate to a motion to exclude evidence, motion for summary judgment or motions that were not dispositive of the case but only of a single issue. And when the appraiser sees that a case has been "remanded," the issues have been sent back to the trial court judge for further proceedings, meaning that the case may be re-tried or findings may be modified.
3. The notable exception to this are tax court opinions, which are governed by unique principles.
4. Purveyors of these databases liken them to jury verdict reporters, relied on by many trial attorney. There is no comparison. Verdict reporters indicate what juries have done, and attorneys use them as guidelines for settlement—in effect, what the market might do. Appraisals, by contrast, are not the market. Only transactions, not reported opinions of courts, indicate what the universe of buyers will do.

CHAPTER 8

The Essential Rules of Evidence

Purpose of This Chapter The goal of the expert witness is to give testimony that reaches the trier of fact. This testimony is evaluated for compliance with the Rules of Evidence. Knowing how counsel and court use and interpret these rules gives the appraiser an understanding of the purpose and process of testimony.

The Rules of Evidence exist to foster fair play in court. Relevant evidence—gathered with regard to the protections to which the parties are entitled, presented in a reliable format, made complete in form and placed in proper context—aids in a fair result.

It is easy to find a copy of the Rules of Evidence pertinent in your jurisdiction—it can be ordered from the official publisher in an annual edition. It is useful to have a set that includes not only the notes of the committee that drafted the Rules, but one with commentary by an editor. These annotated sets can include examples that will provide context for the nonattorney reader. Check your local law school's bookstore for this tool.

This discussion will use the Federal Rules of Evidence as the model. Wording of Rules of Evidence may have some differences in practice areas, but in many states they closely follow the Federal Rules, and where there is no state decision interpreting the Rules, a state court may look to federal court cases for guidance.

These rules are more than the procedures for the court to rule on testimony—they should be read by the expert to determine the minimum standards your testimony must meet—particularly as contained in Rules 702 and 703. Use those rules as a checklist for your testimony, and as a rationale that retaining counsel do what it takes to get you the background data needed for an admissible opinion.

EVIDENCE BASICS

Rule 401. Definition of "Relevant Evidence"
"Relevant evidence" means evidence having any tendency to make the existence of any fact that is of consequence to the determination of the action more probable or less probable than it would be without the evidence.

Rule 402. Relevant Evidence Generally Admissible; Irrelevant Evidence Inadmissible
All relevant evidence is admissible, except as otherwise provided by the Constitution of the United States, by Act of Congress, by these rules, or by other rules prescribed by the Supreme Court pursuant to statutory authority. Evidence which is not relevant is not admissible.

This is the beginning point for all evidence. In order for evidence to be relevant, it is not necessary that it concern a disputed fact. Background, or "storytelling," testimony that provides context is relevant evidence. Duplicative testimony, however, may be ruled inadmissible even though relevant. For this reason, more than one expert on a single issue retained by the same party may not make it to the stand:

Rule 403. Exclusion of Relevant Evidence on Grounds of Prejudice, Confusion, or Waste of Time
Although relevant, evidence may be excluded if its probative value is substantially outweighed by the danger of unfair prejudice, confusion of the issues, or misleading the jury, or by considerations of undue delay, waste of time, or needless presentation of cumulative evidence.

FILLING IN THE BLANKS

Some shortcuts are available when common sense would allow reasonable assumptions.

> *Rule 406. Habit; Routine Practice*
> Evidence of the habit of a person or of the routine practice of an organization, whether corroborated or not and regardless of the presence of eyewitnesses, is relevant to prove that the conduct of the person or organization on a particular occasion was in conformity with the habit or routine practice.

The main aid to the testifying appraiser here is in the definition of routine business practices—review of staff, destruction of obsolete inventory, and other issues. Once established by testimony of a company insider, the appraiser can fill in blanks where evidence on a particular year might not be in evidence.

One of the most common objections to testimony by fact witnesses involves their attempt to provide hearsay testimony. You need to understand what hearsay is, and be aware that experts can rely on hearsay so long as it is within reasonable professional judgment.

Here is the pertinent portion of the Federal Rule:

> *Rule 801. Definitions*
> (c) Hearsay. "Hearsay" is a statement, other than one made by the declarant while testifying at the trial or hearing, offered in evidence to prove the truth of the matter asserted.

In other words, unless it is said on the stand under oath, words are hearsay if they are offered to prove the contents of the statement. Keep in mind that hearsay can be written as well as spoken—for example, your appraisal report is hearsay, and that is why you have to repeat your conclusion of value on the stand, rather than simply having your report marked as an exhibit and read into the record.

Rule 802 specifies that hearsay testimony is not admissible; however, your conclusions are admissible, even though you may have considered hearsay in arriving at your opinion. Your job is to determine that relying on the information is within professional standards of good practice. There are also a number of exceptions to the hearsay rule, and these exceptions deal with circumstances where there is some assumption of credibility, or the opportunity for the opposing party to inquire:

- Prior statements of the witness, when inconsistent and given under oath, or when consistent and offered to rebut an allegation of recent fabrication of the statement
- Admissions of party opponents, when offered in evidence against the party opponent, assuming they were made by authorized representatives
- Recorded recollections, memoranda or records about which the witness once had knowledge but now cannot recall, so long as they have been made contemporaneously with the event
- Records of regularly conducted business activity, records, or data compilations
- Public records and reports
- Learned treatises[1]

Many of these exceptions are designed as time savers for the court. Allowing treatises and public records to come in without a witness to lay foundation avoids the parade of five-minute witnesses authenticating documents. Prior sworn statements, such as deposition testimony, can also be admitted under an exception to the hearsay rule—for this reason, counsel will sometimes read entire deposition transcripts into the record. It's an important reason that you should always read and sign the transcription of your deposition.

TELLING "THE WHOLE TRUTH"

Some rules are designed to aid the witness in telling a complete story.

> *Rule 106. Remainder of Related Writings or Recorded Statements.*
> When a writing or recorded statement or part thereof is introduced by a party, an adverse party may require the introduction at that time of any other part or any other writing or recorded statement which ought in fairness to be considered contemporaneously with it.

Rules like this are designed to prevent "hide the ball" type tactics. You'll see this come up in court when an excerpt from deposition testimony is read into the record or used to impeach a witness with a prior inconsistent statement. As a testifying appraiser, Rule 106 will prevent introduction of only a portion of a report, financial statement, or other information that could create a misleading impression when presented out of context.

The most common exposure you'll have to Rule 106 is when counsel stalks up to the witness chair clutching a book by a noted author on business appraisal (probably one by Shannon Pratt, ASA, MCBA, who is one of the few authors on the topic known to attorneys).[2] Counsel will attempt to impeach your testimony by referring to an isolated paragraph of this book that seems to contradict your appraisal method. Under this rule of completeness, any other portion of the text that is relevant on the topic must be admitted into evidence. Retaining counsel can cover this on redirect testimony, and the additional—and perhaps the more pertinent—portions of the book can be presented to the trier of fact.

Also in the interests of full disclosure, papers you take to the witness stand are subject to examination by all the parties:

Rule 612. Writing Used to Refresh Memory
Except as otherwise provided in criminal proceedings by section 3500 of title 18, United States Code, if a witness uses a writing to refresh memory for the purpose of testifying, either—
(1) while testifying, or
(2) before testifying, if the court in its discretion determines it is necessary in the interests of justice,
an adverse party is entitled to have the writing produced at the hearing, to inspect it, to cross-examine the witness thereon, and to introduce in evidence those portions which relate to the testimony of the witness. If it is claimed that the writing contains matters not related to the subject matter of the testimony the court shall examine the writing in camera, excise any portions not so related, and order delivery of the remainder to the party entitled thereto. Any portion withheld over objections shall be preserved and made available to the appellate court in the event of an appeal. If a writing is not produced or delivered pursuant to order under this rule, the court shall make any order justice

requires, except that in criminal cases when the prosecution elects not to comply, the order shall be one striking the testimony or, if the court in its discretion determines that the interests of justice so require, declaring a mistrial.

This means that any notes that you take to the stand as aids in testimony must be handed over upon request. Care should therefore be taken to make sure that these notes do not contain items such as communications with counsel, or a listing of weaknesses in your report and how to deal with them. This provision will be a bogeyman for those experts who write an incomplete report for "strategic reasons" but must have additional information available on the stand in order to present the opinion. The simplest way to avoid the problem is to write complete reports that do not conceal any information you would want to present while giving expert testimony.

Do you think that, when your direct testimony, cross-examination and redirect testimony is done, you may leave the witness stand? Think again:

Rule 614. Calling and Interrogation of Witnesses by Court
(a) Calling by Court. The court may, on its own motion or at the suggestion of a party, call witnesses, and all parties are entitled to cross-examine witnesses thus called.
(b) Interrogation by Court. The court may interrogate witnesses, whether called by itself or by a party.
(c) Objections. Objections to the calling of witnesses by the court or to interrogation by it may be made at the time or at the next available opportunity when the jury is not present.

Sometimes it will be necessary for the judge to fill in the blanks of counsel's questioning or to clear up an item that may cause jury confusion. In a bench trial, of course, questioning by the court represents inquiry by the trier of fact and is a valuable clue to where the decision may be heading.

Rule 703 (discussed later) allows experts to use information that might not be admissible in evidence. However, this ability to rely on out-of-court evidence does not mean that the information is not subject to disclosure or inquiry. The expert must still establish credibility for the opinion by discussing the data and must be available for cross-examination on the facts that lay its foundation:

Rule 705. Disclosure of Facts or Data Underlying Expert Opinion
The expert may testify in terms of opinion or inference and give reasons therefor without first testifying to the underlying facts or data, unless the court requires otherwise. The expert may in any event be required to disclose the underlying facts or data on cross-examination.

A wise expert will make these disclosures in direct testimony. There are two main reasons for doing so. First, getting this information in on direct avoids a challenge to the admissibility of the conclusion of value that can interrupt the flow of the testimony. Second, forcing opposing counsel to make the inquiry during cross-examination prolongs the length of cross-examination and makes it more likely that the jury will conclude that your testimony has weaknesses that are being exploited.

SPECIAL RULES FOR EXPERTS

Expert witnesses are exempt from certain provisions that pertain to fact witnesses (also known as percipient witnesses). Fact witnesses are limited to testimony that is within their own observation in order to keep within the limits of relevant and credible testimony, and sequestered from information that may color that testimony. Experts, on the other hand, are given latitude in reliance upon their independence from the parties in the case and their status as officers of the court.

Rule 615. Exclusion of Witnesses
At the request of a party the court shall order witnesses excluded so that they cannot hear the testimony of other witnesses, and it may make the order of its own motion. This rule does not authorize exclusion of (1) a party who is a natural person, or (2) an officer or employee of a party which is not a natural person designated as its representative by its attorney, or (3) a person

whose presence is shown by a party to be essential to the presentation of the party's cause, or (4) a person authorized by statute to be present.

Experts are included in the category of "persons whose presence is shown by a party to be essential to the presentation of the party's cause." Rule 615 allows the expert to sit in the courtroom for testimony by other witnesses whose information may be background for the opinion testimony. If you are in the courtroom for this purpose, limit your presence to this purpose. This means you should not sit at counsel table or within note-passing range of counsel, and should not draw attention to yourself during the testimony.

Rule 602. Lack of Personal Knowledge

A witness may not testify to a matter unless evidence is introduced sufficient to support a finding that the witness has personal knowledge of the matter. Evidence to prove personal knowledge may, but need not, consist of the witness's own testimony. The rule is subject to the provisions of Rule 703, relating to opinion testimony by expert witnesses.

Expert witnesses, by contrast, often testify by speculating or drawing conclusions from information presented. They may, for example, testify relying on hearsay testimony, so long as it is of the type usually relied upon by other experts in the field.

Rule 701. Opinion Testimony by Lay Witnesses

If the witness is not testifying as an expert, the witness's testimony in the form of opinions or inferences is limited to those opinions or inferences which are (a) rationally based on the perception of the witness, (b) helpful to a clear understanding of the witness' testimony or the determination of a fact in issue, and (c) not based on scientific, technical, or other specialized knowledge within the scope of Rule 702.

Rule 701 contains the good news and the bad news. The good news is that unless you are accepted by the court as an expert witness, you cannot render an expert opinion. This means that under most circumstances, you cannot be compelled to testify in cases where you have not been retained by a party (and therefore paid for your testimony). For example, if you do the accounting and tax work for the business, you can be called to testify, but your testimony will be limited to the facts of the work you have performed rather than any conclusions that might be drawn from it.

The bad news is that unless you are accepted by the court as an expert witness, you cannot render an expert opinion. This means that if the court has failed to accept your qualifications when you have been tendered as an expert, counsel will be hard-pressed to get your opinion of value into evidence. With some careful questioning counsel may be able to get your thought processes into evidence, but it is unlikely that your valuation will make the record while you testify. Then again, if the court has declined to admit your testimony as expert testimony, counsel may not be anxious to parade your opinion of value.

Rule 702. Testimony by Experts

If scientific, technical, or other specialized knowledge will assist the trier of fact to understand the evidence or to determine a fact in issue, a witness qualified as an expert by knowledge, skill, experience, training or education, may testify thereto in the form of an opinion or otherwise if (1) the testimony is based upon sufficient facts or data, (2) the testimony is the product of reliable principles and methods, and (3) the witness has applied the principles and methods reliably to the facts of the case.

Rule 702 is the threshold test for all expert testimony and the source of the *gatekeeper* obligations assumed by the court under cases such as *Daubert v. Merrell Dow Pharmaceuticals, Inc.*,[3] and *Kumho Tire Co., Ltd. v. Carmichael.*[4] It should also be the litmus test for report and opinion content. Focus on performing a litigation support appraisal with the same level of professionalism, the same quality and quantity of background data and same document content that would be used in a nonlitigation assignment. Some professional organizations contain "departure provisions" in their standards that alter the content requirements or allow for other technical departures if the report is prepared as a litigation assignment. Such departures are a bad idea. Saying that the report is different in format, foundation, or content because the witness was instructed by counsel is a surefire way to raise the specter of bias and possibly have your testimony excluded. Remember, not only do appraisers whose testimony is excluded get no respect, they sometimes don't get paid.

Dealing with this Rule's requirements to use "reliable principles and methods" and applying them reliably is within the control of the appraiser. Most appraisers find that their main problems in following Rule 702 arise when they attempt to accumulate sufficient facts or data to perform an appraisal. The next Rule speaks to this issue:

> *Rule 703. Bases of Opinion Testimony by Experts*
> The facts or data in the particular case upon which an expert bases an opinion or inference may be those perceived by or made known to the expert at or before the hearing. If of a type reasonably relied upon by experts in the particular field in forming opinions or inferences upon the subject, the facts or data need not be admissible in evidence in order for the opinion or inference to be admitted. Facts or data that are otherwise inadmissible shall not be disclosed to the jury by the proponent of the opinion or inference unless the court determines that their probative value in assisting the jury to evaluate the expert's opinion substantially outweighs their prejudicial effect.

Any appraiser who regularly values small, closely held businesses is used to dealing with information of inconsistent *quality;* in the litigation assignment, the *quantity* of data also presents a challenge. Often the lawyer's plan for discovery will not coordinate well with the appraiser's need for complete information. When one lawyer starts stonewalling in document production or the provision of full answers to interrogatories, the other counsel shortly follows suit. Even an appraiser used to getting financial information in a shoebox is hard-pressed when the shoebox is nearly empty. Appraisers retained in marital dissolution cases representing the noninvolved spouse are particularly hard-pressed when counsel elects to hide the ball.

The key point is that the appraiser should not stretch these data beyond the limits of credibility—it is one thing not to have sufficient documentation to meet the enumeration in Revenue Ruling 59–60, and another to have to make a series of guesses in place of data. Discuss with counsel your needs and how the failure of documentation will affect your opinions and result in a scope limitation stated in the report. But follow through and include the scope limitation; the professional standards of most organizations as well as your credibility demand that you do so. Remember, the choice of tactics is out of your control, but the statements in your opinion demand and deserve accuracy.

If the information is not available in conventional financial statements, consider using the testimony of witnesses to supplement the data. Experts can rely on such testimony, and in most cases you will not be given free rein to conduct management interviews if you are not representing the owner or business entity, making depositions your best chance to inquire. Although such testimony is often hearsay (and therefore not admissible in evidence), Rule 703 allows experts to rely on the data as long as they meet a reasonableness standard.

SPECIAL PROTECTIONS FOR CERTAIN COMMUNICATIONS

The Rules also provide for some information to be immune from entry into evidence, whether to facilitate settlement or to facilitate free communication with client, counsel, and consultant.

Proposed Rule 502 deals with tax returns; the purpose of the Rule is to encourage "accurate self-reporting":

> *Proposed Rule 502. Required Reports Privileged by Statute (not yet enacted)*
> A person, corporation, association, or other organization or entity, either public or private, making a return or report required by law to be made has a privilege to refuse to disclose and to prevent any other person from disclosing the return or report, if the law requiring it to be made so provides. A public officer or agency to whom a return or report is required by law to be made has a privilege to refuse to disclose the return or

report if the law requiring it to be made so provides. No privilege exists under this rule in actions involving perjury, false statements, fraud in the return or report, or other failure to comply with the law in question.

If enacted, this Rule will be an issue in many dissolution actions. Until it is incorporated into the Federal Rules, however, tax returns will continue to be presented in civil actions, and will be subject to inquiry.

Rule 408. Compromise and Offers to Compromise
Evidence of (1) furnishing or offering or promising to furnish, or (2) accepting or offering or promising to accept, a valuable consideration in compromising or attempting to compromise a claim which was disputed as to either validity or amount, is not admissible to prove liability for or invalidity of the claim or its amount. Evidence of conduct or statements made in compromise negotiations is likewise not admissible. This rule does not require the exclusion of any evidence otherwise discoverable merely because it is presented in the course of compromise negotiations. This rule also does not require exclusion when the evidence is offered for another purpose, such as proving bias or prejudice of a witness, negativing a contention of undue delay, or proving an effort to obstruct a criminal investigation or prosecution.

Although this Rule can seem incomprehensible, the message is simple—if you heard it in a settlement conference, you can't talk about it later unless it would be otherwise subject to discovery. Since this distinction can be tough to make, consult with retaining counsel if you plan to include any information you heard at settlement talks or read in settlement correspondence in your testimony.

NOTES

1. More about treatises and impeachment with treatises appears in Chapter 5, *infra.*
2. The testifying appraiser is well advised to subscribe to Shannon

Pratt's *Business Valuation Update for Judges and Lawyers*, as it will have much of the information on business appraisal that is being used by the counsel.

3. *Daubert v. Merrell Dow Pharmaceuticals, Inc.*, 113 S.Ct. 2786 (1993).
4. *Kumho Tire Co., Ltd. v. Carmichael*, 119 S.Ct. 1167 (1999). This case and that cited in note 3 are further discussed in Chapter 11, *infra*.

PART THREE

Performing the Assignment

CHAPTER 9

Beginning the Assignment: Initial Information and Client Selection

Purpose of This Chapter You'll never regret the client you did not take, but you may well regret the clients for whom you have performed work. Client selection is one important way to manage practice risks. Once you are retained, getting the necessary information requires you to establish and retain control of the process. Particularly in litigation, there are temptations to provide the appraiser with a lower quality or quantity of materials. This chapter reviews issues important to client selection and data gathering.

BEGINNING THE ENGAGEMENT

The first issue you must consider in every assignment is whether you are competent to perform the work. Qualifications and credentials are discussed in Chapter 4. Here we add consideration of your ability to analyze this industry from available sources. If it is a highly specialized business with little available information about the market, you may find yourself relying too heavily on the owner's subjective information. This will affect the credibility of your opinions.

As a general rule, the appraiser should not do any work until an engagement letter has been signed and the required initial payment received.[1] Even if you have worked with this counsel before, the owner is an unknown quantity and may not be reliable for payment. There may be cases where good relations with a counsel who sends you repeat assignments may justify starting work upon the receipt of a retainer, but the appraiser should view this as a risk/benefit judgment call rather than money in the mail. Remember, checks seem to take weeks to arrive in the mail, while bills seem to arrive the day they are sent!

The stage of the case when you are retained will also affect whether you want big bucks up front. If you are retained when deadlines are looming and your report must be prepared for a scheduled deposition, you can count on having to prepare a large amount of work in a short amount of time. If you will be performing the appraisal as a fixed fee, this timing suggests you should get the majority of the payment before starting work. If you will be working at an hourly rate, you should get a retainer sufficient to cover all your work for the billing cycle plus a portion of the work you anticipate to perform on the next billing cycle. At this stage of the litigation, events can require you to do additional work on short notice. Getting the payment up front decreases your chances of acting as the owner's banker.

What if the client does not want to or cannot afford to make the payment up front? Consider whether the client is sufficiently committed to the litigation to make the required investment, and whether the client has the monetary resources to fulfill a contractual commitment. A no to either of these questions may be a sign you should pass on this assignment.

Reality Check The appraiser takes a call from a business owner who has received a demand letter from a recently departed shareholder. The owner asks the appraiser to take a look at the most recent year's financials and give an opinion on whether any adjustments might be appropriate. The appraiser is asked to set a fee for this limited task, and the owner promises more work on the litigation when this portion of the assignment is complete. *Is anything suspicious going on?*

Maybe. If the owner proposes a limited amount of work for a small fee with the promise of more work once the initial task is complete, consider the possibility that you are being *warehoused*. Once you have done even minor work for an owner, you may have a conflict of interest that will prevent your working for another party in the dispute. It is a typical tactic if you are a specialist in the business type, if you are well known in the courthouse where the suit is likely to be tried, or if you have worked on a similar matter so that your opinion on the subject company or the issues in the case can be predicted.

The best way to avoid warehousing is to decline small assignments that are baited with the promise of bigger work later—agree to start on the small assignment when a nonrefundable retainer for the larger assignment is received up front. If you never hear from the prospect again, you may have defeated the warehousing.

Even if the owner has the ability to pay, warning signs might tell you to pass on this assignment. The first is whether you have actual or perceived conflicts—this is discussed in detail in the next section. The second issue is whether this is a person or entity for whom you would like to work. These conditions are all red flags that you should decline the assignment:

- Counsel intimates the expectation of a work product you cannot or should not deliver.
- You are not provided with necessary information, and your access to information is purposely limited.
- The owner has unreported income, and you are asked to conceal this information, or the owner is unwilling to file amended returns.
- You are not given enough time or budget to do the work needed to support your opinion.
- The owner and retaining counsel will not spend the funds you will need to do extra work in the event of an anticipated *Daubert* challenge.
- The facts of the case are so bad that no matter what you do, you cannot provide testimony that will be helpful.
- Retaining counsel or the owner has misrepresented any information.

View with caution any assignment where other appraisers have been retained, and their opinions will not be used. Although this could be a sign of poor work product from the appraiser, it could mean other things—the expert may not have been paid, the owner could be shopping for a better number, or there may have been issues in the documents that prompted a withdrawal. You have the option of contacting the previous consultants prior to accepting the assignment, and if counsel asks you not to do so, you have your answer.

Another red flag should be whether retaining counsel is the first lawyer on the case. If counsel has been replaced, payment issues or other problems may have existed in the relationship. If you call prior counsel, the reasons for the withdrawal may be privileged and you won't get much information. Ask retaining counsel for an explanation and then rely on your instincts.

Sometimes you'll find you have been listed on an expert witness disclosure before you have been contacted on the case, or before the engagement letter is signed and the retainer is paid. This is, at best, bad manners on the part of counsel (or a symptom that the lawyer is bad at managing deadlines), and at worst an attempt to warehouse. You are not under obligation to accept the assignment if you were not contacted prior to the filing of the disclosure. Some experts even demand an additional fee when this has happened to deter these tactics.

CONFLICTS AND PRIOR WRITINGS

There's more to conflicts than meets the eye. Actual conflicts, of course, should cause an automatic rejection of the assignment. Perceived conflicts can affect the credibility of your testimony, and are deserving of equal attention.

As discussed in Chapter 4, problems can arise when experts perform valuation work concerning businesses for which they have performed other services. It will be easy for a cross-examining counsel to suggest that the expert will have to justify prior assignments by accepting firm work product (such as tax returns) at face value. This applies even when another division of the firm has done the work.

If the business is a repeat client, cross-examining counsel can also make it appear that you must propitiate the owner in order to be assured of additional work. The inference is that the opinion must be slanted in favor of the client. Another reason to refer this work out is that after performing consulting services or other financial services for a business, you will often know where the bodies are buried. Even if these issues may not be relevant to the assignment at hand, there's a risk that you may allude to them in testimony and make serious problems for the owner.

If you have performed valuations of similar businesses, keep these assignments in mind before you accept the engagement. Federal Rules now require you to identify these assignments, and you may have to produce portions of the reports.[2] If these past reports contain statements which could contradict aspects of the current report—such as industry forecasts, competition, or factors in a business that would make it a strong or a weak player in the market—read these carefully and make certain you can credibly distinguish them.

Prior statements in articles or conference presentations can also contain inconsistencies or content you will have to explain. The content of these presentations is fair game at both deposition and trial, and will be carefully scrutinized. Keep copies of all articles in which you are quoted and make sure there is nothing you will have to recant in an assignment.[3]

DOCUMENTATION FOR THE ASSIGNMENT

The standards of all professional associations require the appraiser to determine which documents are necessary to complete the assignment. There is no exception for litigation assignments; indeed, this is an area where the expert is in a better position than counsel to determine what is required. Do not let cost or time concerns affect your judgment about the quantity or quality of documents needed.

In addition to standards, the content of financial information required for appraisals is defined in Revenue Ruling 59–60: five years of information should be obtained whenever possible. When five years of data are not available, include a statement in your report to that effect. It is better to put it in the report than to have to confess it during testimony and give the impression that information has been concealed to strengthen the claims.

Your list of required documents can be attached to your engagement letter. The most frequent problem you'll have is that these documents sometimes won't exist beyond tax returns. This is a problem, but it is not your problem. Make the owner responsible for providing you with financial statements, and don't perform the work until you get them. If you go forward without reliable information, your opinion is little more than "garbage in, garbage out." This does not serve the client. Neither does preparing the financial statements yourself and then performing the valuation. As with performing the accounting work for the business and then performing the appraisal, it can cast doubts on your conclusion.

Counsel or the owner may say that there is no way to objectively substantiate missing records, and that your only option is to go with the figures provided by management. This is a bad idea in any setting, and a terrible idea in the litigation context. In most businesses, there is some provider of goods or services to the business whose records will allow statistical extrapolation based on industry statistics. An accountant or forensic financial analyst engaged for this purpose will be able to create financial statements. For a sandwich shop, they may count the rolls ordered and factor in spoilage; for a dry cleaner, they may go to the supplier of the hangers. For a construction company, they may focus on a raw material supplied for jobs typically done by the contractor and make calculations. In a service industry, they may draw conclusions from postage, number of support staff, or even the photocopies made. If you have been retained by the business operator and do not insist that this work be done, your opinion may be thrown out if another appraiser comes to the stand armed with this type of information. Stand by your guns and do not go forward without some type of objectively verified financial documents.

Hard assets carried on the books may also require separate verification. Particularly in small businesses, there is often no real system for managing the inventory. Obsolete inventory is often carried on the books at original cost, when the real value or the replacement cost is much lower. Trucks or large equipment maintained in poor condition may be closer to their replacement date than the owner states; all of this information must be verified to minimize problems with the appraisal.

The simplest way to define required documents is to tell counsel you need everything that the experts retained by other parties will have. This allows all the experts to prepare reports that can be compared, and if the numbers are close, can aid you in advising counsel on which issues can be settled. If the case does not settle and you proceed to deposition and to trial—you goal is to avoid surprises that could change your opinion.

Remember that many of these records may be kept electronically, and cover the data storage options when you provide your list to counsel or conduct your interviews. If accounting software has been used to keep the records, get access to a copy.

When you receive the records, pay attention to how well the records are maintained—whether they are updated on a consistent schedule, for example. Also take all steps in your control to get assurances that these records have been prepared contemporaneously—if they are re-creations, include a statement in your report that makes that clear. Get a representation letter from retaining counsel on the authenticity of the records.

Interview the records preparation staff whenever possible. If the business has used an outside accountant, arrange for an interview; if you are not retained by the party who can make this possible, get counsel to schedule a deposition and provide a list of topics on which you will need information. This is needed so that you can have some comfort level in the validity of the information on which you will base your valuation.

You will need to know the nature of the business entity—corporation, limited partnership, and so on—but will not usually need to see the corporate documents (with the exception of those related to ownership of shares and issues of control, such as voting). With most small businesses, these will be informal or exist only through the descriptions of the parties. If you do not have access to interviews, make sure retaining counsel covers these issues in discovery (if you are retained too late to have discovery on these matters, discuss this with counsel so that any information that might be available from other experts can be provided to you).

Once you have had a look at the balance sheets for the business, you will have a feel for any other appraisals you will need. If the business has significant equipment or real estate, have appraisals done by qualified appraisers—do not do the work yourself unless you are certified to appraise those assets. This will probably add to the cost of the assignment. It will also add to the credibility of the result.

Your next step is to focus on the business during the time frame that damages are alleged to have been sustained, and to get as much information about this time frame as possible (this is particularly important in lost profits cases). Not only should you look at what business performance was during the time period but you should ask for any projections that had been prepared prior to the damage period, and any documents that establish what business of competitors was during the time period as well as in the industry overall. Be sure to include several years after the business has stabilized

You'll see from this discussion that documents from sources other than the business are important. Often, you will be able to find these documents without the aid of discovery. Drawing up a preliminary list of documentation you think you'll need for the assignment when you are drafting the engagement letter will also help you set the fee and the amount of the initial retainer.

Seeing one group of documents often whets your appetite for more. If they are going to be relevant to the assignment, supplement your lists to the client—this is one good reason for providing in your engagement letter that you will deliver your work product within a defined time (more or less) after the receipt of the last requested piece of information.

NOTES

1. The subject of retainer letters is lengthy and complex; it has been assigned its own Chapter at 6, *infra.*
2. The court, upon proper motion, will provide the expert with an opportunity to *redact* the reports in order to remove information which the client for whom the report was prepared may not consent to disclose.
3. Researching writings and presentations by experts retained by other parties is a valuable part of litigation support for counsel, who often won't know the publications and conferences where this information can be found.

CHAPTER 10

The Consulting Appraiser and the Testifying Appraiser

Purpose of This Chapter Litigation support is not limited to trial or deposition testimony—a consulting expert who works behind the scenes can have dramatic impact on the case. Too many appraisers attempt to be both consultant and testifying appraiser in a single assignment. This chapter examines the differences between the consulting expert and the testifying appraiser and offers guidance on how to separate these roles.

To appreciate the nuances of the role of the appraiser as consultant, we need to define the term *consulting expert*. As used here, a consulting expert is an expert in a particular field who is hired by counsel to assist in the preparation of the client's case, but who is *not* expected to give expert testimony in deposition or at trial.

Experts are occasionally called upon to act as consulting experts, sometimes without realizing that this is the purpose for their retention. It is a legitimate litigation service ancillary to the traditional expert witness–appraiser role.

There are important differences between the expert witness and the consulting expert. Most significantly, the expert consultant is not typically held to the standard of independence and lack of bias to which the expert witness is held, and may, where appropriate, assist retaining counsel as an advocate for the position taken by the client. There are other differences, particularly procedural ones, which are discussed below.

THE CASE FOR A CONSULTING EXPERT

Any number of situations might give rise to counsel's inclination to retain a consulting expert:

- Counsel for a defendant might not think there is a need to hire an appraiser to give expert testimony because the plaintiff has the burden of proof to support the damages, and defendant's counsel thinks that he or she can adequately impeach the plaintiff's expert witness with the assistance of a knowledgeable consulting expert.[1]
- Counsel feels inadequately prepared to depose the opposing expert, and needs the assistance of the consultant to coach and prepare him to take deposition testimony.
- Counsel feels overwhelmed by the economic or valuation issues in the case, and needs the assistance of the consulting expert to understand issues in the valuation.
- Counsel has come too late to the realization that his expert witness is in over his head and needs some outside help in preparing for deposition or trial—including coaching the declared expert witness.
- Wise counsel decides that "two heads are better than one" and wants to hire another appraiser to back up his expert witness.
- Very wise counsel realizes that there is a danger that his expert witness may be perceived as biased if asked to give testimony in court about the work of the opposing expert, and wants to hire another independent consulting expert to review the work of the opposing expert in preparation for trial.

DISCOVERY AND THE WORK OF THE CONSULTING EXPERT

Several procedural issues are of special concern in the engagement of a consulting expert. The first and most commonly encountered question experts have about their role as consultant relates to the discoverability of their work.

The general rule is that everything the expert witness sees, says, uses, relies on, and produces is generally discoverable by opposing parties. This is because the rules of fairness as codified in the Rules of Civil Procedure require that both sides know in advance the evidence that will be presented at trial. Among the reasons for this requirement is the desire to minimize the element of surprise that many lawyers relish, and that often keeps cases from settling rather than going to trial.

By contrast, the work of the nontestifying expert (the consulting expert) is generally *not* discoverable. This is because this information will not be presented as evidence at trial, and because it is covered by special rules protecting the attorney's work product.[2] These rules are intended to maintain the integrity of the adversary process by allowing both sides to prepare their own cases with the freedom to develop their own theory for the case and their own trial strategies (and to experiment with and discard strategies), as long as all the facts are fully disclosed by both sides. The scope of materials covered by the work product exclusion is broad, and can include virtually anything prepared or developed in anticipation of trial. It is easy to see why counsel might want to segregate the work efforts of the expert witness from the work efforts of the consulting expert.

It is unclear in many jurisdictions whether the identity of the nontestifying, consulting expert is discoverable. A split on this issue is illustrated by several reported decisions. In *Ager v. Jane C. Storamanont Hospital*,[3] the court held that the identity of the nontestifying consulting expert was not discoverable, ruling that the disclosure of the consultant would be counter to the protective purposes of the work product rule—including the free development of the legal theories of the case. In contrast, the court in *Baki v. B.F. Diamond Construction*[4] allowed the discovery of the identity of the nontestifying consulting expert because the mere identity of a nontestifying expert does not imply disclosure of any underlying facts or opinions held by the expert—merely his name.

SPECIAL ETHICAL CONSIDERATIONS

The fundamental operative of the expert witness is neutrality, independence, and disinterestedness. The expert's opinion testimony is admissible because the expert can be of assistance to the trier of fact in understanding the evidence or in determining some issue before the court. This rationale implies a high degree of duty on the part of the expert witness to present unbiased, factual information or opinion, independent of the influence of the party or counsel who retained his services. This duty is set forth in the ethical standards of every professional society, and in the Uniform Standards of Professional Appraisal Practice (USPAP), and is the cornerstone of appraiser independence. The consulting expert, on the other hand, if not performing an appraisal, is not bound by the same level of independence, insofar as the expert is consulting with counsel. The consulting expert is free to assist counsel in any way suitable to the purposes that both can agree on, because the expert is not being retained as a disinterested third party and will not need to support an independently derived conclusion of value. Some authorities would argue that aside from the primary duty of honesty and fair play inherent in all business dealings, a consulting expert is free from the standards imposed by appraisal societies because consulting experts do not perform the appraisals. For example, most of the language found in USPAP dealing with consulting refers to the requirements that the appraiser perform the services needed by his client in a competent fashion. An expert retained as a consultant to develop arguments impeaching the proposed testimony of another expert would probably not feel compelled to develop an equal number of arguments in support of that other expert's testimony, as would the expert if testifying at trial.

TASKS INVOLVED IN EXPERT CONSULTING

The tasks a consulting expert can perform cover a wide range, and rely generally on the same skill and expertise which the appraiser would use if she had been retained as an expert witness. However, it is often a wise strategic decision to remove the testifying experts from this role. Having a consultant perform these tasks can allow the testifying expert to focus on the performance of the appraisal free from outside influences, and the expert can maintain the highest degree of nonadvocacy. The consulting services might include the following:

- *The initial analysis of the case.* If consultants are retained early enough in the process, they can give a range of the probability for success and the level of economic risk or return. This is a natural outgrowth of the normal kind of work performed by appraiser experts. The consultant-expert could certainly be retained to conduct preliminary investigation and analysis that could help counsel to make informed decisions about how to proceed with prosecution of the case, defense of the case, or settlement.
- *Assist in the formulation of questions for interrogatories.* Interrogatories are often the first step in the collection of information needed to determine the magnitude of the economic issues, value, or damages that the plaintiff or defendant will face. Appraiser experts are in a good position to help counsel in the formulation of questions or answers to interrogatories as they relate to the economic issues.
- *Assist in the development of lists of documents needed in order for the testifying experts to perform the apraisal.* Often the list of documents prepared by counsel without an expert's assistance is inadequate or poorly focused. Expert appraisers are well qualified to solve this problem because their training and skill in information gathering allows them to focus on information and issues pertinent to the value of the entity.
- *Review documents obtained through discovery to determine their relevance or veracity.* Not every document or piece of information is useful, or even truthful. As it relates to the value or the damages, experienced appraiser experts can assist counsel in the review of documents to see whether they are complete or appear to be trustworthy.
- *Assist in the selection of testifying expert witnesses.* About the best person to judge the qualifications of an appraiser expert is

another appraiser. As an expert appraiser, you know who is well respected in the community, and who has the requisite experience to be credible in giving testimony. This knowledge is valuable to counsel in ensuring that the expert witness hired is qualified, competent, credible, and skillful in giving testimony.

- *Consult with counsel to develop questions for use in taking the depositions of other experts or parties.* Like the formulation of questions for interrogatories, the formulation of questions for expert witnesses for deposition is useful to counsel.[5] Deposition is counsel's opportunity to find out what the expert hired by opposing parties will testify to at trial, and counsel needs to have the right questions to ferret out all the pertinent opinions and their foundation. A consulting expert can provide these services without telegraphing the contents of the appraisal performed by a testifying expert.

- *Review the work of other experts to identify the strengths and weaknesses of the other experts' opinions, and test the work of other experts for compliance with applicable appraisal and ethical standards.* One of the most fundamental tasks usually assigned to consulting experts is the review of the opposing expert's work. Wise counsel will ask a consultant to perform a thorough review of appraisal reports or other work product of experts retained by other parties and to analyze its usefulness in the legal strategy counsel intends to apply. Having a nontestifying expert perform this work allows the testifying expert to say he or she has no opinion about reports prepared by others. Very wise counsel will ask a consultant to review the report prepared by the expert who will offer testimony. A peer review can point out simple errors (such as math errors) or complicated issues (such as selection of method) that could cost the report credibility at trial.

- *Assist counsel in preparing for the direct testimony of testifying expert witnesses.* Another area not often considered by counsel is the use of consulting experts in the preparation and rehearsal of direct testimony by counsel's expert witness. It is uncommon for expert witnesses to have access to good consultants in the preparation of their direct testimony, but given the opportunity to work through trial testimony with another appraiser, most experts would jump at the chance. Good direct testimony is the first line of defense to cross-examination, and the consulting expert is qualified to assist by testing the methodology employed by the expert witness and helping the expert to anticipate cross-examination.

- *Assist counsel in preparing to make and to defend a* Daubert *challenge.* Counsel are bringing *Daubert* challenges with increasing frequency—some legal scholars now believe that the failure to attempt to exclude the testimony of an expert witness may be tantamount to malpractice. If there are significant flaws in the appraisal performed by an opposing expert, or if the expert lacks relevant qualifications, you can provide specifics for the use of counsel. If there are weaknesses in the methods or qualifications of the testifying expert retained by counsel, the consultant can have material ready for counsel's use in responsive argument.

- *Assist counsel in the development of plans for cross-examination of opposing experts.* It is sometimes problematic for the testifying expert to assist in this area without losing the appearance of objectivity, but preparing counsel for cross-examination of opposing experts is tailor-made for the consultant. As a consulting expert, you can assist by preparing questions targeted to give light to the issues in dispute by the experts retained by both sides, and focus on the weaknesses—if any—in the opinion proffered by the other side. A testifying expert may be tempted to find some areas to criticize in the report of the opposing expert in order to justify the preparation of his or her own report; a consultant who has no report to justify can be bluntly honest with counsel on whether the report of an opposing expert should be accepted because it has reached a credible conclusion.

- *Participate in preparation for settlement meetings or mediation.* Counsel may face difficulties in presenting the weak points of the case to the client, and in advising the client to settle for an amount that would be less than might be received at trial, or more than the defendant is willing to pay without rolling the dice in court. Again, the consultant's ability to look at the case without a report to defend and with substantial expertise in appraisal can provide the client with the information that can let the client decide how to manage risk.

The payment structure for a consultant will almost always be an hourly one, but you should get a large retainer up front and keep the billing scrupulously current. An engagement letter with all standard protections for the appraiser is also a must. The hourly rate is set by the market in the practice area, but since this cost will be recovered by a prevailing party, the appraiser will have to be sensitive to client and counsel budgeting.

The most frequent error made by consulting experts is the blurring of the line between the appraiser's work and the attorney's work. It is appropriate for the consultant to prepare a deposition summary of the testimony of the expert witness—it is not appropriate for the consultant to prepare a memo of law. It is appropriate for the consultant to research the availability of other data—it is not appropriate for the consultant to do legal research on the standard of value. Crossing this line exposes the consultant to risk of malpractice claims.

The demeanor of the consultant who attends deposition, settlement conferences, or trial should not interfere with or distract from the counsel's work. Passing notes and making comments gives the impression that counsel is not competent to manage the case without input from the consultant. Even if this is true, the client is not served by having the consultant play too prominent a role.

Sometimes a consulting expert will be asked to stand in for the testifying expert, who may have been damaged at deposition, whose report may have been outclassed by the work product of other experts, or whose testimony may have been ruled inadmissible under *Daubert*. The consultant must bear in mind that once declared as an expert witness, all prior work done by the consultant is open for inquiry. For this reason, it is rarely a good idea to agree to take on testimony (other than as a rebuttal witness) when hired as a consultant. If this situation arises, discuss with counsel all the implications of your providing testimony and amend your engagement letter to cover these circumstances.

NOTES

1. The question of whether the defendant should present appraisal testimony is an important strategic decision. If the defendant presented expert testimony on a lower amount of damages, that testimony would be available for an award to the plaintiff. However, if the plaintiff's expert is impeached, and the court gives that testimony little or no weight, there will be no evidence of damages on the record.

2. Most jurisdictions have codified the circumstances under which the work-product privilege is applicable. For example, Federal Rule of Civil Procedure 26(b)4(B) provides generally that the facts known to and/or held by an expert who is not expected to testify are only discoverable in exceptional and unusual situations, such as where one party has hired all available experts on a subject.

3. *Ager v. Jane C. Stormanont Hsopital,* 622 F.2d 496 (10th Cir. 1980).

4. *Baki v. B.F. Diamond Construction,* 71 F.R.D. 179 (Maryland 1976).

5. The consultant treads a fine line here. You must suggest areas of inquiry with sufficient detail to make sure counsel gets the technical terms and definitions right, but you must not actually write out the questions verbatim; counsel is more skilled than most experts on the phrasing of a question that will overcome an objection.

CHAPTER 11

Preparing the Report—Quality and Admissibility Issues

Purpose of This Chapter The highest-quality report is worthless if it is not admitted and does not reach the trier of fact. And a report or opinion which is admitted might do the client more harm than good if later discredited, as the taint of poor quality may spread to other portions of the case, including to the opinions of other experts. This chapter includes a review of some cases where the admissibility of the report is discussed, and report content essentials.

Any examination of admissibility of expert testimony must emphasize the Supreme Court's opinion in *Daubert v. Merrell Dow Pharmaceuticals, Inc.,*[1] and the more recent opinion in *Kumho Tire Co., Ltd. v. Carmichael.*[2] *Daubert* discussed the special obligations imposed by Federal Rule of Evidence 702[3] upon trial judges to act as "gatekeepers" to determine the admissibility of scientific evidence. The (nonexclusive) criteria of reliability to be applied include the following:

- Can the method be tested, or has it been tested?
- Has the method been subjected to peer review or publication, which aids in detecting flaws in the method?
- What is the known or potential rate of error?

- Are there established standards to control use of the method?
- Is the method generally accepted in the technical community?[4]

The debate among the professions about whether the *Daubert* criteria would apply to nonscientific testimony was resolved in the *Kumho* opinion, which applied the standard to all types of expert testimony to the extent the criteria were applicable, and invited the application of other relevant criteria where the *Daubert* indicia lacked good "fit." Specifics within the *Kumho* opinion may (and should) cause counsel to examine particular practices of business appraisers and contents of their reports, and the expert may assist counsel in preparing for the motion to exclude testimony based on the witnesses' qualifications, methodology, or both.

The holdings of *Daubert/Kumho* are discussed at every conference and written about in nearly every issue of the professional journals. There are good reasons for this. Appraisers who do not do competent, consistent work in conformance with the accepted standards of the profession put themselves at serious risk. For the appraiser who testifies, this could result in exclusion of the opinion. For any appraiser, this could result in a claim of malpractice. As you read these materials, focus on the work product of experts retained by other parties to see how you can issue spot for counsel. Also focus on your own work product to see if your work could be subject to challenge.

DAUBERT AND *KUMHO* STANDARDS AND APPRAISAL ASSIGNMENTS

Despite what the parties or counsel may wish, a litigation report cannot have separate standards or processes than a nonlitigation appraisal assignment. *Daubert* and *Kumbo* standards for the reliability of expert opinion apply to all appraisal assignments.[5]

The objective of that requirement [the *Daubert* gatekeeping requirement] is to ensure the reliability and relevancy of expert testimony. It is to make certain that an expert, whether basing testimony upon professional studies or personal experience, employs in the courtroom the same level of intellectual rigor that characterized the practice of an expert in the relevant field.[6]

REQUIRED SOURCE DOCUMENTS

The initial phases of a business appraisal assignment include the review of financial records on the subject business; throughout the assignment the appraiser continues to analyze and apply information gleaned from these records. When the appraiser relies on inappropriate varieties of information, the entire opinion can fail for lack of a credible basis.

Carefully review the information provided and consider whether it is worthy of credit. When determining which documents to use, the appraiser should remember the "garbage in, garbage out" rule— bad data will yield an unreliable conclusion. If the financial information is questionable, however, the appraiser who will testify should not be the one making major corrections. As discussed in Chapter 9, advise retaining counsel that an independent accountant will have to be obtained to prepare financials and, where appropriate, detailed appraisals of other significant assets. The additional expense involved is part of the cost of getting a reliable opinion.

Counsel may plan to use the testimony of the staffer who prepared the financial statements for the company in order to establish the reliability of these documents. Be certain that you know the formal training of this staffer—in many small companies, this person is merely the person who learned the accounting software, and the staffer will have little training on the formalities of accounting. Be cautious when provided with financial information that has been prepared for a particular purpose, such as review by a potential buyer or to secure financing. Often such information will maximize the dividend-paying capacity of the business, overstate the value of obsolete inventory, or list hard assets at replacement cost rather than their actual worth.

The risk of relying on the wrong type of documents is illustrated in *Target Market Publishing, Inc. v. ADVO, Inc.*[7] In that case, the parties entered into a joint venture to produce and market direct-mail advertising for auto dealers. The venture failed within six months, never made it beyond the first initial market, and never attracted more than fifteen advertisers. In establishing lost profits, the plaintiff's expert used, as a forecasting tool, a marketing *plan* that was not a market *projection*, but rather was used only to establish target revenues. The expert projected that had the contract term continued, the venture would have made $1.4 million in first-year profits.

In attempting to bootstrap their expert's opinion, plaintiffs pointed to *"the long experience and voluminous credentials of the report's author."* In rejecting the expert's opinions as "completely untenable," the court noted the expert's extraordinary assumptions that, contrary to the actual six-month history of the venture, the venture [as it was optimistically described in the market projections] "would penetrate into a total of forty-nine marketing zones, that each zone would generate fourteen advertisers per monthly issue, and that virtually all of those advertisers would pay the full price for their ads." Reviewing the facts against the assumptions, the appellate court agreed with the trial court's assessment that the opinion *"relies upon mere assumptions . . . from which no reasonable inference of lost profits could be drawn,"* leading the court to reject the testimony under *Daubert*. The marketing department's motivation document was not a reliable basis for the forecasting of the appraiser.

It is simple to see how an expert might become enmeshed in this situation. In a recently established business, there are no historical data. In such a circumstance, look to other businesses that offer similar products or services, and rely on their histories for guidance. If that information is not available, you may be wiser to decline the assignment—this may be one of those times when expertise cannot overcome bad facts and the client is better off saving money.

There are some categories of documents that, although they may not be completely representative of the conditions of the business, are nonetheless reliable bases for appraisal projections. The test of such documents applies good common sense. For example, in *Rossi v. Mobil Oil Corp.*,[8] the expert used monthly financial statements prepared by the accountant for the business, which contained expense estimates based on industry averages, and also included data on a combination of businesses, some of which were not involved in the suit. The testimony that relied on these documents was admitted even though the documents were not compilations of "regularly maintained business records."

Experts are entitled to rely on this inadmissable evidence, and the court found the documents met the requirements of Federal Rules of Evidence 703 and 704. This case makes an interesting contrast with the trial court's Memorandum Opinion in *Whelan v. Abell*.[9] The financial expert in that case was found unqualified to testify on damage issues where the expert attempted to rely on financial statements prepared for purpose of a public offering. Flaws in that document rendered it non-compliant with SEC requirements. A credibility problem was certainly created for the witness when he testified that this type of document (i.e., a noncompliant filing!) was "typically relied upon" by experts. It also illustrates why it is a poor idea to do expert work for clients for whom you provide other services. Imagine if the expert in *Whelan* had prepared the SEC filing—as part of its efforts to discredit the expert, counsel for an opposing party would have pointed out that the SEC filing was noncompliant, and the expert would be at risk of suit for that work.

KEEPING APPRAISAL OPINION WITHIN APPRAISAL EXPERTISE

Business appraisers are not a source of one-stop shopping for expert opinions. There are several areas on which the appraiser should *not* agree to render an opinion:

- *The standard of value appropriate to the claim.* Issues of whether goodwill is included in appraisals for the purpose of dissolution of marriage or whether "fair value" v. "fair market value" is the standard in dissenting shareholder cases are legal calls for which information should be provided to the business appraiser.[10] It is not the appraiser's job—nor within the appraiser's expertise—to determine these standards. Failure to provide the business appraiser with the correct standard of value (which will be cited in the report) may render the appraisal conclusion useless.[11]
- *The value of real estate, heavy equipment, fixtures, improvements or other significant assets of the business,* unless the appraiser has the necessary credentials. You may be tempted to use the book

value of these items, the value reported in the property or intangible tax records, or the estimate of management. If the assets represent a significant percentage of the total assets or value of the business, failing to get an independent appraisal for these values can put the opinion at risk. Even if the opinion is ruled admissible by the court, the failure to get an independent appraisal can make the expert appear to be controlled by the client. While obtaining these appraisals adds a level of costs to the assignment, in the case of significant assets, getting these values established is a good investment. Imagine the consequences if you opt not to obtain independent appraisals and take the client's book values for the report, and an opposing party has complete appraisals done which substantially differ from the numbers you have accepted.

- *Interpretation of contractual rights of parties that may give them a right to buy out, first refusal, or appraisal, or that determines liabilities or ultimate facts.*[12] For example, in *Morse/Diesel v. Trinity Industries*,[13] a certified public accountant (CPA) attempted to testify regarding which party was responsible for construction delays and what was the impact of various change orders. The trial court excluded the testimony under Federal Rule of Evidence 703 as there was no foundation for the CPA to have such an opinion. The appellate court agreed with the trial court's statement:

  > [i]n each and every one of the four examples given . . . the proffered testimony is qualitative testimony relating to the reasonableness of including certain work with [*Morse/Diesel's* construction expert's] calculation. I find that this witness is not qualified by knowledge, skill, experience, training or education to render these sorts of qualitative opinions under *Daubert*.[14]

The attempt to use the CPA to bootstrap the construction expert's calculations on damages, or to add testimony lacking from another expert, was unavailing.

SUPERFICIAL TREATMENT OF ISSUES: THE "DOWN AND DIRTY" APPRAISAL

Economic and time factors can also play a part in choices of methodology that can result in the appraisal expert's testimony being excluded for failure to meet *Daubert* and *Kumho* criteria. Most appraisal experts have been asked to take a preliminary opinion to court, often a report prepared for settlement or in early phases of the case before complete information was available. Usually, these requests are motivated by cost controls or poor time management on the part of retaining counsel. A "down and dirty" appraisal used for initial case analysis should not become the opinion rendered at trial. Such initial work (especially when substituted for final work product when money runs short) will rarely employ the methodology that experts in valuation find essential or the "intellectual rigor" discussed in *Kumho.*

Another problem results when experts issue draft reports. Accountants are particularly prone to this practice, as some treat the issuance of a draft as part of the process of getting representation letters. A skilled attorney can make this practice sound as though the number is submitted for client approval. Appraisers whose engagement letter provides for the final payment to be made "upon delivery of the report" are subject to the same challenges. A discussion of how to handle the need for a representation of factual accuracy, and a discussion of draft reports, appears later in this chapter.

While you write the report, you will inevitably print drafts. But these should be internal copies that are not shown to counsel. When a draft is no longer needed, it can be discarded if it is your normal practice to do so. Do not keep drafts in the file and then purge the file before your deposition—doing so can subject you to sanctions.

When the client has no money, or the attorney has not given you enough time to prepare a report worthy of court testimony, give serious thought to declining the assignment. The damage to your credibility may be permanent. Each time you testify in deposition or at trial, you will be asked to name not only the courts that have accepted you as an expert, but those that have not accepted your testimony. Counsel in a locale share transcripts of experts, and you will hear embarrassing testimony and rulings quoted to you again and again.

Do not soft-pedal incomplete work by throwing around appraisal terms. Cloaking incomplete work in technical jargon will not pass a savvy opposing expert. In *Frymire-Brinati v. KPMG Peat Marwick*,[15] the appellees (plaintiffs, below) claimed to be bilked investors in a limited partnership, and alleged that the appellant's certification of partnership financial statements failed to disclose that investments were worth less than represented on the books. Plaintiff's "star witness" used a discounted cash flow analysis to value the partnership projects, determining the projects at 10 times annual cash flow. However, since the historical cash flow of many projects was minimal or even negative cash flow, the expert assigned them a value of zero.

The appellate court determined that the expert testimony was inadmissible because it failed to meet *Daubert's* requirement that the testimony be "not only relevant, but reliable."[16] The trial judge did not conduct any preliminary assessment of the reasoning or methodology used by the expert. The appellate court noted that, had such a preliminary assessment been undertaken, the trial court could not properly have admitted the valuation testimony, as it failed to satisfy the requirements of Federal Rule of Evidence 702.

The specific shortcomings of the expert's method lay in the admittedly surface treatment given to the assignment. The testimony established that normally, to determine market value using a discounted cash flow analysis, the expert considers the *potential* cash flows of the asset, not merely the *historical* cash flow.[17] Under the contrary view taken by the plaintiff's expert, the court noted that "raw land would be worthless and that a large office building in the final stages of construction also has no value even though it is fully leased out and could be sold for a hundred million dollars."[18] Even the expert conceded that his valuation was not an attempt to determine the "market value" of the asset (a fundamental necessity of plaintiff's claims), but merely "a fairly simple pass at what the magnitude of the problem was."[19]

Often, testimony that may be flawed in method or that may lack credibility can be admitted with proper instruction to the trier of fact. However, the *Frymire* appellate court was reluctant to admit the testimony and allow the trier of fact to assign it an appropriate weight, finding it problematic to admit this "fairly simple pass" into evidence simply because it was offered by an expert witness qualified in accounting matters. Ultimately, this lack of conventional methodology persuaded the appellate court that the testimony was not reliable, as the expert "conceded that he did not employ the methodology that experts in valuation find essential."[20] Such a concession prevented the testimony from meeting the criteria for reliability and relevancy set forth in *Daubert*.

Another aspect of the "down and dirty" business appraisal is the assignment which heavily relies on off-the-shelf or personally developed business appraisal software.[21] The quality of appraisal software varies widely, but the major problem with such software is the user. Many users of appraisal software adopt the product as a shortcut for analysis and come to use it as a crutch. Rarely is the template modified by the appraiser, and rarer still is the appraiser who can substantiate the structure or thought processes used by the program. Therefore, if you are going to use canned software, make sure you can credibly address these issues; if not, either do not use the software in the assignment, or get the needed information before you are sworn:

- What are the credentials of the professionals who developed the software?
- Who tested the software?
- Who has peer reviewed it?
- What has been published on it?
- Are there standards governing its use?
- What are the default presets, and how were they determined?
- Is the software generally accepted—how many people use it, and what are their credentials?[22]

If the appraiser cannot answer these questions, the conclusion of value may have no real basis. The trier of fact might conclude that your opinion is worth no more than the opinion of any buyer of the software, and that appraisal is merely filling out forms on a screen. Neither conclusion helps your credibility or gets you paid.

Your lack of information on these topics may also make your report fail to comply with USPAP. The Appraisal Standard Board's Advisory Opinion on the Use of Automated Valuation Models (AVM) provides specific guidelines on the use of AVMs:

An appraiser should have a basic understanding of how the AVM works in its analysis of data . . . the appraiser should know which characteristics [of the data] are analyzed and how the analysis is tested for accuracy and reasonableness. . . .

Even though your report may not be required to comply with USPAP, a knowledgeable counsel is sure to suggest that this is an industry standard, and your failure to comply creates credibility problems.

RISKS OF ORIGINAL OR PERSONALLY DEVELOPED APPRAISAL METHODS

Viewing the expert's opinion as presented to the *Kumho* trial court, the Supreme Court noted there was:

(n)o indication in the record that other experts in the industry use [the expert]'s particular approach or that [other] experts normally make the very fine distinctions necessary to support his conclusions, nor are there references to articles or papers that validate his approach.[23]

Appraisers, weary of searching among the proven approaches for one best suited to an assignment, may be tempted to combine approaches or create an untried approach or method in order to cure what they perceive as deficiencies in the currently sanctioned methodology. Organizations, desirous of recognition or developing a niche, may put their "brand name" on appraisal methods. Authors, wanting to sell books, may invent new theories. Some of these methods are pretty good, and deserve to be adopted. Over time, some of these methods may be evaluated and accepted by the technical community. Until that time, however, the business appraiser uses them at his own risk. Courtroom testimony is not the place to advance new theories that cannot be substantiated in the growing body of business appraisal literature.

In *Moore v. Ashland Chemical*[24] the court discussed that:

[u]nder Rule 702 the "knowledge" of each discipline is both its

principles and methodology and the theories, techniques or inferences produced through its methodology. Thus, the proffered opinion of any expert in a field of knowledge, in order to be evidentially reliable, must either be based soundly on the current knowledge, principles and methodology of the expert's discipline or be soundly inferred or derived therefrom . . . [Moreover], the focus must be on the principles and methodology upon which the expert's opinion is based, not on the merits of the expert's conclusion.[25]

Experts who depart from known principles and methodology, therefore, may develop an incredible (and inadmissible) conclusion, regardless of its apparent merit.

One of the cardinal rules enunciated in the standards of all of the appraisal organizations is that *a valuation conclusion must be replicable.* If the method has not been validated and studied, it may not be a replicable method. It certainly will not pass the "indicia of reliability" criteria set forth in *Daubert. Simple pass* methods, individual or brand-name methods, or software appraisals are no substitute for the developed body of appraisal knowledge.

DOCUMENTING SUBJECTIVE STATEMENTS

Discussing the trial court's rejection of the expert opinion, the Court in *Kumho* focused on the expert's fall-back position—that his subjective analysis (i.e., personal opinion) was the basis for his conclusions. Note that neither the Supreme Court nor the trial court doubted the expert's qualifications. However, they had no comfort level with the expert's repeated subjective judgments.

[T]hese concerns might have been augmented by [the expert]'s repeated reliance on the "subjectiveness" of his mode of analysis in response to questions seeking specific information regarding how he could differentiate between a tire that had actually been overdeflected and a tire that merely looked as though it had been.[26]

[N]othing in either *Daubert* or the Federal Rules of Evidence requires a district court to admit opinion evidence that is connected to existing data only by the *ipse dixit* of the expert.[27]

Statements in reports like "we believe the most representative number to be" are nothing more than the personal opinion of the report's author. As valid as that opinion may be, if it is not sufficiently substantiated, the number will lack force.

In *City of Tuscaloosa v. Harcross Chemicals, Inc.*,[28] the appellate court upheld the exclusion of a CPA's testimony on a bid-rigging conspiracy based on his subjective analysis of bids that were signals to co-conspirators. Not only was the judgment of the witness solely his personal conclusion, but it fell beyond the realm of expertise normally possessed by an accountant. However, testimony within the accountant's competency, particularly his statistical testimony, was allowed to stand where it used "well-established and reliable methodologies."[29]

Prediction of future events also calls the subjective judgment of the business appraiser into question. Any number of future contingencies can be created to affect the value of the business interest. However, the appraiser must be able to show that those contingencies are somewhat likely to occur, and not that they are predicted by management or the product of raw speculation. In *Eisenberg v. Commissioner*,[30] the court rejected a valuation that took into account the ability of a subchapter C corporation to convert to a subchapter S corporation, finding no evidence of such intent and where such an election could produce other consequences, causing the court to characterize such a choice as "practically remote."

Weighting methods to arrive at a conclusion (the averaging of values gained through the various methods) is another sore spot for subjective challenge.[31] In assigning the weights the appraiser must be prepared with subjective data to substantiate the choice,[32] or risk having the weight assignment appear as expert advocacy, or client direction. Either one will taint the conclusion beyond acceptable limits.

CONSIDERING ALL AVAILABLE DATA

Subjectivity can occur when information is *excluded,* as well as when too much unverifiable information is *included.* For example, lack of directly comparable data may also justify failure to employ the market approach. The expert must be prepared to consider data of companies in similar industries, so long as the businesses have comparable characteristics. In *Estate of Hall*,[33] experts for the estate and for the Internal Revenue Service valued a block of stock of Hallmark cards. The estate retained investment banking firms to value the stock. The estate's experts found only one comparable company in the greeting card industry, American Greetings, which was publicly traded (Hallmark was privately held). The estate's experts used other "comparable companies," in the belief that "considering several comparable companies reduced the probability that individual characteristics, temporary market inefficiencies, or aberrations relating to one company might bias the valuation analysis."[34] These companies included "industry leaders" such as McDonald's, Anheuser Busch, IBM, and Coca-Cola, used by one expert for the estate. Another used A.T. Cross Co., Avon Products, Lenox, and a manufacturer of gift wrap items and household products, believing that "these companies provided useful comparisons because they produced brand name consumer goods, were leading companies in their industries, had publicly traded common stock, and had business and financial characteristics similar to Hallmark."[35] It is clear that, given the distinctions between some of these industries, adjustments would be needed—perhaps numerous adjustments.

The expert for the IRS was the senior vice president of a firm specializing in investment analysis and business valuation. In performing his analysis, the IRS expert used only a comparable company, American Greetings, determining that it was the only "reasonably comparable" company because it had a similar product mix and capital structure, and served the same markets. In fact, Hallmark was larger than American Greetings and the IRS expert presumed that Hallmark would command a higher price than American Greetings if its stock were publicly traded. Using this market approach, the expert arrived at a 118 percent ratio of the value of Hallmark stock compared to American Greetings.

Using an income capitalization approach, the expert calculated projected cash flow, then discounted it using a weighted average cost of capital. The expert then calculated a weighted average business enterprise value by assigning the market approach value a 65 percent weight, and the income capitalization approach a 35 percent weight. The same techniques were used to create a minority share valuation under both the market and income capitalization approaches.

The court rejected the precise and painstaking work of the IRS expert. In finding that the data of other industries were of the type on which experts would typically rely, the court emphasized that, more importantly, it was the type of data on which *buyers* would reasonably rely: "It is inconceivable to us that a potential buyer of Hallmark stock would consider only one alternative 'comparable,' i.e., American Greetings stock,"[36] and found that the IRS's expert had defined "similar" characteristics, in effect, as identical ones. What seems an unorthodox approach was accepted because it was well documented and rationally presented.

Wary of adjustments, business appraisers, particularly those with rigid technical or financial backgrounds, may shy away from these "similar companies" or from the market approach altogether. However, the skill—and sometimes the fortitude—to make these adjustments is an essential part of the business appraisal process. Reluctance to do so reflects a misguided attempt "to infuse a talismanic precision into an issue which should frankly be recognized as impractically imprecise."

EVALUATING DATA FROM OUTSIDE SOURCES

As is the case with business appraisal software, the appraiser should not blindly insert the data into the spreadsheet, push a button and wait for the magic number to be revealed. The business appraiser should have a thorough understanding of the contents of the data and their proper use—including which discounts can be properly applied.

In *Estate of Jung*,[37] one of the issues was whether cash flow was to be distributed to a controlling interest. The court examined expert testimony based on the Capital Asset Pricing Model (CAPM). The tax court concluded that the use of a minority discount was not proper when using comparables of publicly traded stock:

> What is important for purposes on the minority discount question is that the basic data these experts used are the data of stock

market trading, which is almost entirely the data of trading in minority interests. Thus, this element of the discount rate also suggests that ordinarily the DCF approach results in minority interest value. . . . The expert notes that the prospective controlling investor will control the total available cash flow of the acquired corporation. However, this explanation does not persuade us that the discount rate . . . implies control, because this rate of return is developed from data that reflect the actions of minority investors and generally not the actions of controlling investors.

Therefore, particularly when using public data, the application of such a discount can, in fact, represent a double-counting. If you want to insist that this is not the case, you had better be prepared with technical literature to back up the claim.

You must also make counsel aware that each database defines its data points differently, and the combining of data from various sources into a single spreadsheet or statistical model may not yield reliable results, again rendering it unworthy of credit.

Remember that you will be responsible for laying the foundation for the admissibility of the data. Therefore, do not use data in your report unless you are prepared to testify how the data are harvested, authenticated, and updated. If there are articles or studies on the data, be familiar with them and the qualifications of the authors.

A number of excellent research services are available to business appraisers, but they must be correctly used. As with data, the appraiser must be familiar with the background of persons who have performed the research, the sources consulted, and the aging of the information.

USING THE REPORT'S AUTHOR AS THE EXPERT WITNESS

It is common practice, particularly in larger appraisal or accounting firms, for the delegation of assignments to result in a work product far removed from the expert witness who offers the valuation conclusion. The report may be the product of a technician in another department or even another office in a different state. Even in smaller firms, junior staff often produce work that is then offered through the testimony of an older, more experience appraiser who is comfortable on the witness stand. In court, the attorney or client may desire another appraiser to testify and offer the opinion of another expert (perhaps the initial appraiser is not a skilled witness or has no wish to testify, or the parties have discontinued their relationship for a variety of reasons). The primary objection faced in these situations, of course, is that the report is hearsay.[38] As you'll see from the following discussion, simply having the chosen "mouthpiece" sign the report is no solution. It is important for the expert witness to also be the author of the opinion or report.

Take, for example, the attempt at presenting expert testimony in *Tokio Marine & Fire Insurance Co., Ltd. v. Norfolk & Western Railway Co.*,[39] The court held automobile appraisal evidence inadmissible when presented by an expert witness, even though the witness had participated in the preparation of the appraisal and had offered input. However, the court found that the conclusions of the appraisal were those of another member of the same firm, who did not testify. Where the appraisal report "as a whole" was not the opinion of the witness offering expert testimony, the testimony is not admissible, but was excluded by the court as hearsay. *One expert may not give the opinion of another expert who does not testify.*[40] A valid objection against mouthpiece testimony is that the opposing party has no opportunity to cross-examine the person who performed the work for flaws in the methodology or other information that may defeat the admissibility of the testimony under the *Daubert* criteria.

MAKING THE REPORT COMPREHENSIVE AND COMPLETE

A threshold question in any report preparation is the nature of the report. There are only two levels of ~~reports~~ appraisals under USPAP—Complete Appraisal and Limited Appraisal. The limited appraisal is distinguished only by the invocation of the Departure Provision in the performance of the scope of the work, not in the contents of the report. The scope of work, therefore, must be clearly delineated in your report.

Reporting the results of the appraisal is organized into three levels under USPAP:

- ~~Self-contained~~ Appraisal report
- ~~Summary appraisal repor~~t
- Restricted use appraisal report

The standards of most appraisal organizations also delineate levels of report content. Some also attempt to carve out exceptions if the report is intended for use in litigation. Do not utilize these exceptions. Your appraisal methods and work product in litigation settings should not differ from reports prepared for other purposes. Changing the rules for litigation assignments is one of the surest ways to look like an advocate.

Retaining counsel may ask you for a bare-bones report that states your conclusion of value and little else. This is bad practice; don't agree to this. Your conclusion must be replicable if it is to comply with professional standards, and have a demonstrably reliable foundation to be admitted in court. If you do good work there will be nothing to hide in your appraisal report. The most credible appraisal reports have the process fully explained and documented.

Do not issue drafts—no matter what. Counsel may ask to see a draft of the report. Just say no. Nothing good can come from passing a draft report around. If additional information is provided that may change your conclusion before the issuance of the final report, the draft report has created expectations that now must be changed. An owner who does not like the number in the draft may not pay for the production of the final report. If you revise the report after you have issued the draft, you can be discredited on the stand.

Some appraisers issue drafts in order to obtain representations that the facts recited in the report are accurate. If this is your intent, then provide the draft section of the report with the description of the business—and provide only that section. There is simply no legitimate or helpful reason to send your numbers around until your conclusions are final.

A sample table of contents for an appraisal report appears at the end of this chapter. This table of contents should not change because the report is written as a litigation assignment; good practice does not change because a report may be the basis for courtroom testimony.

The report should always demonstrate a good writing style, and completely present the reasoning behind the appraiser's selection of subjective analytical values such as the following:

- The capitalization rate
- The discount rate
- Company-specific risk premia
- Adjustments for liquidity and control
- Selection of appraisal approaches and methods
- Selection of guideline companies and data

The competent appraiser must be able to clearly communicate both the value conclusion and the underlying rationale.

Keep the intended audience in mind. The report will probably be marked as evidence and read by the trier of fact. Ideally, the report should incorporate an *executive summary*—a brief synopsis of the entire report. Try to limit this to a single page. When your report is marked as an exhibit at trial, the trier of fact will be able to review a single page for the essence of your opinion, and have the backup available that contains the detailed analysis. Within the body of the report, keep the organization tight. Use headings for all the sections. Use sequential numbering of paragraphs within each section (in Section 4, for example, the second topic discussed should be numbered as 4.2). Number each page of the report and have a detailed table of contents in the front of the report. Place all graphs and charts in the relevant section of the report so that the reader does not have to flip to the appendices to find this information —if you aren't sufficiently facile with software to do this, get help. Use graphics at the relevant portion of the report, and label each graph as relating to the section in which it is included. This allows more than one graph to be included in a section of the report without confusion. Labels on graphs and exhibits should avoid shortcuts that may not be understood by a reader with limited background on financial analysis.

The principal sources of information should be set out in the report, and should be carefully selected. As you write the report, anticipate that counsel for an opposing party will read these sources and search for content inconsistent with your opinion. Make sure that your sources match the date of valuation. Any Internet resources you use should be checked for the age of the material and the site's policy for updating content. Information for trade associations should also be for the correct time period. All of this background information should be retained in your file.

Be scrupulously accurate with all facts about the subject company.[41] Do not solve this problem by issuing a draft of the entire report for client approval. Do, however, send the portion of the report with a description of the company, its history, the ownership of the interests, and the interest being appraised to the owner before it is included in the report, and get written assurances that it is accurate. Particularly if you have been retained by the company or the controlling owners, you may be tempted to describe the company in glowing terms. Avoid this impulse; it will look like bias. The fewer adjectives in your report, the better.

The most subjective portions of the appraisal are, of course, the ones that will be the focus of most inquiry when you testify. Remember the *ipse dixit* rule and state in the report why the numbers, weighting, or data you have selected are the most credible. Substantiate your forecast of future earnings as much as possible—and (heeding the lesson of *Target Marketing*) don't take the projections of management at face value.

You should include in your report all approaches and methods that you considered, even though you may have ultimately given them no weight. Be certain to state why you selected one method over another. If you did not use any method or approach, include the reasons that it was not employed. If you did not have sufficient information to use a method or approach, be prepared to detail the steps you took to attempt to secure the needed information.

If you have selected the income approach, one area that deserves special attention is the section on the selection of the capitalization rate or discount rate. Because this always involves some degree of interpretation and subjectivity, this section must be thoroughly documented. Avoid general statements about the selection, and include all the reasons for the selection of the discount rate.

If you have selected the market approach, pay particular attention to your use of data. A number of writings suggest that data are not time sensitive,[42] and some court cases even suggest that data pertaining to transactions that took place after the date of valuation can be used. However, the reliability and relevancy of the data must be thoroughly supported. Avoid "cherry picking" the available data, which can appear as mere manipulation for a predetermined range of values.

And values are indeed a range—admit the possibility of other numbers in your report as well as your testimony. After the appraiser has applied all the necessary methods, the result will be an array of indicated values. It is vital to point out to the reader the reasons you relied on or had more confidence in one indicated value over another.

There are two ways to learn how to write good reports. The first is to enter a peer review accreditation process: Submit your work product and resubmit after reading the critique of the reviewers. The second is to read the work product of other appraisers. Once you have received your professional credentials, become a reviewer for the accreditation process. Participate in the report review workshops, which are offered by organizations, including the Institute of Business Appraisers and the National Association of Certified Valuation Analysts. A number of the books referenced in Chapter 5 contain sample appraisal reports or individual sections of reports. Several collections of reports also give examples of reports for a variety of assignments, standards of value, and percentages of interest valued. After you have worked on a number of litigation assignments, you will also have access to the reports of other experts

A word to the wise—*read* these reports, but do not *copy* them. Sooner or later, someone will catch you at it.

Although it is true that business appraisal is not an exact science (and in fact, not a science at all), there are, nevertheless, accepted and defined rules, approaches and methods. Adherence to these methods and to the common body of knowledge is the best policy for the attorney and the business appraiser.

Do not overlook the simple issues in report preparation—appearance is as important as content.[43]

- Use bright, good quality paper.
- Use a readable font and terminal digit numbering.[44]
- Number the pages of the appendices for ease of reference in testimony.
- Incorporate the exhibits into the body of the report—put the graphs on the page where the text explains them. This is extra work but makes the report more useful to the reader.
- Include an executive summary in the front of the report—a jury taking the report back into the jury room, a judge flip-

ping through the report, or an attorney using the report at deposition will be able to easily find the essentials of your opinion.

- Have the report proofread (including the grammar!) and the math checked carefully. If you do this yourself, take a break of at least a week after finishing the report and doing the final proofread. This allows your head to clear and lessens the possibility that you will skim over errors. It is better to have a second set of eyes proofreading your work.
- Pay particular attention to your boilerplate. Few things are more embarrassing than finding an error, and then realizing that you have incorporated it into every report issued this year.

Reading this material is not as valuable as having your reports undergo peer review (though it is less painful to the ego just to read the material). Apply for a professional credential that offers peer review (remember, "peer review" is defined as a written critique of your work product, not a pass/fail process based on a report prepared with supplied information in an artificial assignment). Do not doctor the reports you submit to approach perfection—let them be examples of your typical work product, including the size of the company and the purpose of the valuation. Even if you may not be ready for accreditation, the targeted feedback will make you a better appraiser.

TWO SAMPLE TABLES OF CONTENTS FOR BUSINESS APPRAISAL REPORTS[45]

Sample 1

1. Disclosures and Description of the Assignment
   1.1 Subject of the Appraisal
   1.2 Restrictions to Alienation
   1.3 Brief Description of the Subject Company.
   1.4 Nature and Purpose of the Appraisal
   1.5 Use of the Appraisal Restricted
   1.6 Summary Report
   1.7 Standard of Value—Fair Value

Sample 2

1   Description of the Assignment
     1.1 Subject of the Appraisal
     1.2 Summary Description of the Subject
     1.3 Purpose and Use of the Appraisal
     1.4 Standard of Value
     1.5 Date of Valuation
     1.6 Ownership and Control
     1.7 Scope of the Assignment
     1.8 Definitions
     1.9 Principal Sources of Information
     1.10 Assumptions and Limiting Conditions

2   Economic Conditions and Industry Data
     2.1 Overview of the National Economy
     2.2 Overview of the State and Local Economies
     2.3 History and State of the Specialty Surgery Profession
             2.3.1   Specialty Surgery Profession Demographics: City
     2.4 Implications for the Practice

3   Survey of the Subject Firm
     3.1 History
     3.2 Form of Organization
     3.3 Restrictions on Sale of Subject Interest
     3.4 Prior Ownership Transactions
     3.5 Subsidiaries and Affiliates
     3.6 Management
     3.7 Sales and Marketing
     3.8 Patient Base
     3.9 Competition
     3.10 Location
     3.11 Tour of the Center and Interview of Dr. Miller

4   Financial Performance of the Practice
     4.1 Financial Statements
     4.2 Financial Statement Analysis
     4.3 Summary of Analysis
     4.4 Adjustments to Financial Statements

NOTES

1. *Daubert v. Merrell Dow Pharmaceuticals, Inc.*, 113 S.Ct. 2786 (1993).
2. *Kumho Tire Co., Ltd. v. Carmichael*, 119 S.Ct. 1167 (1999).
3. *See* Chapter 8, *supra.*
4. Although the *Daubert* standard focuses on a Federal Rule of Evidence, states whose Rules of Evidence are modeled upon or have similar language to Rule 702 are allowing trial courts the discretion of applying these criteria. See e.g., *Leaf v. Goodyear Tire & Rubber Co.*, 590 N.W.2d 525 (Iowa 1999), which stated that the observations in *Daubert* will be helpful to a court in assessing reliability of evidence in complex cases, and Iowa trial courts accordingly may use the criteria at their discretion.
5. The professional standards of some business appraisal societies attempt to distinguish between "advocacy" appraisals and other assignments, allowing departures from standards—with disclosure in the report—at the directives of counsel or the discretion of the appraiser. These standards are in direct contrast to the standards of objectivity and nonadvocacy throughout the appraisal profession, and in seeming contradiction to the holdings in *Daubert* and *Kumho Tire*. The application of "intellectual rigor" in any appraisal assignment should, by definition, exclude advocacy of anything but the correctness of the appraisal result. It is a disservice to counsel to accept direction that can reduce the chances of the opinion being admitted into evidence.
6. *Kumho Tire*, 119 S.Ct. at 1167.
7. *Target Market Publishing, Inc. v. ADVO, Inc.*, 136 F.3d 1139 (7th Cir. 1998).
8. *Rossi v. Mobil Oil Corp.*, 710 F.2d 821 (Temp Emergency Ct. App. 1983).
9. *Whelan v. Abell*, 1997 U.S. Dist. Lexis 9794 (Dist. Ct. DC 1997).
10. A scathing commentary on the overstepping of an economic expert can be read in *City of Tuscaloosa v. Harcross Chemicals*, 158 F.3d 548, 567. Although the testimony of this particular expert was not even challenged on these grounds, the court noted that the "testimony does indeed appear to warrant exclusion: specifically, [the expert]'s opinions regarding the legal standards applicable to the case are outside of his competence as an economist and should be excluded. The same is true of [his] characteriza-

tions of pieces of documentary evidence as tending to show collusion; such judgments are for the court to make at summary judgment and for the trier of fact to make at trial. Furthermore, we point out that [his] professed market definition is clearly wrong." The court also noted that the expert's opinion may have been "one with an apparent eye toward litigation," perhaps explaining their pains to critique the expert unasked.

11. Retaining counsel will sometimes ask the appraiser to suggest the standard of value, feeling that the appraiser is in a better position to know. Since this is a legal determination, suggesting the standard of value is high-risk behavior. You are better off preparing a report which uses alternate standards of value, or having the court define the standard before the report is issued. This is another circumstance where a representation letter is good risk management.

12. Rule 704 states that experts may not render opinions on the ultimate facts of the case.

13. *Morse/Diesel v. Trinity Industries,* 67 F.3d 435 (2nd Cir. 1995)

14. *Morse,* 67 F.3d at 444.

15. *Frymire-Brinati v. KPMG Peat Marwick,* 2 F.3d 183 (7th Cir. 1993).

16. *Frymire, supra* at 186, citing *Daubert,* 113 S.Ct. at 2786

17. Often it seems that when cutting corners to save money on appraisals, the forecast for the company is the first to go. Without a decent forecast it is easy for an attorney to make the opinion sound like guesswork. No potential buyer would purchase a business without considering how much money could be made in the future, yet business appraisers often omit this step.

18. *Frymire,* 2 F.3d at 186.

19. *Id.*

20. *Id.*

21. Software that contains report templates or is described by the supplier as "appraisal software" is distinguished from spreadsheet software or data mining software. The first category contains more problems for the appraiser.

22. *Generally accepted* means that professionals throughout the industry use the software. If the only people who use the software are members of a single organization which promotes the software, it will fail the "generally accepted" test.

23. *Kumho,* 119 S.Ct. 1178.

24. *Moore v. Asland Chemical,* 126 F.3d 679 (5th Cir. 1997): *appeal after remand,* 151 F.3d 269 (5th Cir. 1998).
25. *Moore,* 126 F.3d 687, 688.
26. *Kumho,* 119 S.Ct. 1177.
27. *Kumho,* 119 S.Ct 1179, quoting *General Electric Co. v. Joiner,* 118 S.Ct. 136, 512 (1997).
28. *City of Tuscaloosa v. Harcross Chemicals, Inc.,* 158 F.3d 548 (11th Cir. 1998).
29. *City of Tuscaloosa,* 158 F.3d 565.
30. *Eisenberg v. Commissioner,* 155 F.3d 50 (2nd Cir. 1998)
31. It is also true that appraisers can also be criticized for failing to use all the approaches to valuation. See, e.g., *Estate of Bennett,* TCM 1993-34; *Estate of Campbell,* TCM 1991-615; and *Estate of Andrews,* 79 TC 938 (1982). However, these criticisms are generally not for failure to use a weighted approach, but rather for failure to consider the applicability of all available approaches—a different abuse of subjectivity.
32. For a review of the dangers of weighted methods, *see* the discussion regarding *Estate of Hall, infra.* In that case, the weighting was an issue along with the expert's subjective exclusion of other data which were arguably comparable although clearly distinguishable from the subject business by many characteristics.
33. *Estate of Hall,* 92 T.C. 312 (1989).
34. *Estate of Hall,* 92 T.C. at 326.
35. *Estate of Hall,* 92 T.C. at 325.
36. *Estate of Hall,* 92 T.C. at 339.
37. *Estate of Jung,* 101 T.C. 412 (1993).
38. *Federal Rule of Evidence 801: Definitions*
   [c] Hearsay
   "Hearsay" is a statement, other than one made by the declarant while testifying at the trial or hearing, offered in evidence to prove the truth of the matter asserted.
   Federal Rule of Evidence 802: Hearsay Rule
   Hearsay is not admissible except as provided by these rules or by other rules prescribed by the Supreme Court pursuant to statutory authority or by act of Congress.
39. 1999 US App. Lexis 476 (4th Cir. 1999).

40. *Tokio Marine, supra,* citing *Weaver v. Phoenix-Home Life Mutual Insurance Co.,* 990 F.2d 154 (4th Cir. 1993); *6816.5 Acres of Land v. U.S.,* 411 F.2d 834 (10th Cir. 1969).
41. Although an attorney may not be able to learn all of the appraisal methods in order to cross-examine you, the attorney can certainly pick up on factual inaccuracies in your report.
42. *See, e.g., How to Use the IBA Market Database,* a collection of technical essays by Raymond C. Miles, published by the Institute of Business Appraisers, Inc.
43. The report is a better marketing tool than a brochure; work product that demonstrates quality services can get you appraisal work from everyone who reviews it.
44. The sample appraisal report table of contents at the end of this chapter demonstrates terminal digit numbering—it is a numbering system used in key words to index cases and will have a comfort level with counsel.
45. These Tables of Contents appear in the *Business Appraisal Reports Library,* a set of eight sample reports published by the IBA Press. They are used by permission of the Institute of Business Appraisers.

CHAPTER 12

Teaching the Attorney about Business Appraisal

Purpose of This Chapter Counsel may be experienced in litigation but inexperienced in business appraisal. It is one of the most important jobs of the litigation support professional to teach the attorney the essentials of the expert's business so that the attorney can be an effective advocate.

LAWYERS ARE FROM MARS

One of the reasons that attorneys need appraisers as expert witnesses is that lawyers often have limited education in finance, economics, and accounting. Ask any room full of attorneys about their undergraduate majors, and you will generally find that most lawyers took four-year degrees in political science, English, communications, history, or psychology. There is no mandatory undergraduate course of study for law school, and the only finance-oriented courses taught in most law schools are business law, corporations, and taxation—all of which are electives, and are generally taken by law students who do not anticipate trial work. Ask any room full of appraisers about their undergraduate majors, and you will generally find that appraisers took four-year degrees in accounting, economics, finance, statistics, or business administration. Business school majors probably did not hang out with the liberal arts majors at your college; they probably had little in common. However, in the litigation support setting, these two groups need to interact, and the liberal arts majors—now lawyers—need to grasp issues for which they have little background and sometimes minimal ability.

Judges are lawyers who have been promoted, and their background is unlikely to include training in finance or accounting. In fact, many trial court judges have risen through the criminal defense ranks and have limited civil trial experience. Teaching lawyers to teach the court requires an even higher level of knowledge on the part of attorneys—and more work for the appraiser.[1]

The most effective way to assist an attorney in understanding how appraisal testimony fits into the case is to get retained as early as possible in the life of the suit. This allows the appraiser to track the technical descriptions in pleadings in discovery, with an eye toward the proofs that will be presented in support or defense of damages, drafting the initial demand letters and planning the documents to be reviewed. It is cheaper for the lawyer to use experts for this work than to pay someone else to gain superficial knowledge of the technical area.

If you want to present the lawyer with a book on the subject, select one that can be understood by someone with little background. Gary Trugman's *Understanding Business Valuation*, Shannon Pratt's *The Lawyer's Business Valuation Handbook*, or Raymond C. Miles's *Basic Business Appraisal* are all good choices.[2] Most of the time, however, lawyers will only skim these books, unless they anticipate handling a number of cases where the knowledge can be recycled. You will have to be the principal source of tutelage.

SAMPLE AREAS OF CONFUSION

Degrees of Reliability of Financial Documents

Counsel may not know the difference between audited, reviewed, or compiled financial statements. You might have to explain the difference between a balance sheet and an income statement, and the difference between cash and accrual accounting methods. Above all, you will need to emphasize the low quality of internally generated information and the lack of its representative faithfulness.

Adjustments to Financial Statements

It is a common cost- or time-saving measure for counsel to ask the appraiser to take the financial statements at face value and apply the discounts to the income as reported by the owner. In the appraisal of small or mid-size businesses, failing to normalize the earnings can result in an inaccurate appraisal. Fair-market value would reflect the earnings capacity of the company, not the income reported by the owner. Removing common entries that reflect control group perquisites, for example, is a necessary step in the process. Discuss with counsel whether the business will have additional income if expenses are recharacterized in sample areas:

- Travel
- Entertainment
- Leased cars, insurance, and other auto expenses
- Family members on the books
- Above-market rents for office space or equipment
- Owner's salary over market rates

The other effects of these adjustments will also have to be carefully reviewed with counsel, particularly if these adjustments will create tax issues for the business or the owners. Be prepared to discuss with counsel the impact of these adjustments on the tax status of the business, the interests of other shareholders or partners, and the impact on a potentially innocent spouse. The nature of the claim can also make identification of actual and available income important. For example, if the appraiser is retained by plaintiff's counsel in a case where punitive damages are sought, determining the actual income (as opposed to reported income) of the business supplies needed information on which the award of punitive damages can be based.

Keep in mind that a courtroom is a public place and that, unless the judge closes the session to the public, anyone—including representatives of the IRS—can listen to the testimony. In some states the IRS routinely monitors divorce trials for information on how the reported income of the business differs from the actual income that a nonoperating spouse seeks to claim.

Types of Risks That Can Affect the Strength of a Business

Again, because most lawyers have limited experience in financial analysis, do not throw around terms like *levels of value* and *elements of risk* without providing a context. Be prepared to explain the following:

- *Internal risk*—differences in expense projections and actual cost; failure of sales to materialize, fluctuation in cost of goods sold.
- *External risk*—changes in the industry such as consolidation or the spinoff or breakup of larger competitors
- *Financial risk*—risk that projected earnings before taxes will not materialize even though the projected EBIT is realized. This is the interest expense. Counsel needs to understand that significant interest expense represents significant risk. Leverage is in addition to financial risk.
- *Liquidity risk*—a fact of life in small businesses, this quantifies whether the owner will be able to sell quickly and for a reasonable fee (and the answer, generally, is no).

Difference between a Discount and a Capitalization Rate

Counsel may treat these the same and confuse the terms. The definitions in the literature will be of limited assistance to the attorney. Here are the definitions used in AICPA business appraisal courses or in books authored by Shannon Pratt:

- *Discount rate*—a yield rate used to convert anticipated future payments or receipts into present value.
- *Capitalization rate*—any divisor (usually expressed as a percentage) that is used to convert income into value.

To a liberal arts major turned lawyer, this will make little sense. Be prepared to provide some examples and walk through a calculation of a premium and a discount rate.

Use of Last Year's or Next Year's Earnings to Value a Business

Counsel may not understand how a speculative number can be used, or be able to reconcile using future earnings that Revenue Ruling 59-60's pronouncement that the best indication of what a business will do in the future is what it has done in the past.

Discounts or Premiums for Minority, Marketability, and Other Factors

Lawyers may not intuitively grasp that the value of a minority interest is worth less than the percentage of ownership. The effect of other factors may also strike counsel as so subjective that it will have no credibility. For that reason, the distinct nature of each premium or discount and the factors that led to the selection of the discount or premium need to be laid out for counsel. In addition to minority or marketability discounts, these can include the following:

- Blockage discounts
- Key person discounts
- Litigation risk discounts
- Portfolio discounts
- Trapped-in capital gains discounts

Appraisers who have not kept up with treatment of discounts in current literature will have a tendency to combine the marketability and minority factors into a single discount.

Counsel will also need to understand that whether some discounts are taken will depend on the data used by the appraiser. For example, a discount for lack of marketability may not be appropriate where the appraiser has used private company data in the application of the market approach.

Application of Data on Large Privately Owned Companies to Small or Mid-size Privately Owned Companies

For many business categories, there is little similarity when the characteristics of a large company in an industry are compared to a small or mid-size company in the same industry. However, because of the relative ease in gathering data on large companies, many appraisers give counsel information about a large company for consideration in the appraisal of a company that is radically different in size. Counsel will need to be educated that the finance characteristics of these businesses are radically different, making data on large companies inapplicable to small companies. For example, in large, privately owned companies, personal guarantees are less likely to be required; technology is more likely to be appropriate or up to date; management structure will be organized, and company policies will be documented. Small businesses, on the other hand, are often based on return on labor, not return on investment—the owner is interested in salary and paying off the acquisition debt. This will lead to a discussion of seller's discretionary cash flow, of significant impact in appraisal of a small business.

The temptation to make comparisons with publicly held companies raises concerns. For example, counsel will have some familiarity with factors affecting stock value and will seek to apply this information to the appraisal of small businesses. Counsel may already be thinking about examples to use for the court or jury, and will want the brand-name recognition that using publicly traded stocks can provide, or counsel might want to focus on data from the stock market because there is a perception of greater comfort factor. Counsel must be taught the significant differences between large companies and small to mid-size businesses:

- There is a significant difference in liquidity and how illiquidity depresses value.
- Publicly traded businesses are affected by different market factors (for example, people don't go to the corner sub shop for the same reasons they buy stock in McDonald's Corporation).
- The valuation of closely held businesses is more intuitive and subjective.

The subjectivity of the valuation of closely held businesses may create doubts for counsel; be prepared to reference treatises and articles about how to perform appraisals competently, and stick with the literature. This will allow counsel to bolster your methods with established technical references and cross-examine other experts on any departures from the body of knowledge.

Reality Check After going through this information, counsel feels that use of information from the publicly traded market will cause less jury confusion and be more readily accepted by the trier of fact. Accordingly, counsel instructs you to use these data in your report. However, you believe that data from the private sector are a more reliable indicator of value. What do you do?

What you should not *do:* Do not let counsel dictate the appraisal conclusion by specifying the data to be used—particularly when it is information that you would give less weight. At the same time, if counsel has reservations about the methods or data you select, this is a situation you must resolve before testimony. Consider performing two appraisals, or having another appraiser perform the appraisal using public company data. The second option is the better one, as you will not have to present both opinions, and the jury is free to weight the testimony according to its perceptions. If you do perform two appraisals, be prepared to have an opinion as to which number is the better representative of the actual value of the business—even if it does not fit with the wishes of client or counsel. Giving the jury no indication of your opinion deprives them of the benefit of your experience, and does not assist them in reaching a just result—remember, a just result is the correct one, not the outcome desired by any party.

GENERAL CAUTIONS FOR ADVISING COUNSEL

Be careful to apply the information you supply in the context of the case. Once counsel understands these issues, the next step is to select the material elements of the appraisals of other experts that are incorrect or incredible. This allows counsel to apply the knowledge to the essentials of the case.[3] If you are not comfortable performing this review and giving testimony, a consulting appraiser should perform this function.[4] It is a disservice to expect counsel to apply this information in a vacuum and select the issues that impact the appraisal conclusion.

The education of counsel should lead to counsel's increased confidence in the appraiser's conclusion. It may also lead to counsel's increased reliance upon the appraiser for input on other aspects of the case that may only marginally involve the expert's opinion. Take on this additional role with caution. Clearly define the limits of your competence and do not exceed them. It is one thing to write a memo for counsel defining the issues—it is another, more complicated, matter to write a direct examination for counsel, even a direct examination of your own testimony. To compose verbatim questions of the cross-examination of another expert is fraught with risk. Ask yourself if you can set up a *Daubert* challenge of another expert when you have not even read the opinion in that case, let alone the dozens of opinions of other courts which have interpreted that holding and applied it to the testimony of appraisal or accounting experts.

Just as the appraiser should not accept counsel's direction on appraisal issues when doing so would affect independence, the appraiser should not agree to be ghost counsel. Your appraisal education has not prepared you for this role, and your malpractice insurance may not protect you if you assume it.

NOTES

1. A good gift for the attorneys on your list of regular clients is a subscription to Shannon Pratt's *Business Valuation Update for Judges and Lawyers*, published by Business Valuation Resources. It is targeted to the legal profession's use of business appraisers.
2. The publishers for these books are given in Chapter 5, *supra.*
3. More on reviewing the reports of experts retained by other parties appears in Chapter 14, *infra.*
4. The pros and cons of performing reviews of reports of other experts when you will be giving testimony on your own work product are detailed in Chapter 10, *supra.*

CHAPTER 13

The Business Appraiser at Deposition

Purpose of This Chapter Your performance at deposition is the most crucial segment of a litigation support assignment. By competently and confidently presenting your conclusion, you can establish yourself as an advocate for only your opinion, and assist the parties in resolving the dispute by clearly setting out your valuation conclusion. You can also assist counsel in preparing for the deposition of the appraiser for opposing parties, and in getting important information for your report from the depositions of fact witnesses. This chapter examines some common areas of inquiry, how to prepare for deposition, and how to get your conclusion into the transcript even if the attorneys can't figure out the right questions to ask.[1]

The first reaction of many expert witnesses upon receiving a notice for deposition is panic. The report may not be finished, the scheduling may be inconvenient, and the list of documents to be produced looks daunting. Often you will not have heard from retaining counsel since the signing of the engagement letter, and you will not have reviewed your report with the attorney or the owner.

There are many purposes for taking your deposition. First, it locks you into the opinions you will render at trial. If at trial you add data or opinions not expressed in your deposition, an opposing counsel can claim surprise. For this reason you should not agree to a deposition unless your work is complete. Tell retaining counsel that the deposition will have to be reset, and stand firm.

Second, your deposition creates a record that can be used in lieu of your live testimony in the event that you are unavailable for trial. For this reason, you have to keep your answers precise. Always think of how they will appear on a written transcript. Practice giving organized answers that can read well as paragraphs, with a topic sentence and good structure.

Third, your deposition is your first impression on the opposing party's counsel. Your demeanor, confidence, and professional competence can impress counsel that your conclusion is worthy of weight, or can label you as a made-to-order hack who does slipshod work. A credible deposition that presents thorough work, and testimony that is frank about your conclusions, can help to settle the case by clearly presenting the issues where the experts will differ—and, more importantly—where they agree. Counsel is rarely hankering to go to trial. Trials are disruptive to the attorneys' practices and personal lives, and giving the resolution of the dispute to the trier of fact deprives the parties of control. If a case settles favorably after your deposition, you stand a good chance of getting future engagements from the counsel (and may be called by the opposing party's counsel on other cases), and you can establish a reputation in the community as an expert whose work can aid in the cost-effective resolution of disputes.

PREPARING FOR DEPOSITION

Establish a system for dealing with deposition preparation. When you receive a notice for deposition, your routine should involve the following steps:

- Advise retaining counsel to reset the deposition if your work is not complete.
- Confirm your availability and have the deposition rescheduled if you have a conflict.
- Check the payment status under your engagement letter and have the necessary funds deposited in your account.[2]

- Schedule a meeting with counsel to prepare for your deposition.
- Review the list of documents requested in the subpoena duces tecum.
- Organize your file for easy access at the deposition.
- Update your curriculum vitae.

Some important things *not* to do in preparation for deposition: Do not remove documents from the file. Do not delete any computer records. Do not destroy any documents. Doing so after you have been noticed for deposition or received a subpoena can subject the retaining party to serious sanctions and may lead to your opinion being inadmissible in court.

Legends abound on the topic of experts being required to bring their computer or all electronic files to deposition—these instances are rare even in high-profile, big-ticket litigation. You are normally asked to bring your work papers and your report to the deposition. You should also bring a curriculum vitae that complies with Federal Rule of Civil Procedure 26. Even if you are not testifying in a case where this Rule is applicable, stating your qualifications in an organized and detailed format will provide an organization for this questioning, and make the point to deposing counsel that your qualifications as well as your opinions are open for review. You are only obligated to produce what is currently in your custody or control, even if other items are listed in the subpoena duces tecum—there should be an enumerated list. You are not required to be an interpreter of vague requests—just use your common sense. If something has not been requested, don't produce it. The single exception to this is that even if you are not subpoenaed for deposition, or if there is no document list requested, you must bring your report and any supporting documentation. You may want to try to testify without your report for reference, but it will make your deposition much longer and can create problems if you inadvertently omit information.

You may face opposition from retaining counsel when you attempt to schedule a preparatory session. For cost savings, retaining counsel may say that a prep session is not required, or that it can be done a few minutes prior to the deposition. The authors recommend that the appraiser insist on a prep conference—even by telephone, if necessary. Ideally, however, this meeting should be in person. At the meeting, retaining counsel should review your file. If counsel intends to claim a work product privilege for any of the documents in your file, those documents should be marked in the file. It is embarrassing and a time waste to sit at deposition while your retaining counsel reviews your file and pulls out documents.

At the preparation conference, you should discuss the following:

- The type of questions that will be asked by deposing counsel
- Questions—if any—retaining counsel will ask
- Any "magic words" that must be used to assist in the admissibility of testimony—these can be definitions of the standard of value, elements of the claim, or other issues that have come up in the discovery
- Privileged information in the file
- What should be brought to the deposition
- Update on current status of litigation, including recent pleadings and discovery
- A review and update of your qualifications
- Any prior contrary opinions for which you might be on record
- Statements in your prior writings—articles, books, presentations (all can be found by opposing counsel)

At your deposition, you will probably be asked if you met with retaining counsel. Do not be defensive about this question—it is a normal part of the process for an expert witness to meet with counsel prior to deposition. Advise the deposing attorney that you had a meeting to review your planned testimony. As for all deposition questions, telling the truth is not only your ethical obligation, it is easier to remember. If retaining counsel thinks the inquiry is straying into privileged issues, he or she will interpose an objection. If you think that the inquiry is straying into privileged issues and retaining counsel is not paying attention, you might want to deliver a swift kick under the table.

Some lawyers will attempt to restrict your testimony in deposition by asking you to soft-pedal or even conceal parts of your opinion in order to diminish the weaknesses of the case. From the standpoint of the appraiser, any such concealment is flagrantly unethical. Do not risk your reputation or the wrath of the court by agreeing to hide the ball. The facts of the case are not your problem, and your conclusion, if honestly reached, should cause you no shame. If counsel does not like your conclusions, counsel is free to retain another expert. Establish yourself as someone whose silence cannot be purchased.

You cannot rehearse your deposition testimony because you cannot anticipate each question, but you can be prepared for the usual areas of inquiry. As you prepare, review the important details in the case so the information can be answered without shuffling through your papers:

- When you were first contacted by retaining counsel
- When you were retained as an expert
- When you requested records and when they were received
- How much time was spent on the project
- When you formed an opinion of value that was not changed by subsequently provided information
- Whether you issued drafts to counsel or checked preliminary opinions with counsel
- Others who assisted in the performance of the work and their qualifications
- Your fee arrangement and payment status

Inquiring about financial arrangements is customary in deposition and should not raise your blood pressure—if you were not getting paid for your time, you would not be an expert witness, would you? If you have not been paid at the time of the deposition, deposing counsel may later imply that your payment was contingent upon satisfactory testimony, so insist that the owner bring all fees up to date, and preferably, pay you in advance for the estimated time of your testimony.

GIVING A DEPOSITION

Take note of the fact that retaining counsel does not represent you, at deposition or at any other time. The decision to answer questions at deposition is yours alone. If the inquiry goes into areas that are not germane to your opinion or the issues in litigation, decline to answer pending a court ruling. The attorney who represents your practice can bring a *motion for protective order* on those issues, either at the time the subpoena duces tecum is received or after your deposition has been concluded and you have unanswered questions. Some deposing counsel will include impertinent inquiry as a dominance tactic—asking for your annual income, tax returns, credit status, and so on. This is low-class tactics and you should refuse to play along. However, a mild inquiry on whether you are on medication should not be taken as implying anything—if you are on any medication that might make recollection difficult, or cause fatigue, there may be problems with using your testimony later. Generally, lawyers who make such inquiries are just doing their job.

Unless you reside out of the county or parish where the case has been filed, you may have the option of holding the deposition at your office. Although this eliminates your travel time, it is not always the best idea. Not only can it be disruptive to staff, but holding the deposition at your office can prolong proceedings—you can be asked to go to the library for texts, pull material from other files, or even run spreadsheet calculations when you are surrounded by all your normal tools. If you bring to deposition only your working file, you have the relevant information but less opportunity for counsel to wander through your practice.

The most important person in the room at your deposition is the court reporter. These individuals are highly trained and endlessly abused by attorneys. Taking down testimony is mentally exhausting, and a little courtesy will take you a long way. Before your deposition begins, give the reporter your card so he or she can get the correct spelling of your name. Spell out proper names during your testimony. Keep an eye on the reporter as you testify—unless the reporter's fingers are on the keys, there is not testimony making it into the transcript! This means that when the reporter stops to sip coffee, change paper, or turn over the audiotape, you need to stop talking. And unless your deposition testimony is being videotaped, nonverbal or grunting responses also won't work in the transcript. Yes or no cannot be misinterpreted. When you are looking at a document, name the document—if it has been marked as an exhibit, use the exhibit number.[3]

Never answer a question without pausing to think and organize your answer. This pause also allows for the reporter to complete taking down the question, and gives retaining counsel time to interpose an objection. Listen to the nature of the objection and react, if necessary. At deposition, most objections will be short and will relate to the form of the question. However, if retaining counsel makes a *speaking objection*—a long statement about the questioning—chances are the information is also for your benefit. After the objection is made, you can answer the question unless the question is vague, or the objection was so lengthy you forgot the question. In that case, the reporter can read it back to you from the tape.

Sometimes attorneys will engage in heated colloquy. Sit back and ignore the sniping. Don't enter into the fray, and never become argumentative during your deposition. It undermines your credibility and makes you lose focus. A deposition can go any length of time, but you are not a hostage. When you need a break, a bite to eat, or when you become fatigued, stand on your rights and take a break. If deposing counsel insists that you continue, state on the record that your testimony may be misleading or unclear if you don't have the chance to recharge your batteries. Only a jerk would make you continue beyond this point.

Typically, an expert deposition will begin with a review of your qualifications. Deposition is never the time to conceal information, and as soon as you are asked about your qualifications, present your curriculum vitae. It will be marked as an exhibit and counsel will read it and enquire. This is one of the areas where your testimony can be rehearsed. You should be able to give a cogent summary of your experience, education and professional credentials.

You should also be able to recite much of the following information on the case without much reference to the file:

- The standard of value
- The nature of the business
- Familiarity with the business or product line
- Terms of art and their definitions

Often the deposing counsel will have seen your report for the first time at the deposition. This may mean that their questioning will not be well organized, and that the right questions will not be asked. Make sure that your opinion of value gets onto the record, even if you have to bring it up yourself.

Remember that the deposing counsel may have little training

in appraisal matters—for this reason some of the questions may not make much sense. If you do not understand a question, ask to have it rephrased, and explain your confusion. Take the opportunity to replace the unartful question with correct terminology. If you do this with tact, counsel will generally appreciate the information (he does not want to look stupid in print any more than you do).

Take your time to read documents handed you by counsel, even if they come from your own file. Do not get rattled by attorneys who attempt to rush. Look at each page if you have to. Even your notes in the margins can be reviewed and questioned. Your private notes are not private if they are part of your investigative process—keep this in mind as you assemble your work file.

Here are some things you should *not* do at deposition:

- *Do not* make value statements regarding the parties or their actions. It makes you appear biased.
- *Do not* argue with counsel or lose your temper. It will always come back to haunt you on the witness stand.
- *Do not* deny that you would have liked more information, if you were not provided with five years' financial information in a reliable format. Remember, if you did not get the information, a potential buyer would not have it available, either. This is the way small businesses work.
- *Do not* cover up for the owner on tax issues. If you made adjustments that reallocate income to the client, all you can do is advise retaining counsel of the issue.
- *Do not* respond to pauses by counsel. If there is no question pending, sit and wait for one. Pauses are sometimes an attempt by counsel to draw out information or discover the areas of your testimony that make you squirm.
- *Do not* recalculate your numbers based on information provided at the deposition. A new fact may impact too many portions of the report. Once you change your number based on a hypothetical from counsel, you'll find more and more outlandish scenarios presented for your consideration.[4]
- *Do not* assume a deposition persona—becoming a teacher, academic, or actor. It rarely comes across well. Act like yourself—again, it is easier to remember.
- *Do not* ask for breaks to talk with counsel—you'll be asked

about them when you get back. Do not talk with counsel about the testimony on any break or at lunch.

- *Never* guess or speculate on information in order to provide a response to a question. The three most powerful words you can utter in deposition are "I don't know." When asked if additional information would change your opinion, saying "I don't know" cuts off further inquiry on the point. When asked your opinion about the liability or character of the parties, saying you have no idea reinforces your independence. Be careful, however, to say "I don't know" only when you don't. It is not a substitute for "I can't recall." And if it is information you *should* know, acknowledge that it might change your opinion—but still decline to quantify the impact while you are testifying.

Once the party who has set your deposition has completed questioning, other parties in the case may ask questions. Technically, if these parties have not also served you with a subpoena for deposition, their inquiry should be limited to the scope of questioning by the subpoenaing party. However, broad latitude is generally permitted in order to avoid additional depositions. Retaining counsel will ask questions last. These should be cleanup in nature, dealing with any opinions you have failed to give while questioned by other counsel.

When the deposition is over, you may think you have done well— there may have been no challenges to your opinion and little controversy. You have missed the point. A deposition is for fact gathering, and the impeachment of your qualifications, methods, conclusions, and credibility will take place at trial. However, if you have done your best, the case may settle as a result of your testimony.

REVIEWING THE DEPOSITION

At the conclusion of your deposition, you will be given the option to read and sign the transcript or to waive reading and signing. If you wish to read and sign, you will often have to go to the reporter's office to do so. You should bill for this review time. It is always best to read your testimony. You cannot alter the substance of your answers during this review; its purpose is to look for errors in transcription. Your accent or the pace of your speech may make taking down your testimony difficult, and where so much of your testimony will concern numbers, it is worth a careful reading to make sure they were accurately taken down.

If, after you have read the transcript, you find that one of your answers was substantively incorrect (even though correctly transcribed), you have an obligation to correct the error. Prepare a letter to all counsel with the correct statement (as a courtesy, discuss this with retaining counsel prior to sending, but do not be talked out of your ethical duty). It is not necessary to explain the reason for the change other than to say that your answer was in error. Although you will obviously have to deal with the change at trial, better to deal with an honest admission than to admit on the stand that your opinion is incorrect.

ASSISTING WITH THE DEPOSITION OF OPPOSING PARTY EXPERTS AND OTHER WITNESSES

The best role for the appraiser to play in the deposition of opposing party's experts is to teach counsel the issues of the appraisal so that counsel can do a competent job, and to prepare counsel on the reports of other appraisers. Clearly, the ability to do this is going to depend on whether you have been retained in the case before the depositions of the other experts, and whether you can see the report prior to the deposition.

The author's personal preference is that you not attend the depositions of other experts. You are not a member of retaining counsel's team unless you have been retained as a consultant and will not be giving testimony.[5] It is hard to appear as an impartial appraiser when you are sitting at counsel's elbow and passing notes. It also reflects poorly on counsel to imply that he or she cannot take a deposition absent significant coaching.

This is not to say that you should not review the work of other appraisers and discuss them with counsel. You can be on standby by telephone if counsel has questions, and can prepare a work-product memo for counsel on issues that can be explored during deposition. Your review of the reports issued by experts retained by opposing parties will also lead you to treatises that may contradict the methods or other portions of the reports. Provide these references to counsel, and explain the contradictions. Do not, however, suggest questions to counsel. Allow retaining counsel to decide which issues to explore at deposition and which to save for trial.

Depositions of fact witnesses may also require your input, particularly if these witnesses have information that you need for the appraisal and that has not been obtainable through other discovery. At these depositions, the attendance of the expert poses less of a problem, since these depositions may be the closest you can get to employee or management interviews. However, you should still remain unobtrusive. Do not pass notes, make comments, or talk during the deposition. If you make your own notes, be aware that they will be subject to discovery during your deposition testimony or at trial.

NOTES

1. Source material for this chapter includes information from *How to Excel During Depositions: Techniques for Experts that Work*, by Steven Babitsky, Esq. & James J. Mangraviti, Jr., Esq. Published by SEAK Inc. Legal and Medical Information Systems, Falmouth, Mass, 1999. SEAK has a number of publications and videotapes that are valuable for litigation support professionals, and that present high-quality expert testimony workshops and seminars.

2. Deposing counsel is generally responsible to pay your fees associated with attending the deposition, but not for your preparation time. Deposition fees are calculated portal to portal, or by a daily rate if that is your routine billing practice. In some practice locales these costs are reimbursed to your counsel at the conclusion of the suit, but more often they are paid by deposing counsel at the time of or shortly after your deposition. Confirm local practice with retaining counsel, and do not be shy about advising of the amount of the check that should be brought to the deposition. No one expects you to testify for free.

3. If portions of your file are marked as exhibits, have copies made before you leave the deposition. The reporter may need to retain the marked copies, and you do not want to have an incomplete file.

4. This is an area where expert testimony is markedly different from the testimony of fact witnesses; expert witnesses can be asked to respond to hypothetical facts.
5. See Chapter 12, *infra*.

CHAPTER 14

Reviewing the Reports of Other Experts

Purpose of This Chapter Whether you are retained as a testifying or as a consulting expert, you will need to be prepared to review and comment on the reports of experts retained by other parties. Focusing on the technical aspects of the appraisal allows you to avoid personal issues and provides information for counsel to use in cross-examination of other experts. This chapter examines some of the areas that deserve scrutiny in the work product of other appraisers, and perhaps a checklist to avoid problems in your own work product.

The first essential in reviewing the reports of other experts is to define the purpose of the review. It is *not* to find fault for the purpose of challenging the opinion at trial on minutiae or even on significant issues. The first purpose of report review should be to point out similarities between the reports of the experts on which no additional investigation, expense, or argument is necessary.

The second purpose of report review is to point out strengths of the report of an appraiser retained by another party—especially where they disagree with the report you have prepared—that might change your opinion. This requires humility, honesty, and an unwavering commitment to serve the truth. Remember that you are seeking a correct result, not a desired result. Admitting that your conclusion should change fulfills the expert's duty to be a servant of the court. This commitment harkens back to the message in the Preface—you cannot do a good job at expert witnessing unless your head is in the right place.

The third purpose of report review is to expose flaws in the report. In taking this step, the appraiser must be careful to focus on the *material* errors in the report. Point out all errors to counsel; this allows the lawyer to get an impression of the overall competency of the witness. If the report is fraught with minor errors, demonstrates a failure to check the math, relies on support staff to perform key functions, or uses a cavalier approach to standards, it reveals minor infractions that could be compounded. This information will help counsel determine the worth of the report. This information can be used for settlement and case strategy. However, unless you point out which errors are material, counsel may become lost in minutiae and miss the real value of the case.

During cross-examination of other experts, counsel will need to focus on only two or three errors in the report. To prolong cross-examination allows the trier of fact to become sympathetic to an attacked expert, allows an expert skilled at testimony to repeat his or her conclusion, and dilutes the power of the cross-examination. That is why you have to prioritize the issues you find in the review process.

The result of the review process is an evaluation of the worth, veracity, and credibility of the opponent's report so that settlement talks can be initiated and the risks at trial can be anticipated. An ancillary result is to point out flaws in your own work product that may be repeated in the report of other experts. Be careful about suggesting a point of inquiry about which you are also in error!

COMPARING APPLES TO APPLES

Review the report prepared by the other appraisers to see if they are comparable to the report you have prepared (or, if you are a consulting expert, by the expert testifying for the party who has retained you). Pay particular attention to the following:

- The standard of value
- The date of valuation
- The description of the interest to be valued

- The documents and data to which the appraiser had access from the business[1]

If any of this information is materially different from your report, there may be issues that need to be resolved through motions in limine, arguments of counsel to the trier of fact, or jury instruction. Provide counsel with a list of these differences and their impact upon the conclusions of the appraisers.

COMPLYING WITH STANDARDS

Review the report to determine its compliance with professional standards. In doing so, do not limit yourself to the standards of the organizations to which the expert belongs—as a member of a profession, focus on professional standards. Only a fool would argue that it is not a good idea to comply with USPAP.

SUPPORTING SUBJECTIVE ANALYSIS

Bald conclusions without support do not lead to a credible opinion; more importantly, under professional standards, they do not lead to a replicable opinion. Several problems are created by bare-bones reports. First, they leave the impression that the emperor has no clothes, and that is why the underlying information has been omitted (i.e., there is no objective evidence to support a capitalization or discount rate). Second, these reports make depositions longer because the information has to be extracted verbally. Third, the reviewer of the report will have to do significant guessing to determine the rationale behind the conclusions. This costs the report credibility and the author has lost a chance to demonstrate command of the appraisal process. Fourth, bare-bones reports may create an evidence problem if the court finds the opinion lacks foundation.

Here are samples of statements that should raise a red flag during your report review:

- "After considering all relevant factors, we have concluded that a subjective risk factor of 11.2 percent is appropriate for the subject."

- "In the opinion of the appraiser, a capitalization rate of 25 percent will be suitable for the subject."
- "The average control premium observed in the _____ study was 35 percent, so this is what we will use for the subject."
- "Average annual growth rate for the last five years is 8.9 percent, so we will project future income at this rate."
- "We used management's opinion of value for the hard assets."
- "We have selected the excess earnings approach as the best indicator of value."
- "We assigned a weighting of 5-4-3-2-1 to the last five years' earnings."
- "We gave greatest weight to the income approach."

All of these questions will prompt counsel to ask "Why?" If the "Because" is not laid out in the report, the opinion is not sufficiently supported.

Support of subjective factors must include logical elements:

- Discussion of applicable empirical information
- Description of range of probable values
- Discussion of *why* the value for the subject falls where the appraiser believes it does—listing all of the factors taken into consideration
- Comparison to appraisal literature

When this information is not in the report, review the empirical information and the literature for data and writings which are inconsistent with the appraiser's opinions.

COMPLYING WITH THE BODY OF KNOWLEDGE SET FORTH IN THE LITERATURE

All appraisers who testify will eventually have to face impeachment with a treatise. This is a process during which the appraiser is presented with a book, asked to admit that it is authoritative and recognized throughout the profession, and then peppered with language from the book by cross-examining counsel. The reviewing appraiser should be able to provide counsel with information in treatises that is inconsistent with the report, and demonstrate to counsel the impact in the report's conclusions from the deviation from accepted appraisal theory.

The body of knowledge contained in the books and periodicals is listed in Chapter 5; this information is added to over time. However, every article appearing in a technical journal does not alter the body of knowledge, nor does every presentation at a conference (and some presentations deliberately raise controversial issues) rise to the level of accepted practice. Provide the materials to counsel, and be careful to distinguish from what is considered accepted theory and what is a developing area of appraisal professional development.

Most often, departure from the literature occurs in personally crafted methods, or methods that are fraught with subjective options. Brand-name methods, blends of accepted methods, or methods proprietary to the appraiser may borrow from elements that are accepted throughout the profession. However, when they are combined into a new approach, they might contain challenged elements. Just because a method is not documented in the literature, however, does not mean it will lack logic. Provide information so that counsel can impeach with the treatise, but also have an opinion about whether the method (however unorthodox) has yielded a reasonable conclusion.

SHORTCUTS IN THE APPRAISAL PROCESS

Reacting to direction of counsel or to time and budget constraints, appraisers sometimes take shortcuts in the process that impact the quality and credibility of the work product.

- There is no industry analysis in the report. Without a comparison to the industry cohort, the appraiser may not demonstrate the strength of the company for placement in the universe of comparable companies for the application of a market approach, or may not be able to quantify risk for the assignment of a capitalization rate.
- There are no interviews or site inspections. Sometimes this is not possible without court order, but if the appraiser has not attempted to get access to the site or to interview management, the conclusion lacks important information.

- Appraisal includes no trending or economic forecast. Without a look at the future of the business and a good analysis of historical performance, rates and discounts can be little more than numbers plucked from space. Every good appraiser knows that the value of an interest in any business is based on the amount of money the owner can expect to receive in the future. Without a forecast, how is it possible to pick such a number?
- Financial statements and other information from the company have not been adjusted. Taking this information at face value can prevent the appraiser from having an accurate picture of the financial condition of the company.
- The value of real estate, equipment, leases, or other significant assets has not been substantiated with independent appraisals.

INCONSISTENCIES WITH THE AUTHOR'S PRIOR WRITINGS

Speeches, published articles, and even other reports authored by an appraiser can provide prior inconsistent statements. If the other appraiser is published or has given presentations, be familiar with this material so that you can advise counsel if the appraiser seems to be departing from a process or position that can be documented. Make sure the contradiction is directly applicable to the contents of the report, and that it affects the appraisal conclusion.

USE OF APPRAISAL SOFTWARE

In addition to spreadsheet and data mining software, the appraiser may have used report formatting or report writing software, available from several reputable publishers and appraisal organizations. Brief counsel on the mechanics and specifics of the software to assure that it is reputable and that you know counsel knows enough about the software to have used it correctly.

IGNORING ACTUAL INCOME IN FAVOR OF REPORTED INCOME

In businesses such as restaurants, convenience stores, service stations, repair shops, or any establishment taking payments in cash, unreported income is a real possibility. If the appraiser has not dealt with this in the report, a reviewing appraiser must point this out to counsel and provide some examples of how the income could be traced. Change of income over time (as the dispute is anticipated or the divorce is contemplated by the parties) also merits scrutiny.

Reality Check In reviewing the report of another appraiser, it is apparent that the parties have substantially reported their income. For either party to adjust the income would present tax consequences and potential liabilities.

What should you do? This is never a pleasant situation for the appraiser to face. After informing counsel, the appraiser must decide whether to remain in the assignment. Under no circumstances should the appraiser agree to testify that the income as reported by the parties is the actual income of the business. If you choose to remain in the assignment, the counsel should meet and have the parties stipulate the income which the appraisers for both parties are to use. Counsel may also decide that the case needs to be settled so that none of the witnesses have to deal with taking the stand and testifying to the level of income reported by the parties and how it differs from actual income.

Often in the report review process, you will find errors in your own report. Do not attempt to conceal these errors; you will only be forced into admitting them on the stand, and your opinion will suffer as a result. If you have already been deposed, you should advise counsel that your opinions have changed. If you have not yet been deposed, you should provide a revised report and be prepared to answer at deposition that you have reviewed information that changed your initial opinion. Concealment will only draw attention to the issue.

Appraisal organizations sometimes receive ethics complaints from parties who have been involved in litigation and who are turning in opposing appraisers for violation of standards. It is often clear that the idea for making such a complaint has not originated with the complainant, but from an appraisal expert. Do not play this game. There is no credit to be reflected on you for bad tactics. Rather, provide counsel with the appropriate information based on a competent review, and do your best to make sure that the errors you criticize do not appear in your own work product.

NOTES

1. If your review demonstrates that the other appraiser had access to documents with which your party has not been provided, throw up a flag. Counsel will need to get these documents and should be prepared to have the experts do additional work to determine whether this information will affect their opinions.

CHAPTER 15

The Business Appraiser in Trial

Purpose of This Chapter The vast majority of cases settle prior to trial, allowing the parties to retain some measure of control and manage their risk. When settlement fails, the expert witness has the opportunity to present and defend the opinion of value. This chapter discusses preparation and how to handle direct testimony and cross-examination at trial.[1]

All of the material regarding deposition preparation from Chapter 13 is pertinent to trial preparation. Trial testimony is a natural extension of your performance at deposition, and allows you to explain (and, if needed, to defend) the information you gave at deposition.

In your assignments as a litigation appraiser, you will certainly be faced with going to trial without first giving a deposition. In such circumstances you will have less information about the opposing counsel's theory of the case and points of potential inquiry. Preparation in those instances is doubly important. You may also find that the counsel who deposed you will not be the counsel who is conducting your trial cross-examination; the deposition will have been taken by a junior attorney who may be acting as second chair at the trial.[2]

PREPARING FOR TRIAL

In addition to thoroughly reviewing your report, you should review your deposition testimony and discuss with retaining counsel any issues that you find may be the basis for further inquiry, or any weak points in either your report or your testimony. This is a time to be accurate and honest, not to hope that the opposing counsel will gloss over your flaws.

Also, review with counsel developments in the case that may affect your opinion. Discuss the case with counsel, but do not be prepared to be a mouthpiece for counsel's theory. Your sole job at trial is to be an advocate for the conclusion you reached in your appraisal, and to explain to the trier of fact why that conclusion should be given credit.

The usual admonitions apply to trial testimony—go well rested, well dressed, and at the top of your game. Insist on a preparation meeting with counsel prior to your trial testimony. During a fast-moving trial this may have to take place in the evening, so keep your schedule clear. Well in advance of trial, however, you should provide to counsel a copy of all materials that you will use or refer to during your testimony. Counsel will generally have a schedule for production of all trial exhibits, and if you do not have this information available by the disclosure date, do not count on being able to use them in trial.

This also applies to any demonstrative exhibits you will be using in connection with your testimony. Although a demonstrative exhibit is not marked in evidence, the source documents on which it is based must be admissible for the exhibit to have a foundation.

At the prep conference, you may be able to run through your testimony. Some counsel will have a script of questions prepared so you can go over your answers to each question. Others will have areas of inquiry for your review. If you are not given such a list, be prepared to go over with counsel the following anticipated areas of direct testimony:

- *Your qualifications*—essential for the court to admit your opinion testimony
- *The scope of your assignment*—the definition of value, the interest appraised, and the date of valuation

- *Data reviewed and processes used in your analysis*—including estimates of time spent on the various tasks
- *Your conclusion and the substantiations for your opinion*

Make certain that counsel understands each of these areas so that he or she can be prepared to elicit the appropriate information from you on direct.

In addition to getting an idea of the date and time you will be needed, find out which witnesses will have testified before you and what facts they will have established in their testimony. This allows you to know whether you will be responsible for laying groundwork about the business or whether you can assume that information is before the court.

TRIAL TESTIMONY—DIRECT TESTIMONY

If you do not have experience in trial testimony, go to the courthouse and watch some trials to get familiar with what happens. The clerk's office will have a list of the scheduled trials, and you can generally tell the nature of the case based on the style, or (if the system divides the judge's assigned cases into civil, criminal and domestic cases) to whom the matter is assigned. You can also contact the counsel for the case and ask when their experts will be giving testimony so that you can see opinion evidence and cross-examination.

Your trial performance begins when you enter the courthouse. The judges, attorneys, and jurors will use the same elevators, hallways, and bathrooms that you do. Accordingly, keep your demeanor detached and professional at all times. Do not discuss any aspect of the case in a public area. Do not hobnob with the counsel. Limit your remarks to anyone wearing a "Juror" badge to a simple smile and greeting. Do not sit at counsel table or pass any note to counsel when you are in the courtroom. If you are in the courtroom before or after your testimony, make yourself unobtrusive.

At the beginning of trial, one of the parties may choose to "invoke the Rule," or the court may invoke the Rule on its own motion. This "Rule" applies to the exclusion of witnesses, and provides that witnesses shall not be in the courtroom until they give their testimony. The purpose of this exclusionary rule is to avoid contaminating the testimony of fact witnesses (also known as percipient witnesses, because they testify on the perceptions of their senses). Because expert witnesses testify on matters other than the facts of the case, this Rule is sometimes not applied; some courts also take the position that expert witnesses are party representatives, and so should be exempted from the exclusionary rule. Confirm with counsel whether you should enter the courtroom or remain outside until called.

Knowing and observing the nuances of courtroom etiquette demonstrates your confidence and your respect for the process. The layout of the courtroom will usually be a spectator gallery, separated from the remainder of the courtroom by a railing in which there may be a swinging gate. This railing is referred to as *the bar* (hence the phrase "admitted to the bar"), and you do not cross that boundary without leave of court.

The work area will include counsel tables, a raised bench for the judge, desks for the clerk and sometimes the bailiff, a witness stand and a jury box. These work stations will be arranged in a square with a blank space in the middle—this is the *well.* It is bad form to walk through the well; walk around the border of the space to get to the witness stand.

In bench trials with limited witnesses and only two parties, the trial may be held in chambers. In these cases there will generally be a long table terminating at one end by the judge's desk; counsel will be on either side of the table. Although the proceedings will seem less formal, do not alter your demeanor in this altered setting.

After you have been sworn and given your name, counsel will generally begin with inquiry about your qualifications to testify. In a bench trial this may be an abbreviated process, but in a jury trial the inquiry may be prolonged. At some point, opposing counsel may stipulate to your qualifications. Sometimes this will end this topic of inquiry; however, if your qualifications are substantially better than the other experts who will testify, opposing counsel may be attempting to shut down this portion of your testimony.

You may be asked about any of these areas of *qualifications*:

- Profession—employment, nature of the firm, length of service with the firm
- Other occupations or professional positions

- Professional designations and how many attempts it took to achieve them
- Member of professional associations
- Names of all the professional associations
- Standards adhered to in general practice and in the instant assignment
- Professional education in appraisal
- Books or articles written on appraisal
- Books read on appraisal
- Awareness of standards for business appraisal—whether they were met in this assignment
- History of disciplinary proceedings
- History of claims for professional negligence
- History of courtroom testimony
- Types of businesses subject of appraisals
- Types of businesses subject of courtroom testimony
- Types of clients (plaintiff or defendant)
- Relationship with counsel
- Percentage of work which is litigation

This is the easiest part of your testimony, and the portion that you should rehearse most carefully.

At the end of your recital of qualifications, retaining counsel will ask if you have rendered an opinion. This prepares you for being *tendered to the court* as an expert. The court may ask if opposing counsel has any inquiry, and you can anticipate inquiry on all of the above points, as well as any conflicts issues, lack of qualifications, retainer arrangements, and whether you have ever been tendered as an expert and were not accepted by the court. At this point, you may feel your adrenalin begin to flow. Fight this, as it will cause you to lose control. You need to maintain a neutral attitude during your testimony in order to be effective. Never, never engage in any emotional exchange with counsel, or allow heated arguments to affect your demeanor on the stand.

Once the court has decided to admit your testimony, get your opinion in early—and often. Your testimony should begin with a description of the assignment; then walk the court through what was done to carry it out. Bring out that the appraiser had access to necessary information, and also that it was credible and trustworthy. Most important is your explanation of the methods used in determining value. It is very important to be able to explain this credibly—and to do so using commonly understood terms.

Many experts spend time developing complicated anaolgies to explain appraisal terms. Unfortunately, these often are not helpful to a jury. The jury will focus on the analogy and not on the appraisal. Opt instead for defining the terms in plain language and applying them to the assignment at hand.

Do what you can to humanize the company. If it produces a product, bring a sample along. Mention the places where the product is offered, or how long the company has been in business. Establish rapport with the trier of fact by relating the business to their common experience.

Above all, be yourself. Do not act professorial—authority figures talk down to jurors. Talk directly to the jurors or (in a bench trial) to the court with an open expression and appropriate gestures. Let them know you found the assignment interesting. Admit any problem areas with the assignment; if you would have liked to have had more information, say so openly. This will enhance your credibility.

Anything you bring to the witness stand is fair game for counsel to examine. This applies to notes, to your report (so watch the marginalia) and to your deposition transcript. If you wish to use exhibits, get the court's permission to leave the stand and go to the easel—and to return to your seat. It is not possible in most courtrooms to set up an easel where it can easily be viewed by everyone, so just give it your best efforts.

Exhibits will first be marked for identification and then, when they are admitted into evidence, they will be assigned a sequential number. Refer to these documents by their exhibit number so that the transcript of the trial will be clear. If the trier of fact does not have a copy of the document, be sure to read aloud the portion of the document about which you will testify.

At the end of your direct testimony, remain on the stand (no matter how much you would like to flee!). Cross-examination will come next.

CROSS-EXAMINATION

Make it clear to retaining counsel that you expect to be revived after cross if necessary—and do not accept their incompetence as an excuse. If you have adequately informed your counsel of adverse data, reports, treatises, or other material that may contradict the conclusion you reached, your counsel will be well prepared.

Be prepared for attacks on your qualifications without taking it personally—no one is perfect, including you. If this is your first time testifying (or even your first appraisal), be prepared to reiterate the care with which you performed the assignment without sounding defensive. Be prepared for a challenge that your qualifications or methodology may make your testimony inadmissible under *Daubert*, and sit impassively while that argument rages around you. In many trials, these challenges are becoming pro forma and may not indicate any lack of qualifications or breach of good practice.

It is impossible to suggest all areas of inquiry on cross-examination; since most of the problems will result from the way in which you performed the valuation, it is too late to fix them now! All that can be done is to deal with these problems in a way that preserves your credibility—and ends the cross-examination as soon as possible.

There are three types of answers you can give in response to a question on cross-examination—a helpful response, a neutral response, and a damaging response. Good witnesses never give damaging responses, even when they have to admit that they made mistakes. Be prepared for the fact that your report will contain mistakes—from serious breaches in methodology to embarrassing math errors. If one is pointed out, admit it immediately. Express regret, correct the mistake and move on. A counsel who belabors the point will irritate the trier of fact.

If you are asked about the qualifications or the conclusions of other experts, avoid any personal commentary. Simply aver that you disagree with the conclusion and focus on your own conclusion—do not dwell on a list of negative comments.

If you are asked if your numbers could be different and still be correct, admit the possibility. Appraisal is an art, not a science. Use the opportunity to explain your process and the facts you reviewed to bolster your opinion. Digging in and insisting that the discount rate is 28 and could not possibly be 29 is not helpful—or realistic.

Make your responses on cross-examination as organized and cogent as your answers on direct. This will require you to stop, think, and organize your responses—a difficult job when all you want to do is end the cross-examination and get off the stand. Practice speaking in paragraphs with topic sentences in both direct testimony and cross-examination.

Occasionally, counsel will attempt to cut you off before you have finished your answer, or ask a question with the instruction to "answer yes or no" when that response will not be responsive. This is a control play; do not agree to play the game. Advise counsel that your answer might mislead the court if phrased in that way, or advise that you need to complete your answer in order to avoid misleading the court. The judge will generally come to your rescue—no one wants to leave a misleading answer on the record. A counsel who insists on your continuing is, in effect, volunteering to mislead the jury.

Know your limits in testimony and do not exceed them. When fatigue sets in, ask for a break. Do not agree to do math on the stand if you might make a mistake. Bring a calculator and use it. If offered a calculator you do not know how to use, opt for your own, and explain to counsel that all calculators work differently. If you are testifying in a jury trial, the jurors will sympathize.

Above all, do not lose your focus. This is not your case. You are in court to represent your opinion and to demonstrate your competence and credibility. Keep your answers responsive to the question, to maintain as much control in cross-examination as you had in direct testimony. If you use the opportunity in cross-examination answers to reiterate your conclusion, wise counsel will eventually give up.

REDIRECT

Redirect testimony should be short. New areas cannot be introduced (just as on cross-examination counsel should be limited to the areas of inquiry on direct testimony). Redirect is a time to clean up any areas of confusion that may have been raised during cross examination. It is also the last time for you to get your number on the record—don't miss the chance.

NOTES

1. An excellent book which expands on this topic is by Roberto Aron and Johnathan L. Rosner, Esquire, *How to Prepare Witnesses for Trial,* 2nd edition. West Group, 1998.
2. In large or complex cases, a number of lawyers may assist main trial counsel by dealing with experts (and therefore learning technical issues), handling the legal arguments such as the charging conference, managing voluminous documents and other functions. You may also face a different counsel if the attorney who deposed you has been rotated off the case or left the law firm.

APPENDIX A

Professional Certifications

AMERICAN INSTITUTE OF CERTIFIED PUBLIC ACCOUNTANTS (AICPA)

201 Plaza Three, Jersey City, NJ 07311-3881
Phone: (201) 938-3000
Fax: (201) 938-3399
Web site: *www.aicpa.org*

Certification Offered

CPA/ABV—Accredited in Business Valuation
Prerequisite: AICPA member with current CPA license
Courses/exams: One-day exam
Experience requirement: Involvement in at least ten business valuation engagements
Reaccreditation requirement: Every three-year period: evidence of five business valuation engagements and 60 hours of related continuing professional education

AMERICAN SOCIETY OF APPRAISERS (ASA)

P.O. Box 17265, Washington, DC 20041
Phone: (703) 478-2228
Fax: (703) 742-8471
Web site: *www.appraisers.org*

Certifications Offered

AM—Accredited Member
Educational requirement: College degree or equivalent
Courses/exams: Completion of four courses of three days each,
with successful completion of one half-day exam following
each of the three courses and a full-day exam following BV204,
or successful completion of an all-day challenge exam; successful completion of an ethics exam
Reports: Submission of two actual appraisal reports to satisfac-
tion of board examiners
Experience requirement: Two years full-time or full-time-equivalent
work (e.g., five years of 400 hours business appraisal work per
year equals one year full-time equivalent)
Related experience offset: One full year of the experience requirement is granted to anyone who has any of the following three
designations with five years of practice in that respective field:
certified public accountant (CPA), chartered financial analyst (CFA), or certified business intermediary (CBI).

ASA—Accredited Senior Appraiser
Has met all requirements listed plus an additional three years
of full-time or full-time-equivalent experience.

FASA—Fellow of the American Society of Appraisers
Has met all requirements listed plus is voted into the college of
fellows on the basis of technical leadership and contribution to
the profession and the society.

INSTITUTE OF BUSINESS APPRAISERS (IBA)

P.O. Box 17410, Plantation, FL 33318
Phone: (954) 584-1144
Fax: (954) 584-1184
Web site: *www.go-iba.org*

Certifications Offered

AIBA—Accredited by IBA

Course/experience: IBA-8001 eight-day workshop OR possess business appraisal designation from AICPA, ASA, or NACVA
Exam: Four-hour exam
Reports: Submit one report per peer review.
Other requirements: Provide references of character and fitness.
Continuing education: Submit proof of continued professional development with 24 hours of advanced BV education every 24 months OR submit another report for peer review OR pass CBA exam and enter CBA review process OR demonstrate completion of 10 business appraisal assignments in two years.

CBA—Certified Business Appraiser

Educational requirement: Four years of college or equivalent
Courses/exams: Exam of six hours
Reports: Submission of two business appraisal reports demonstrating professional level of competence
Experience requirement: Five years of full-time experience or equivalent OR 85 hours appraisal education

MCBA—Master Certified Business Appraiser

CBA designation plus 15 years experience and professional references

BVAL—Business Valuator Accredited for Litigation

Educational requirement: Business appraisal designation from IBA, AICPA, ASA, or NACVA

Course/exams: Seven-day litigation support and expert testimony workshop with four-hour exam

Other requirements: Two letters of reference from lawyers OR 16 hours of education in the areas of law appraiser will testify in

Award for Service

FIBA (*Fellow of the Institute of Business Appraisers*) has met all requirements listed plus is voted into the college of fellows on the basis of technical leadership and contribution to the profession and the institute

NATIONAL ASSOCIATION OF CERTIFIED VALUATION ANALYSTS (NACVA)

1245 East Brickyard Road, Suite 110, Salt Lake City, UT 84106
Phone: (801) 486-0600
Fax: (801) 486-7500
Web site: *www.nacva.com*

Certifications Offered

CVA—Certified Valuation Analyst

Prerequisite requirement(s): Hold a valid Certified Public Accountant (CPA) certificate and/or license issued by a legally constituted state authority.

Educational requirement: Must complete a four-hour pre-read and NACVA's five-day training program.

Examination: A four-hour proctored exam and a 30- to 50-hour take-home/in-office comprehensive exam.

Experience requirements: Hold a valid Certified Public Accountant (CPA) certificate and/or license issued by a legally constituted state authority.

Periodic recertification requirement: Requirements for Continuing Professional Education (CPE); training at NACVA's course titled "Report Writing, Ethics and Standards—Raising the Bar"; participating in NACVA's Quality Enhancement program.

GVA—Government Valuation Analyst

Prerequisite requirement(s): Government-employed valuator with four-year college degree (i.e., a minimum of a BA, BS, or similar degree); and have a minimum GS-12 or comparable rating.

Educational requirement: Must complete a four-hour pre-read and NACVA's five-day training program.

Examination: A four-hour proctored exam, and a 30- to 50-hour take-home/in-office comprehensive exam.

Experience requirements: Be currently employed by a federal or state government agency and have the combined equivalent of two years' full-time experience in business valuation.

Periodic recertification requirement: Requirements for Continuing Professional Education (CPE); training at NACVA's course titled "Report Writing, Ethics and Standards—Raising the Bar"; participating in NACVA's Quality Enhancement program.

AVA—Accredited Valuation Analyst

Prerequisite requirement(s): Hold a business degree from an accredited college or university. Pass a prequalification examination focused on subject matter related to accounting fundamentals and forensic accounting concepts as might be applicable in business valuation theory and practice. Applicants holding a CFA (Certified Financial Analyst) or CMA (Certified Management Accountant) designation or those having obtained a master's (or higher) degree in accounting can exempt out of the prequalification examination.

Educational requirement: Must complete a four-hour pre-read and NACVA's five-day training program.

Examination: A four-hour proctored exam, and a 30- to 50-hour take-home/in-office comprehensive exam.

Experience requirements: Two years or more full-time or equivalent experience in business valuation and related disciplines (such as merger and acquisition work, securities analyst for a major brokerage concern, economic loss analysis, etc.); or having performed 10 or more business valuations where the applicant's role was significant enough that they were referenced in the valuation report or a signatory on the report; OR being able to demonstrate substantial knowledge of business valuation concepts, having published works on the subject; completed graduate work in the field; obtained accreditation from another recognized business valuation accrediting organization.

Periodic recertification requirement: Requirements for Continuing Professional Education (CPE); training at NACVA's course titled "Report Writing, Ethics and Standards—Raising the Bar"; participating in NACVA's Quality Enhancement program.

THE CANADIAN INSTITUTE OF CHARTERED BUSINESS VALUATORS (CICBV)

2777 Wellington Street West, 5th Floor, Toronto,
   Ontario, M5V 3H2
Phone: (416) 204-3396
Fax: (416) 977-8585
E-mail: admin@ciebv.ca
Web site: *www.businessvaluators.com*

Designation Offered

CBV—Chartered Business Valuator

Educational requirement: College degree, accounting designation or equivalent

Courses/exams: Successful completion of a program of six courses including assignments and examinations for each course plus the required experience. This is followed by the writing of the Membership Entrance Examination (final examination). Writing of this examination can be challenged without successful completion of the six courses, provided the applicant has at least five years of full-time experience in the field of business valuations.

Experience requirement: Two years of full-time experience or the equivalent of part-time obtained over a five-year period, attested to by a sponsoring CICBV member.

FCBV—Fellow of Canadian Institute of Chartered Business Valuators

Recognizes members who have rendered outstanding service to the business valuation profession, or whose achievements in their professional lives or in the community have earned them distinction and have brought honor to the profession. Designation is granted only upon receipt of a nomination, recommendation by the Fellowship Selection Committee, and approval by the Board.

Professional Standards

AICPA STATEMENT ON CONSULTING SERVICES STANDARDS 1

Consulting Services: Definitions and Standards

Introduction

1. Consulting services that CPAs provide to their clients have evolved from advice on accounting-related matters to a wide range of services involving diverse technical disciplines, industry knowledge, and consulting skills. Most practitioners, including those who provide audit and tax services, also provide business and management consulting services to their clients.

2. Consulting services differ fundamentally from the CPA's function of attesting to the assertions of other parties. In an attest service, the practitioner expresses a conclusion about the reliability of a written assertion that is the responsibility of another party, the asserter. In a consulting service, the practitioner develops the findings, conclusions, and recommendations presented. The nature and scope of work is determined solely by the agreement between the practitioner and the client. Generally, the work is performed only for the use and benefit of the client.

3. Historically, CPA consulting services have been commonly referred to as management consulting services, management advisory services, business advisory services, or management services. A series of Statements on Standards for Management Advisory Services (SSMASs) previously issued by the AICPA contained guidance on certain types of consulting services provided by members. This Statement on Standards for Consulting Services (SSCS) supersedes the SSMASs and provides standards of practice for a broader range of professional services, as described in paragraph 5.

4. This SSCS and any subsequent SSCSs apply to any AICPA member holding out as a CPA while providing consulting services as defined herein.

Definitions

5. Terms established for the purpose of SSCSs are as follows:

Consulting services practitioner. Any AICPA member holding out as a CPA while engaged in the performance of a consulting service for a client, or any other individual who is carrying out a consulting service for a client on behalf of any Institute member or member's firm holding out as a CPA.

Consulting process. The analytical approach and process applied in a consulting service. It typically involves some combination of activities relating to determination of client objectives, fact-finding, definition of the problems or opportunities, evaluation of alternatives, formulation of proposed action, communication of results, implementation, and follow-up.

Consulting services. Professional services that employ the practitioner's technical skills, education, observations, experiences, and knowledge of the consulting process.[1] Consulting Services may include one or more of the following:

---

[1] The definition of consulting services excludes the following:

   a. Services subject to other AICPA Technical Standards such as Statements on Auditing Standards (SASs), Statements on Standards for Attestation Engagements (SSAEs), or Statements on Standards for Accounting and Review Ser-

a. *Consultations,* in which the practitioner's function is to provide counsel in a short time frame, based mostly, if not entirely, on existing personal knowledge about the client, the circumstances, the technical matters involved, client representations, and the mutual intent of the parties. Examples of consultations are reviewing and commenting on a client-prepared business plan and suggesting computer software for further client investigation.

b. *Advisory services,* in which the practitioner's function is to develop findings, conclusions, and recommendations for client consideration and decision making. Examples of advisory services are an operational review and improvement study, analysis of an accounting system, assistance with strategic planning, and definition of requirements for an information system.

c. *Implementation services,* in which the practitioner's function is to put an action plan into effect. Client personnel and resources may be pooled with the practitioner's to accomplish the implementation objectives. The practitioner is responsible to the client for the conduct and management of engagement activities. Examples of implementation services are providing computer system installation and support, executing steps to improve productivity, and assisting with the merger of organizations.

d. *Transaction services,* in which the practitioner's function is to provide services related to a specific client transaction, generally with a third party. Examples of transaction services are insolvency services, valuation services, preparation of information for obtaining financing, analysis of a potential merger or acquisition, and litigation services.

---

vices (SSARS). (These excluded services may be performed in conjunction with Consulting Services, but only the Consulting Services are subject to the SSCS.)
b. Engagements specifically to perform tax return preparation, tax planning/advice, tax representation, personal financial planning or bookkeeping services; or situations involving the preparation of written reports or the provision of oral advice on the application of accounting principles to specified transactions or events, either completed or proposed, and the reporting thereof.
c. Recommendations and comments prepared during the same engagement as a direct result of observations made while performing the excluded services.

e. *Staff and other support services,* in which the practitioner's function is to provide appropriate staff and possibly other support to perform tasks specified by the client. The staff provided will be directed by the client as circumstances require. Examples of staff and other support services are data processing facilities management, computer programming, bankruptcy trusteeship, and controllership activities.

f. *Product services,* in which the practitioner's function is to provide the client with a product and associated professional services in support of the installation, use, or maintenance of the product. Examples of product services are the sale and delivery of packaged training programs, the sale and implementation of computer software, and the sale and installation of systems development methodologies.

Standards for Consulting Services

6. The general standards of the profession are contained in Rule 201 of the AICPA Code of Professional Conduct (ET section 201.01) and apply to all services performed by members. They are as follows:

Professional competence. Undertake only those professional services that the member or the member's firm can reasonably expect to be completed with professional competence.

Due professional care. Exercise due professional care in the performance of professional services.

Planning and supervision. Adequately plan and supervise the performance of professional services.

Sufficient relevant data. Obtain sufficient relevant data to afford a reasonable basis for conclusions or recommendations in relation to any professional services performed.

7. The following additional general standards for all consulting services are promulgated to address the distinctive nature of consulting services in which the understanding with the client may establish valid limitations on the practitioner's performance of services. These Standards are established under Rule 202 of the AICPA Code of Professional Conduct (ET section 202.01).

Client interest. Serve the client interest by seeking to accomplish the objectives established by the understanding with the client while maintaining integrity and objectivity.[2]

Understanding with client. Establish with the client a written or oral understanding about the responsibilities of the parties and the nature, scope, and limitations of services to be performed, and modify the understanding if circumstances require a significant change during the engagement.

Communication with client. Inform the client of *(a)* conflicts of interest that may occur pursuant to interpretations of Rule 102 of the Code of Professional Conduct (ET section 102.03),[3] *(b)* significant reservations concerning the scope or benefits of the engagement, and *(c)* significant engagement findings or events.

8. Professional judgment must be used in applying Statements on Standards for Consulting Services in a specific instance since the oral or written understanding with the client may establish constraints within which services are to be provided. For example, the understanding with the client may limit the practitioner's

---

[2] Article III of the Code of Professional Conduct describes *integrity as* follows:
"Integrity requires a member to be, among other things, honest and candid within the constraints of client confidentiality. Service and the public trust should not be subordinated to personal gain and advantage. Integrity can accommodate the inadvertent error and the honest difference of opinion; it cannot accommodate deceit or subordination of principle."
Article IV of the Code of Professional Conduct differentiates between *objectivity* and *independence* as follows:
"Objectivity is a state of mind, a quality that lends value to a member's services. It is a distinguishing feature of the profession. The principle of objectivity imposes the obligation to be impartial, intellectually honest, and free of conflicts of interest. Independence precludes relationships that may appear to impair a member's objectivity in rendering attestation services."

[3] Rule 102-2 on Conflicts of Interest states, in part, the following:
"A conflict of interest may occur if a member performs a professional service for a client or employer and the member or his or her firm has a significant relationship with another person, entity, product, or service that could be viewed as impairing the member's objectivity. If this significant relationship is disclosed to and consent is obtained from such client, employer, or other appropriate parties, the rule shall not operate to prohibit the performance of the professional service..."

effort with regard to gathering relevant data. The practitioner is not required to decline or withdraw from a consulting engagement when the agreed-upon scope of services includes such limitations.

Consulting Services for Attest Clients

9. The performance of consulting services for an attest client does not, in and of itself, impair independence.[4] However, members and their firms performing attest services for a client should comply with applicable independence standards, rules, and regulations issued by the AICPA, the state boards of accountancy, state CPA societies, and other regulatory agencies.

Effective Date

10. This statement is effective for engagements accepted on or after January 1, 1992. Early application of the provisions of this statement is permissible.

AMERICAN SOCIETY OF APPRAISERS BUSINESS VALUATION STANDARDS PREAMBLE APPROVED BY THE ASA BOARD OF GOVERNORS, SEPTEMBER 1992[5]

1. To enhance and maintain the quality of business valuations for the benefit of the business valuation profession and users of business valuations, the American Society of Appraisers, through its Business Valuation Committee, has adopted these standards.

2. The American Society of Appraisers (in its Principles of Appraisal Practice and Code of Ethics) and the Appraisal Foundation (in its Uniform Standards of Professional Appraisal Practice) have

---

[4] AICPA independence standards relate only to the performance of attestation services; objectivity standards apply to all services. See footnote 2.

[5] Reprinted with the permission of the American Society of Appraisers.

established authoritative principles and a code of professional ethics. These standards include these requirements, either explicitly or by reference, and are designed to clarify and provide additional requirements specifically applicable to the valuation of businesses, business ownership interests or securities.

3. These standards incorporate, where appropriate, all relevant business valuation standards adopted by the American Society of Appraisers through its Business Valuation Committee.

4. These standards provide minimum criteria to be followed by business appraisers in the valuation of businesses, business ownership interests, or securities.

5. If, in the opinion of the appraiser, circumstances of a specific business valuation assignment dictate a departure from any provisions of any Standard, such departure must be disclosed and will apply only to the specific departure.

6. These Standards are designed to provide guidance to ASA Appraisers conducting business valuations and to provide a structure for regulating conduct of members of the ASA through Uniform Practices and Procedures. Deviations from the Standards are not designed or intended to be the basis of any civil liability; and should not create any presumption or evidence that a legal duty has been breached; or create any special relationship between the appraiser and any other person.

BVS-I General Requirements for Developing a Business Valuation

I. Preamble

A. This standard is required to be followed in all valuations of businesses, business ownership interests, and securities by all members of the American Society of Appraisers, be they Candidates, Accredited Members (AM), Accredited Senior Appraisers (ASA), or Fellows (FASA).

B. The purpose of this standard is to define and describe the general requirements for developing the valuation of businesses, business ownership interests, or securities.

C. This standard incorporates the general preamble to the Business
   Valuation Standards of the American Society of Appraisers.

II. The Valuation Assignment Shall Be Appropriately Defined

A. In developing a business valuation, an appraiser must identify and
   define the following:
   1. The business, business ownership interest, or security to be
      valued
   2. The effective date of the appraisal
   3. The standard of value
   4. The purpose and use of the valuation
B. The nature and scope of the assignment must be defined. Acceptable scopes of work would generally be of three types as delineated below. Other scopes of work should be explained and
   described.
   1. Appraisal
      a. The objective of an appraisal is to express an unambigu-
         ous opinion as to the value of the business, business own-
         ership interest, or security, which is supported by all pro-
         cedures that the appraiser deemed to be relevant to the
         valuation.
      b. An appraisal has the following qualities:
         (1) It is expressed as a single dollar amount or as a range.
         (2) It considers all relevant information as of the ap-
             praisal date available to the appraiser at the time of
             performance of the valuation.
         (3) The appraiser conducts appropriate procedures to
             collect and analyze all information expected to be
             relevant to the valuation.
         (4) The valuation is based upon consideration of all con-
             ceptual approaches deemed to be relevant by the ap-
             praiser.
   2. Limited Appraisal
      a. The objective of a limited appraisal is to express an esti-
         mate as to the value of a business, business ownership
         interest, or security, which lacks the performance of ad-
         ditional procedures that are required in an appraisal.
      b. A limited appraisal has the following qualities:
         (1) It is expressed as a single dollar amount or as a range.

(2) It is based on consideration of limited relevant information.

(3) The appraiser conducts only limited procedures to collect and analyze the information which such appraiser considers necessary to support the conclusion presented.

(4) The valuation is based on the conceptual approach(es) deemed by the appraiser to be most appropriate.

3. Calculations

a. The objective of calculations is to provide an approximate indication of value based upon the performance of limited procedures agreed upon by the appraiser and the client

b. Calculations have the following qualities:

(1) They may be expressed as a single dollar amount or as a range.

(2) They may be based on consideration of only limited relevant information.

(3) The appraiser performs limited information collection and analysis procedures.

(4) The calculations may be based on conceptual approaches as agreed upon with the client.

III. Information Collection and Analysis

The appraiser shall gather, analyze, and adjust relevant information to perform the valuation as appropriate to the scope of work. Such information shall include the following:

A. Characteristics of the business, business ownership interest or security to be valued including rights, privileges and conditions, quantity, factors affecting control and agreements restricting sale or transfer.

B. Nature, history and outlook of the business.

C. Historical financial information for the business.

D. Assets and liabilities of the business.

E. Nature and conditions of the relevant industries which have an impact on the business.

F. Economic factors affecting the business.

G. Capital markets providing relevant information, e.g., available rates of return on alternative investments, relevant public stock transactions, and relevant mergers and acquisitions.
H. Prior transactions involving subject business, interest in the subject business, or its securities.
I. Other information deemed by the appraiser to be relevant.

IV. Approaches, Methods, and Procedures

A. The appraiser shall select and apply appropriate valuation approaches, methods, and procedures.
B. The appraiser shall develop a conclusion of value pursuant to the valuation assignment as defined, considering the relevant valuation approaches, methods, and procedures, and appropriate premiums and discounts, if any.

V. Documentation and Retention

The appraiser shall appropriately document and retain all information and work product that were relied on in reaching the conclusion.

VI. Reporting

The appraiser shall report to the client the conclusion of value in an appropriate written or oral format. The report must meet the requirements of Standard 10 of The Uniform Standards of Professional Appraisal Practice. In the event the assignment results in a comprehensive written report, the report shall meet the requirements of BVS-VH.

BVS-II Financial Statement Adjustments

I. Preamble

A. This standard is required to be followed in all valuations of businesses, business ownership interests, and securities by all members of the American Society of Appraisers, be they Candidates, Accredited Members (AM), Accredited Senior Appraisers (ASA), or Fellows (FASA).

B. The purpose of this standard is to define and describe the requirements for making financial statement adjustments in valuation of businesses, business ownership interests, and securities.
C. This present standard is applicable to appraisals and may not necessarily be applicable to limited appraisals and calculations as defined in BVS-I, Section II.B.
D. This standard incorporates the general preamble to the Business Valuation Standards of the American Society of Appraisers.

II. Conceptual Framework

A. Financial statements should be analyzed and, if appropriate, adjusted as a procedure in the valuation process. Financial statements to be analyzed include those of the subject entity and any entities used as guideline companies.
B. Financial statement adjustments are modifications to reported financial information that are relevant and significant to the appraisal process. Adjustments may be necessary in order to make the financial statements more meaningful for the appraisal process. Adjustments may be *appropriate* for the following reasons, among others: (1) To present financial data of the subject and guideline companies on a consistent basis; (2) To adjust from reported values to current values; (3) To adjust revenues and expenses to levels which are reasonably representative of continuing results; and (4) To adjust for nonoperating assets and liabilities and the related revenue and expenses.
C. Financial statement adjustments are made for the purpose of assisting the appraiser in reaching a valuation conclusion and for no other purpose.

III. Documentation of Adjustments

Adjustments made should be fully described and supported.

BVS-III Asset-Based Approach to Business Valuation

I. Preamble

A. This standard is required to be followed in all valuations of businesses, business ownership interests, and securities by all members of the American Society of Appraisers, be they candidates, Accredited Members (AM), Accredited Senior Appraisers (ASA), or Fellows (FASA).

B. The purpose of this standard is to define and describe the requirements for the use of the Asset-Based Approach to business valuation and the circumstances in which it is appropriate.

C. This present standard is applicable to appraisals and may not necessarily be applicable to limited appraisals and calculations as defined in BVS-I, Section II.B.

D. This standard incorporates the general preamble to the Business Valuation Standards of the American Society of Appraisers.

II. The Asset-Based Approach

A. In business valuation the Asset-Based Approach may be analogous to the Cost Approach of other disciplines.

B. Assets, liabilities, and equity relate to a business that is an operating company, a holding company, or a combination thereof (mixed business).

1. An operating company is a business that conducts an economic activity by generating and selling, or trading, in a product or service.

2. A holding company is a business that derives its revenues by receiving returns on its assets which may include operating companies and/or other businesses.

C. The Asset-Based Approach should be considered in valuations conducted at the *total entity level* and involving the following:

1. An investment or real estate holding company.

2. A business appraised on a basis other than as a going concern.

Valuations of particular *ownership interests* in an entity may or may not require the use of the Asset-Based Approach.

D. The Asset-Based Approach should not be the sole appraisal approach used in assignments relating to operating companies appraised as going concerns unless it is customarily used by sellers and buyers. In such cases, the appraiser must support the selection of this approach.

BVS-IV Income Approach to Business Valuation

I. Preamble

A. This standard is required to be followed in all valuations of businesses, business ownership interests, and securities by all members of the American Society of Appraisers, be they Candidates, Accredited Members (AM), Accredited Senior Appraisers (ASA), or Fellows (FASA).
B. The purpose of this standard is to define and describe the requirements for use of the income approach in valuation of businesses, business ownership interests, and securities, but not the reporting therefor.
C. This present standard is applicable to appraisals and may not necessarily be applicable to limited appraisals and calculations as defined in BVS-I, Section II.B.
D. This standard incorporates the general preamble to the Business Valuation Standards of the American Society of Appraisers.

II. The Income Approach

A. The income approach is a general way of determining a value indication of a business, business ownership interest or security using one or more methods wherein a value is determined by convening anticipated benefits.
B. Both capitalization of benefits methods and discounted future benefits methods are acceptable. In capitalization of benefits methods, a representative benefit level is divided or multiplied by a capitalization factor to convert the benefit to value. In discounted future benefits methods, benefits are estimated for each of several future periods. These benefits are converted to value by the application of a discount rate using present value techniques.

III. Anticipated Benefits

A. Anticipated benefits, as used in the income approach, are expressed in monetary terms. Depending on the nature of the business, business ownership interest or security being appraised and other relevant factors, anticipated benefits may be reasonably represented by such items as net cash flow, dividends, and various forms of earnings.

B. Anticipated benefits should be estimated considering such items as the nature, capital structure, and historical performance of the related business entity, expected future outlook for the business entity and relevant industries, and relevant economic factors.

IV. Conversion of Anticipated Benefit

A. Anticipated benefits are convened to value using procedures that consider the expected growth and timing of the benefits, the risk profile of the benefits stream and the time value of money.

B. The conversion of anticipated benefits to value normally requires the determination of a capitalization rate or discount rate. In determining the appropriate rate, the appraiser should consider such factors as the level of interest rates, rates of return expected by investors on relevant investments, and the risk characteristics of the anticipated benefits.

C. In discounted future benefits methods, expected growth is considered in estimating the future stream of benefits. In capitalization of benefits methods, expected growth is incorporated in the capitalization rate.

D. The rate of return used (capitalization rate or discount rate) should be consistent with the type of anticipated benefits used. For example, pretax rates of return should be used with pretax benefits; common equity rates of return should be used with common equity benefits; and net cash flow rates should be used with net cash flow benefits.

BVS-V Market Approach to Business Valuation

I. Preamble

A. This standard is required to be followed in all valuations of businesses, business ownership interests, and securities by all members of the American Society of Appraisers, be they Candidates,

Accredited Members (AM), Accredited Senior Appraisers (ASA), or Fellows (FASA).

B. The purpose of this standard is to define and describe the requirements for use of the market approach in valuation of businesses, business ownership interests, and securities, but not the reporting therefor.

C. This present standard is applicable to appraisals and may not necessarily be applicable to limited appraisals and calculations as defined in BVS-I, Section II.B.

D. This standard incorporates the general preamble to the Business Valuation Standards of the American Society of Appraisers.

II. The Market Approach

A. The market approach is a general way of determining a value indication of a business, business ownership interest or security using one or more methods that compare the subject to similar businesses, business ownership interests, and securities that have been sold.

B. Examples of market approach methods include the guideline company method and analysis of prior transactions in the ownership of the subject company.

III. Reasonable Basis for Comparison

A. The investment used for comparison must provide a reasonable basis for the comparison.

B. Factors to be considered in judging whether a reasonable basis for comparison exists include the following:

1. Sufficient similarity of qualitative and quantitative investment characteristics.

2. Amount and verifiability of data known about the similar investment.

3. Whether the price of the similar investment was obtained in an arm's length transaction, or a forced or distress sale.

IV. Manner of Comparison

A. The comparison must be made in a meaningful manner and must not be misleading. Such comparisons are normally made through the use of valuation ratios. The computation and use of such ratios should provide meaningful insight about the pricing of the subject considering all relevant factors. Accordingly, care should be exercised in the following:

1. Selection of underlying data used for the ratio.
2. Selection of the time period and/or averaging method used for the underlying data.
3. Manner of computing and comparing the subject's underlying data.
4. The timing of the price data used in the ratio.

B. In general, comparisons should be made using comparable definitions of the components of the valuation ratios. However, where appropriate, valuation ratios based on components that are reasonably representative of continuing results may be used.

V. Rules of Thumb

A. Rules of thumb may provide insight on this value of a business, business ownership interest or security. However, value indications derived from the use of rules of thumb should not be given substantial weight unless supported by other valuation methods and it can be established that knowledgeable buyers and sellers place substantial reliance on them.

BVS-VI Reaching a Conclusion of Value

I. Preamble

A. This standard is required to be followed in all valuations of businesses, business ownership interests, and securities by all members of the American Society of Appraisers, be they Candidates, Accredited Members (AM), Accredited Senior Appraisers (ASA), or Fellows (FASA).
B. The purpose of this standard is to define and describe the requirements for reaching a final conclusion of value in valuation of businesses, business ownership interests, or securities.
C. This present standard is applicable to appraisals and may not necessarily be applicable to limited appraisals and calculations as defined in BVS-I, Section II.B.

D. This standard incorporates the general preamble to the Business Valuation Standards of the American Society of Appraisers.

II. General

A. The conclusion of value reached by the appraiser shall be based on the applicable standard of value, the purpose and intended use of the valuation, and all relevant information obtained as of the appraisal date in carrying out the scope of the assignment.
B. The conclusion of value reached by the appraiser will be based on value indications resulting from one or more methods performed under one or more appraisal approaches.

III. Selection and Weighing of Methods

A. The selection of and reliance on the appropriate method and procedures depends on the judgment of the appraiser and not on the basis of any prescribed formula. One or more approaches may not be relevant to the particular situation. More than one method under an approach may be relevant to a particular situation.
B. The appraiser must use informed judgment when determining the relative weight to be accorded to indications of value reached on the basis of various methods or whether an indication of value from a single method should dominate. The appraiser's judgment may be presented either in general terms or in terms of mathematical weighting of the indicated values reflected in the conclusion. In any case, the appraiser should provide the rationale for the selection or weighing of the method or methods relied on in reaching the conclusion.
C. In formulating a judgment about the relative weights to be accorded to indications of value determined under each method or whether an indication of value from a single method should dominate, the appraiser should consider several factors:
   1. The applicable standard of value
   2. The purpose and intended use of the valuation
   3. Whether the subject is an operating company, a real estate or investment holding company, or a company with substantial non-operating or excess assets

4. Quality and reliability of data underlying the indication of value
5. Such other factors which, in the opinion of the appraiser, are appropriate for consideration

IV. Additional Factors to Consider

As appropriate for the valuation assignment as defined, and if not considered in the process of determining and weighting the indications of value provided by various procedures, the appraiser should separately consider the following factors in reaching a final conclusion of value:

A. Marketability, or lack thereof, considering the nature of the business, business ownership interest or security, the effect of relevant contractual and legal restrictions, and the condition of the markets.
B. Ability of the appraised interest to control the operation, sale, or liquidation of the relevant business.
C. Such other factors that, in the opinion of the appraiser, are appropriate for consideration.

BVS-VII Comprehensive Written Business Valuation Report

I. Preamble

A. This standard is required to be followed in the preparation of comprehensive, written business valuation reports by all members of the American Society of Appraisers, be they Candidates, Accredited Members (AM), Accredited Senior Appraisers (ASA), or Fellows (FASA).
B. The purpose of this standard is to define and describe the requirements for the written communication of the results of a business valuation, analysis or opinion, but not the conduct thereof.
C. This standard incorporates the general preamble to the Business Valuation Standards of the American Society of Appraisers.

II. Signature and Certification

A. An appraiser assumes responsibility for the statements made in the comprehensive, written report and indicates the acceptance of that responsibility by signing the report. To comply with this standard, a comprehensive, written report must be signed by the appraiser. For the purpose of this standard, the appraiser is the individual or entity undertaking the appraisal assignment under a contract with the client

B. Clearly, at least one individual is responsible for the valuation conclusion(s) expressed in the report. A report must contain a certification, as required by Standard 10 of the *Uniform Standards of Professional Appraisal Practice* of The Appraisal Foundation, in which the individuals responsible for the valuation conclusion(s) must be identified.

III. Assumptions and Limiting Conditions

The following assumptions and/or limiting conditions must be stated:

1. Pertaining to bias—a report must contain a statement that the appraiser has no interest in the asset appraised, or other conflict, which could cause a question as to the appraiser's independence or objectivity or if such an interest or conflict exists, it must be disclosed.

2. Pertaining to data used—where appropriate, a report must indicate that an appraiser relied on data supplied by others, without further verification by the appraiser, as well as the sources which were relied on.

3. Pertaining to validity of the valuation—a report must contain a statement that a valuation is valid only for the valuation date indicated and for the purpose stated.

IV. Definition of the Valuation Assignment

The precise definition of the valuation assignment is a key aspect of communication with users of the report. The following are key components of such a definition and must be included in the report:

1. The business interest valued must be clearly defined, such as "100

shares of the Class A common stock of the XYZ Corporation" or "a 20% limited partnership interest in the ABC Limited Partnership." The existence, rights and/or restrictions of other classes of ownership in the business appraised must also be adequately described if they are relevant to the conclusion of value.

2. The purpose and use of the valuation must be clearly stated, such as "a determination of fair market value for ESOP purposes" or "a determination of fair value for dissenter's fight purposes." If a valuation is being done pursuant to a particular statute, the particular statute must be referenced.

3. The standard of value used in the valuation must be stated and defined. The premise of value, such as a valuation on a minority interest or a control basis, must be stated.

4. The appraisal date must be clearly defined. The date of the preparation of the report must be indicated.

V. Business Description

A comprehensive, written business valuation report must include a business description which covers all relevant factual areas, such as the following:

1. Form of organization (corporation, partnership, etc.)
2. History
3. Products and/or services and markets and customers
4. Management
5. Major assets, both tangible and intangible
6. Outlook for the economy, industry and company
7. Past transactional evidence of value
8. Sensitivity to seasonal or cyclical factors
9. Competition
10. Sources of information used

VI. Financial Analysis

A. An analysis and discussion of a firm's financial statements is an integral part of a business valuation and must be included. Exhibits summarizing balance sheets and income statements for a period of years sufficient to the purpose of the valuation and the nature of the subject company must be included in the valuation report.

B. Any adjustments made to the reported financial data must be fully explained.

C. If projections of balance sheets or income statements were utilized in the valuation, key assumptions underlying the projections must be included and discussed.

D. If appropriate, the company's financial results relative to those of its industry must be discussed.

VII. Valuation Methodology

A. The valuation method or methods selected, and the reasons for their selection, must be discussed. The steps followed in the application of the method or methods selected must be described and must lead to the valuation conclusion.

B. The report must include an explanation of how any variables such as discount rates, capitalization rates or valuation multiples were determined and used. The rationale and/or supporting data for any premiums or discounts must be clearly presented.

VIII. Comprehensive, Written Report Format

The comprehensive, written report format must provide a logical progression for clear communication of pertinent information, valuation methods and conclusions and must incorporate the other specific requirements of this standard, including the signature and certification provisions.

IX. Confidentiality of Report

No copies of the report will be furnished to persons other than the client without the client's specific permission or direction unless ordered by a court of competent jurisdiction.

Definitions

Adjusted book value: The book value that results after one or more asset or liability amounts are added, deleted or changed from the respective book amounts.

Appraisal: The act or process of determining value. It is synonymous with valuation.

Appraisal approach: A general way of determining value using one or more specific appraisal methods. (See *asset-based approach, market approach* and *income approach* definitions.)

Appraisal method: Within approaches, a specific way to determine value.

Appraisal procedure: The act, manner, and technique of performing the steps of an appraisal method.

Appraised value: The appraiser's opinion or determination of value.

Asset-based approach: A general way of determining a value indication of a business's assets and/or equity interest using one or more methods based directly on the value of the assets of the business less liabilities.

Book value: (1) With respect to assets, the capitalized cost of an asset less accumulated depreciation, depletion or amortization as it appears on the books of account of the enterprise. (2) With respect to a business enterprise, the difference between total assets (net of depreciation, depletion and amortization) and total liabilities of an enterprise as they appear on the balance sheet. It is synonymous with net book value, net worth and shareholder's equity.

Business appraiser: A person who, by education, training and experience, is qualified to make an appraisal of a business enterprise and/or its intangible assets.

Business enterprise: A commercial, industrial, or service organization pursuing an economic activity.

Business valuation: The act or process of arriving at an opinion or determination of the value of a business or enterprise or an interest therein.

Capitalization: (1) The conversion of income into value. (2) The capital structure of a business enterprise. (3) The recognition of an expenditure as a capital asset rather than a period expense.

Capitalization factor: Any multiple or divisor used to convert income into value.

Capitalization rate: Any divisor (usually expressed as a percentage) that is used to convert income into value.

Capital structure: The composition of the invested capital.

Cash flow: Net income plus depreciation and other noncash charges.

Control: The power to direct the management and policies of an enterprise.

Control premium: The additional value inherent in the control interest, as contrasted to a minority interest, that reflects its power of control.

Discount for lack of control: An amount or percentage deducted from a pro rata share of the value of 100 percent of an equity interest in a business, to reflect the absence of some or all of the powers of control

Discount rate: A rate of return used to convert a monetary sum, payable or receivable in the future, into present value.

Economic life: The period over which property may be profitably used.

Effective date: The date as of which the appraiser's opinion of value applies (Also referred to as *appraisal date, valuation date,* or *as of date*).

Enterprise: See *business enterprise.*

Equity: The owner's interest in property after deduction of all liabilities.

Fair market value: The amount at which property would change hands between a willing seller and a willing buyer when neither is under compulsion and when both have reasonable knowledge of the relevant facts.

Going concern: An operating business enterprise.

Going concern value: (1) The value of an enterprise, or an interest therein, as a going concern. (2) Intangible elements of value in a business enterprise resulting from factors such as having a trained work force; an operational plant; and the necessary licenses, systems, and procedures in place.

Goodwill: That intangible asset that arises as a result of name, reputation, customer patronage, location, products and similar factors that have not been separately identified and/or valued but that generate economic benefits.

Income approach: A general way of determining a value indication of a business, business ownership interest or security using one or more methods wherein a value is determined by converting anticipated benefits.

Invested capital: The sum of the debt and equity in an enterprise on a long-term basis.

Majority control: (1) Ownership position greater than 50% of the voting interest in an enterprise. (2) The degree of control provided by a majority position.

Market approach: A general way of determining a value indication of a business, business ownership interest or security using one or more methods that compare the subject to similar businesses, business ownership interests or securities that have been sold.

Marketability discount: An amount or percentage deducted from an equity interest to reflect lack of marketability.

Minority interest: Ownership position less than 50 percent of the voting interest in an enterprise.

Minority discount: A *discount for lack of control* applicable to a minority interest.

Net assets: Total assets less total liabilities.

Net income: Revenue less expenses, including taxes.

Rate of return: An amount of income (loss) and/or change in value realized or anticipated on an investment, expressed as a percentage of that investment.

Replacement cost new: The current cost of a similar new item having the nearest equivalent utility as item being appraised.

Report date: The date of the report. May be the *same* as or different from the *appraisal date.*

Reproduction cost new: The current cost of an identical new item.

Rule of thumb: A mathematical relationship between or among a number of variables based on experience, observation, hearsay or a combination of these, usually applicable to a specific industry.

Valuation: See *Appraisal.*

Valuation ratio: A factor wherein a value or price serves as the numerator and financial, operating or physical data serve as the denominator.

Working capital: The amount by which current assets exceed current liabilities.

SBVS-I The Guideline Company Valuation Method

I. Preamble

A. This statement is required to be followed in all valuations of businesses, business ownership interests, and securities by all members of the American Society of Appraisers, be they Candidates, Accredited Members (AM), Accredited Senior Appraisers (ASA), or Fellows (FASA).

B. The purpose of this statement is to define and describe the requirements for the use of guideline companies in the valuation of businesses, business ownership interests or securities.

C. This statement incorporates the general preamble to the Business Valuation Standards of the American Society of Appraisers.

II. Conceptual Framework

A. Market transactions in businesses, business ownership interests or securities can provide objective, empirical data for developing valuation ratios to apply in business valuation.

B. The development of valuation ratios from guideline companies should be considered for use in the valuation of businesses, business ownership interests or securities, to the extent that adequate information is available.

C. Guideline companies are companies that provide a reasonable basis for comparison to the investment characteristics of the company being valued. Ideal guideline companies are in the *same* industry as the company being valued; but if there is insufficient transaction evidence available in the same industry it may be necessary to select companies with an underlying similarity of relevant investment characteristics such as markets, products, growth, cyclical variability and other salient factors.

III. Search for and Selection of Guideline Companies

A. A thorough, objective search for guideline companies is required to establish the credibility of the valuation analysis. The procedure must include criteria for screening and selecting guideline companies.
B. Empirical data from guideline companies can be found in transactions involving either minority or controlling interests in either publicly traded or closely held companies.

IV. Financial Data of the Guideline Companies

A. It is necessary to obtain and analyze financial and operating data on the guideline companies, as available.
B. Consideration should be given to adjustments to the financial data of the subject company and the guideline companies to minimize the difference in accounting treatments when such differences are significant. Unusual or nonrecurring items should be analyzed and adjusted as appropriate.

V. Comparative Analysis of Qualitative and Quantitative Factors

A comparative analysis of qualitative and quantitative similarities and differences between guideline companies and the subject company must be made to assess the investment attributes of the guideline companies relative to the subject company.

VI. Valuation Ratios Derived from Guideline Companies

A. Price information of the guideline companies must be related to the appropriate underlying financial data of each guideline company in order to compute appropriate valuation ratios.
B. The valuation ratios for the guideline companies and comparative analysis of qualitative and quantitative factors should be used together to determine appropriate valuation ratios for application to the subject company.

C. Several valuation ratios may be selected for application to the subject company and several value indications may be obtained. The appraiser should consider the relative importance accorded to each of the value indications utilized in arriving at the valuation conclusion.

D. To the extent that adjustments for dissimilarities with respect to minority and control, or marketability, have not been made earlier, appropriate adjustments for these factors must be made, if applicable.

RECOMMENDATIONS ON INTERNAL REVENUE SERVICE VALUATION POLICIES AND PROCEDURES

Executive Summary

In July of 1998, the IRS established a Review Team of employees from various branches of the Service to examine and comment on existing IRS valuation practices and policies. Part of the impetus for the establishment of this team was a report published by the American Society of Appraisers in 1997 regarding IRS valuation policies.

The IRS Review Team considers it essential that all interest groups involved with valuation issues, such as the American Institute of Certified Public Accountants (AICPA), American Society of Appraisers (ASA), National Association of Certified Valuation Analysts (NACVA), Institute of Business Appraisers (IBA), The Appraisal Foundation, etc., be contacted for their input and involvement.

The scope of the Review Team's investigation included the following:

- Review of information on valuation in the existing Internal Revenue Code, regulations, procedures, rulings, publications, etc.
- Review of current IRS valuation practices
- Review of current industry valuation practices and guidelines including the Uniform Standards of Professional Appraisal Practice (USPAP)
- Review of current levels of taxpayer compliance in valuation issues based on the experience of IRS personnel involved in valuation issues

- Consultation with in-house stakeholders involved in valuation issues
- Consideration of existing concerns that have been raised by both internal and external stakeholders in valuation issues

The IRS Review Team concluded that the IRS needs to assume a leadership role in valuation. This role should include developing strategy for pre-filing activities, providing guidance and education, and establishing policy with the involvement and input of internal and external stakeholders.

The Review Team considered the IRS's responsibility to keep taxpayer burden to a minimum while ensuring reasonable tax compliance. The Review Team concluded that the following recommendations would improve the IRS valuation process and provide better customer service to taxpayers and appraisers.

Items Recommended by the IRS Review Team

1. Establish an IRS Valuation Policy Council to set direction for valuation policy that cuts across functional lines.
2. Establish an Issue/Industry Specialist position(s) for valuation issues within the Industry Specialization Program that also provides support to the IRS Valuation Policy Council.
3. Have the Valuation Policy Council consider areas that could enhance our communication on valuation:

   - Develop guidelines for valuing real property interests.
   - Update Revenue Ruling 59-60 providing guidelines for valuing business interests.
   - Develop guidelines for valuing personal property in the estate and gift tax area.

4. Require taxpayers to substantiate their valuation opinions in accordance with the guidelines under item 3 above for all federal tax purposes.
5. Produce a vehicle to provide guidance to taxpayers on valuations for all federal tax purposes incorporating information from all

IRS valuation guidelines (regulations, rulings, procedures, publications, etc.).

6. Create a form similar to Form 8283 (Non-cash Charitable Contributions) for all other federal tax valuations.
7. Review and develop clear and concise guidelines for appraisal reports prepared by IRS personnel.
8. Recommend that counsel consider revising the estate and gift tax regulations to update and remove obsolete material.

Items Not Recommended by the IRS Review Team

1. Adoption the Uniform Standards of Professional Appraisal Practice (USPAP) for all appraisals.
2. Revision of IRS appraisal filing requirements and threshold amounts.
3. Revision of the IRS definition of "qualified" appraiser.

Discussion of IRS Review Team Recommendations

In administering the tax laws, the IRS must balance taxpayer compliance requirements with the burden placed on the taxpayer to comply. Before committing resources, the IRS must be reasonably convinced that it will reap a substantial benefit in overall tax compliance to warrant the expenditure and additional taxpayer burden.

In considering proposed actions, the Review Team identified long term as well as relatively short term projects to deal with particular areas. For example, the estate tax regulations date from 1958 and have some obsolete material. While a regulation project would be a long-term consideration, the Review Team judged that updating and consolidating the existing IRS material and publishing additional revenue procedures and publications would be a more expeditious method of implementation.

The Review Team concluded that although the IRS has considerable written materials applicable to valuation in the form of regulations, revenue procedures, and publications there is no one source, particularly in the estate and gift tax area, that consolidates the information for taxpayers and appraisers. It is this inaccessibility that we believe significantly contributes to the confusion in the valuation area.

The IRS Review Team's recommendations and proposed actions are set forth below:

1. *Establish an IRS Valuation Policy Council to set direction for valuation policy that cuts across functional lines.* The IRS should form a National Valuation Policy Council to set direction and oversee the implementation of valuation policies and utilization of IRS resources. The Council would be comprised of primary stakeholders such as Small Business Self-Employed Division (SBSE), Large and Mid-Size Business Division (LMSB), Chief Counsel, Appeals, Tax Exempt and Government Entities Division (TEGE), Communications & Liaisons (C&L), etc. The Council determines valuation activities and sets priorities, most importantly it looks for process improvements to effect compliance and to better utilize resources. The Council uses the expertise of the Industry Specialization Program (see below). It also solicits input from the appraisal industry and taxpayer groups such as the American Bar Association (ABA) and Tax Executive Institute (TEI).

2. *Establish an Issue/Industry Specialist position(s) for valuation issues within the Industry Specialization Program that also provides support to the IRS Valuation Policy Council.* The valuation function of the IRS is decentralized. The commissioner's emphasis on consolidating resources and restructuring the way the IRS does business creates an excellent opportunity to study the most effective way to efficiently manage the IRS valuation operation.

   The IRS Review Team envisions a centralized function with appraisal expertise to provide the following services:

   • Play a public role in the valuation community.
   • Collaborate with chief counsel on valuation issues and projects.
   • Facilitate dispute resolution and mediation.
   • Provide valuation expertise.
   • Advise on technical issues such as discounts, 338 elections, etc.

- Advise taxpayer and field personnel on valuation methodology.
- Assist in selection of expert witnesses.
- Support the IRS Valuation Policy Council.
- Support valuation training activities.
- Develop taxpayer education vehicles such as publications, Web sites, etc.

Special consideration needs to be given to the feasibility of utilizing the Issue/Industry Specialization Program. The IRS Review Team recommends the centralization and coordination of IRS valuation services to provide expertise to all functions for uniformity and consistency of approach.

3. *Actions that could enhance our communication on valuation policy and should be considered by the Valuation Policy Council:*

- *Develop guidelines for valuing real property interests.* The IRS has revenue rulings and revenue procedures for valuing artwork, and business interests. It would be beneficial to provide guidelines, such as a revenue ruling or a revenue procedure, for valuing all types of real estate.

   The lack of consistency in providing general guidance for the valuation of property such as art and business interests and not providing similar guidelines for such a basic property category as real estate can be frustrating. Accordingly, the Assistant Commissioner Examination should consider working with Chief Counsel to identify guidance opportunities for valuing all types of real estate.

- *Update Revenue Ruling 59-60 providing guidelines for valuing business interests.* As part of the review of USPAP, the IRS Review Team made a comparison of Revenue Ruling 59-60's "Factors to Consider" with USPAP Standard 9's (the business valuation standard) "Data to be Included When Relevant" and found them to be very similar to each other. Only the "dividend paying capacity" factor from Revenue Ruling 59-60 is not specifically covered by USPAP Standard 9.

   While there may be similarities with USPAP, Revenue Ruling 59-60 is 40 years old. It should be updated to include more detail on subjects such as discounted cash flow, regression analysis, and additional valuation methods.

- *Develop guidelines for valuing personal property in the estate and gift tax area. (A proposed revenue procedure is currently in the Office of Chief Counsel for valuing personal property).* The substantiation requirements for charitable contributions of art are more stringent in the income tax area than in the estate and gift tax area. While appraisals by disinterested, qualified individuals are required in the estate tax regulations for personal property valued over $3,000, the regulations would be clarified by this new revenue procedure. IRM 42(16)4, Valuation Assistance for Cases Involving Works of Art, already requests most of the same information listed in the contribution requirements from taxpayers as necessary for Art Panel review. Guidance applicable to estate tax, that provides specific information and guidelines, would significantly improve the valuation process for taxpayers, appraisers, and IRS personnel. This guidance would provide uniformity in the personal property area. A draft proposed revenue procedure was submitted to the office of chief counsel and has, as yet, not been issued.

4. *Require taxpayers to substantiate their valuation opinions in accordance with the guidelines under item 3 above for all federal tax purposes.* There was much debate among the Review Team members on this recommendation. Information obtained from the IRS Statistics of Income (SOI) group confirmed that less than 10 percent of gift tax and less than 50 percent of estate tax returns are taxable. Several members of the Review Team who are routinely involved in reviewing estate and gift tax returns for audit stated that formal appraisals are routinely being submitted by experienced individuals who generally follow appraisal guidelines.

It was argued that to require by regulation formal appraisals on *all* estate and gift tax returns, when all indicators are that compliance is already taking place (except as already required by regulation, i.e., adequate disclosure requirements), would create an increase in taxpayer burden that would outweigh any potential compliance advantages. Therefore, the Review Team initially considered requiring formal appraisals and applying the definition of qualified appraiser/appraisal from Section 170 to *only* taxable estate and gift tax returns or above a specific dollar threshold. However, the Review Team concluded, after input from the Estate and Gift Tax Program, that these requirements may be unnecessarily burdensome or too restrictive.

5. *Produce a new IRS vehicle to provide guidance to taxpayers on valuations for all federal tax purposes incorporating information from all IRS valuation guidelines (regulations, rulings, procedures, etc.).* IRS valuation materials are found in several different places such as the regulations, revenue rulings, procedures, and publications. Some of these procedures and rulings are intended more for the appraiser than the taxpayer. This can be confusing and creates uncertainty for both the appraiser and the taxpayer.

    The IRS currently has *Publication 561—Determining the Value of Donated Property* as its guide to assist taxpayers and appraisers; however, it deals only with *donated* property. The IRS Review Team concludes that there is a need to provide a comprehensive publication, or other form of vehicle, on valuation that would include estate and gift tax to assist appraisers and taxpayers. This would create a more customer oriented approach to dealing with valuation matters.

6. *Create a form similar to Form 8283 (Non-cash Charitable Contributions) for all other federal tax valuations.* Form 8283 is an appraisal summary form which taxpayers must submit with their return on non-cash contribution deductions in excess of $500. It provides a summary of the property donated, specific information on the property (such as purchase price and date), a declaration by the appraiser, and signature of the donee. A redesigned summary form for the other valuation areas could provide a uniform and easily accessible format for appraisal review. It could summarize the items involved and provide other data such as taxable basis, allocation of purchase price, whether the asset was sold or distributed, and other applicable information. It would be signed by the person who prepared the valuation.

7. *Review and develop clear and concise guidelines for appraisal reports prepared by IRS personnel.* Taxpayers should be provided IRS valuation reports that are professional, credible, and provide clear

reasons to support the recommended changes. The IRS should review the existing materials providing guidance on valuation report standards. They should be updated as necessary to provide consistency, clarity and quality.

8. *Recommend that Counsel consider revising the estate and gift tax regulations to remove or update obsolete material.* Many of the estate and gift tax regulations pertaining to personal property are outdated. Obsolete sections should be revised (e.g., the $100 threshold for listing household property which should be raised).

Items Considered but Not Recommended

After serious consideration, the IRS Review Team does not recommend the following:

• Adoption of USPAP standards for all appraisals at this time
• Revision of appraisal filing requirements and threshold amounts
• Revision of the definition of qualified appraiser

Adoption of USPAP

As stated in its foreword, The Appraisal Standards Board (ASB) of The Appraisal Foundation develops, publishes, interprets, and amends USPAP on behalf of appraisers and users of appraisal services. USPAP may be altered, amended, interpreted, supplemented, or repealed by the ASB after exposure to the appraisal profession. USPAP provides general guidelines to appraisers on the development and reporting of real property, personal property and business appraisals. It contains a Preamble, Ethics Provision, Competency Provision, Departure Provisions, and Definition section followed by the ten standards that address the specific property being appraised. USPAP is applicable to all types of appraisal situations and is not specifically targeted to federal tax.

When compared with current IRS requirements, there is agreement on a number of crucial elements. Both recognize that an appraisal report answers a valuation question pertaining to a specific property as prepared by a disinterested third-party professional with sufficient knowledge about the property and its market.

An appraisal for tax purposes is a specific type of appraisal. An appraisal for federal tax purposes needs to conform to certain IRS requirements that are delineated in the income tax, and estate and gift tax regulations of the Internal Revenue Code and explained more fully in our procedures and publications. Consequently, some of the IRS requirements, particularly in the personal property area, have more specificity than the applicable USPAP standards.

However, both emphasize:

- Description and identification of the property
- Purpose of the appraisal
- Assumptions and limiting conditions
- Basis for the valuation
- Statement about the appraiser's disinterestedness

The property being valued for tax purposes can be any type of property, including real estate, fine art, business interests, intangibles, yachts, automobiles, etc. As a result, the IRS must provide general guidelines to allow taxpayers access to the best appraisal for their specific situation.

As previously noted, USPAP is considered a living document that responds to the changing needs of professional appraisers and users of professional appraisal services. The Appraisal Standards Board (ASB) does not have the authority to enforce compliance with USPAP. Although many state and federal agencies enforce USPAP through laws, regulations, and ordinances, and many organizations require that their members comply with USPAP, it is questionable as to what enforcement powers these organizations have, and to what extent they are invoked. Not all appraisal organizations adopt the USPAP standards. For example, while USPAP has standards for Business Valuations, these standards have not been adopted by appraisal organizations that have business valuation sections.

It is imperative that the IRS retain control of the appraisal standards and prescribed requirements for federal tax purposes. IRS adoption of USPAP for all valuations would allow the Appraisal Foundation to set standards, which may or may not conform to IRS needs.

With the constant changes being made to USPAP it would be extremely difficult to have the public as well as IRS personnel trained and kept up to date on these changes. In addition, it becomes even more difficult to visualize what remedies the IRS would have if USPAP were adopted and an appraiser violated one of these standards. The IRS is not authorized to enforce USPAP. New regulations and code provisions would be necessary to set up a specific penalty. The IRS would not be able to disclose violations to state appraisal regulatory officials or the various appraisal organizations because of disclosure restrictions.

Other members of the valuation community have expressed concern about the IRS adopting USPAP at this time. Chris Rosenthal is an AICPA representative on the Business Valuation Professional Task Force that made recommendations to the Appraisal Standards Board on USPAP revisions. In the August 1999 edition of *Shannon Pratt's Business Valuation Update*, Mr. Rosenthal indicated that the IRS's adoption of USPAP at this time would be premature. When asked why, he went on to say:

> There are two reasons. First, it's undergoing changes, and we think it would be better when more changes have been made reflecting more input. Second, many valuation professionals, including CPAs, don't understand USPAP, and we still have a lot of educating to do. . . . USPAP is still struggling to find its identity in the appraisal profession.

The IRS strongly encourages utilizing methodologies or guidelines that will produce better quality appraisals. The IRS is not opposed to USPAP in itself and, as previously discussed, our requirements and procedures in many cases agree with USPAP. However, the IRS cannot endorse USPAP as the *only* means and standard.

Revision of Appraisal Filing Requirements and Threshold Amounts

The IRS Review Team looked closely at the regulations under Internal Revenue Code Section 170 with respect to the appraisal requirements for noncash charitable contributions. Our aim in reviewing this section of the Code was to see if it could be applied to the estate and gift tax filing requirements.

While initially, consistency between the code sections appealed to the team, it became apparent upon further consideration that the differences in the type of tax and the sensitivity to taxpayer burden allow for these inconsistencies. While an argument for consistency appears logical, appraisal filing requirements and thresholds appropriately vary depending on the type of tax being administered.

Income tax deals with income and deductions and has a relatively low starting point for taxable income. However, the return filing requirements on estates (a transfer tax) does not start until the gross estate exceeds $650,000 (for 1999). The return filing requirements on gifts (a transfer tax) does not start until a gift exceeds $10,000 per donee. Consequently, to impose the income tax appraisal filing requirements on all estate and gift tax returns would be an additional burden on taxpayers. It has not been demonstrated that the benefits to the IRS would outweigh this additional burden.

To illustrate, all estate and gift tax returns are individually inspected for audit potential. Information obtained from the IRS Statistics of Income (SOI) group confirms that less than 50 percent of estate tax returns and less than 10 percent of gift tax returns are taxable. In FY97, there were 97,013 estate tax returns filed nationwide and of those 11,207 were selected for audit which represents an 11.6 percent audit coverage. Likewise 267,183 gift tax returns were filed nationwide for FY97 and 2,076 returns were selected for audit which represent approximately 1 percent audit coverage.

IRS substantiation requirements for documenting valuation issues are dependent on the type of tax and the value claimed. In general, the IRS has more stringent reporting requirements in areas such as charitable contributions. As substantial numbers of tax non-compliance situations were identified, it became necessary to increase specific requirements. However, in order to keep taxpayer burden to a minimum, the additional requirements were only applicable to those situations identified with compliance problems.

The income tax appraisal requirements for charitable contributions are applicable to all types of property. A qualified appraisal by a qualified appraiser is required for an item or group of similar items of donated property when the deduction is more than $5,000. A specific IRS Form (Form 8283, Non-cash Charitable Contributions) must be completed and attached to the return for all deductions of more than $500. The form is completed and signed by the taxpayer's appraiser and donee. Detailed instructions are also provided in the instructions for preparing returns as well as in Publication 17 (Your Federal Income Tax), Publication 561 (Determining the Value of Donated Property), and Publication 526 (Charitable Contributions).

Estate tax regulations require that all assets be valued. However, while the regulations discuss in general what should be taken into consideration, no specific "qualified" appraisal is required to be filed for business or real estate valuations. Estate tax regulations only require an appraisal for the valuation of personal property. Appraisals by disinterested, qualified individuals are required by the estate tax regulations for personal property valued over $3,000. A proposed revenue procedure applicable to estate and gift tax in the personal property area which would provide uniformity with the income tax regulations is currently in the Office of Chief Counsel.

The Review Team concluded that it was not appropriate to apply the appraisal standards of Code Section 170 to the Estate and Gift Tax Program. However, the attachment of a summary form similar to Form 8283 would be helpful.

Revising Requirements for the Definition of Qualified Appraiser

The IRS has purposely kept its definition of an "appraisal" and its requirements for an "appraiser" broad because it recognizes that there are many individuals from different disciplines who are capable of providing an opinion as to the value of certain kinds of property and who routinely do so. Examples of these include certified public accountants, economists, art dealers, stamp collectors, professors from academia, auction personnel, real estate dealers and financial analysts.

For the IRS to summarily dismiss these persons "by definition" from providing an appraisal that would be an acceptable work product, and in some instances a superior work product, would not be in the best interest of tax compliance or in the best interest of the taxpayer. It is much better for the IRS, and for the taxpayer, to be as inclusive as possible rather than to be so restrictive that it eliminates persons who can provide the expertise needed.

The IRS provides broad general requirements for tax preparation purposes. It does not restrict tax preparation to CPAs or attorneys. The reason for this approach is that the IRS is best served by having taxpayers file their own returns. It recognizes that there is a wide variety of qualified people with sufficient education or experience to prepare returns. To eliminate them from tax preparation by having unduly restrictive requirements would not be in the best interests of taxpayers or the government.

The IRS intent is for appraisal reports to adequately support the value claimed. An appraisal is an opinion of value based on facts. It is the facts upon which the opinion is based which is important to the IRS. The IRS already recognizes, in its definition of a qualified appraiser, that for a report to be credible the person preparing the report must have certain education, experience, and background in the subject area to perform the appraisal. Consequently, the Review Team has concluded that it is in the interest of taxpayers and the IRS to maintain the definition of qualified appraiser.

Summary

Within the valuation profession there is much debate on issues such as what constitutes a qualified appraisal and a qualified appraiser and the adoption of USPAP. In addition, there may also be different points of view among tax practitioners and taxpayers in general regarding any changes to IRS appraisal policies. Whatever action the IRS takes on the above recommendations, the Review Team considers it crucial that the input and involvement of all stakeholders (both internal and external) be solicited.

The IRS is responsible for reviewing appraisals. The IRS is concerned with the appraised value and the supporting information that validates the appraised value and not necessarily the form, the theory, whether or not they follow USPAP, or to what organization the appraiser belongs. We are seeking a balance between requiring taxpayers to provide enough information for the IRS to conduct a fair and objective review without being too onerous.

In summary, the IRS needs to continue to review its own organizational structure to determine the best way to ensure taxpayer compliance, keep taxpayer burden to a minimum and effectively manage its work force. Finally, it needs to ensure that input from all interested parties be considered in these recommendations.

IRS Review Team Members

Michael J. Coyne
Chairperson
Associate Chief Appeals,
Virginia–West Virginia District

Karen E. Carolan
Chief, Art Appraisal Services and Chair, Commissioner's
    Art Advisory Panel

Bernard Crinigan
Engineering and Valuation Group Manager
Northern California District

Barbara Platt
Estate & Gift Tax Group Manager
Rocky Mountain District

Jeffrey Schutzman
Appraisal Group Manager
Manhattan District

Dorothy A. Taylor
National Engineering Program Manager

INTERNATIONAL GLOSSARY OF BUSINESS VALUATION TERMS

To enhance and sustain the quality of business valuations for the benefit of the business valuation profession and the users of the services of its practitioners, the below identified societies and organizations whose members provide business valuation services have adopted the definitions for the terms included in this glossary.

The performance of business valuation services requires a high degree of skill, and imposes upon the valuation professional a duty to communicate the valuation process and conclusion, as appropriate to the scope of the engagement, in a manner that is clear and not misleading. This duty is advanced through the use of terms whose meanings are clearly established and consistently applied throughout the profession.

If, in the opinion of the business valuation professional, one or more of these terms needs to be used in a manner that materially departs from the enclosed definitions, it is recommended that the term be defined as used within that valuation engagement.

This glossary has been developed to provide guidance to the business valuation practitioners who are members of the listed societies, organizations, and others performing valuations of business interests or securities by further memorializing the body of knowledge which constitutes the competent and careful determination of value and, more particularly, the communication of how that value was determined.

Departure from this glossary is not intended to provide a basis for civil liability and should not be presumed to create evidence that any duty has been breached.

> American Institute of Certified Public Accountants
> American Society of Appraisers
> The Canadian Institute of Chartered Business Valuators
> National Association of Certified Valuation Analysts
> The Institute of Business Appraisers

Adjusted book value: The value that results after one or more asset or liability amounts are added, deleted, or changed from their respective financial statement amounts.

Appraisal: See *valuation.*

Appraisal approach: See *valuation approach.*

Appraisal date: See *valuation date.*

Appraisal method: See *valuation method.*

Appraisal procedure: See *valuation procedure.*

Asset (asset-based) approach: A general way of determining a value indication of a business, business ownership interest, or security by using one or more methods based on the value of the assets of that business net of liabilities

Benefit stream: Any level of income, cash flow, or earnings generated by an asset, group of assets, or business enterprise. When the term is used, it should be supplemented by a definition of exactly what it means in the given valuation context.

Beta: A measure of systematic risk of a security; the tendency of a security's returns to correlate with swings in the broad market.

Blockage discount: An amount or percentage deducted from the current market price of a publicly traded security to reflect the decrease in the per share value of a block of those securities that is of a size that could not be sold in a reasonable period of time given normal trading volume.

Business: See *business enterprise.*

Business enterprise: A commercial, industrial, service, or investment entity, or a combination thereof, pursuing an economic activity.

Business valuation: The act or process of determining the value of a business enterprise or ownership interest therein.

Capital asset pricing model (CAPM): A model in which the cost of capital for any security or portfolio of securities equals a risk-free rate plus a risk premium that is proportionate to the systematic risk of the security or portfolio.

Capitalization: A conversion of a single period stream of benefits into value.

Capitalization factor: Any multiple or divisor used to convert anticipated benefits into value.

Capitalization rate: Any divisor (usually expressed as a percentage) used to convert anticipated benefits into value.

Capital structure: The composition of the invested capital of a business enterprise; the mix of debt and equity financing.

Cash flow: Cash that is generated over a period of time by an asset, group of assets, or business enterprise. It may be used in a general sense to encompass various levels of specifically defined cash flows. When the term is used, it should be supplemented by a qualifier (for example, "discretionary" or "operating") and a definition of exactly what it means in the given valuation context.

Control: The power to direct the management and policies of a business enterprise.

Control premium: An amount (expressed in either dollar or percentage form) by which the pro rata value of a controlling interest exceeds the pro rata value of a noncontrolling interest in a business enterprise, that reflects the power of control.

Cost approach: A general way of estimating a value indication of an individual asset by quantifying the amount of money that would be required to replace the future service capability of that asset.

Cost of capital: The expected rate of return (discount rate) that the market requires in order to attract funds to a particular investment.

Discount: A reduction in value or the act of reducing value.

Discount for lack of control: An amount or percentage deducted from the pro rata share of value of one hundred percent (100%) of an equity interest in a business to reflect the absence of some or all of the powers of control.

Discount for lack of marketability: An amount or percentage deducted from the value of an ownership interest to reflect the relative absence of marketability.

Discount rate: A rate of return (cost of capital) used to convert a monetary sum, payable or receivable in the future, into present value.

Economic life: The period of time over which property may generate economic benefits.

Effective date: See *valuation date.*

Enterprise: See *business enterprise.*

Equity net cash flows: Those cash flows available to pay out to equity holders (in the form of dividends) after funding operations of the business enterprise, making necessary capital investments, and reflecting increases or decreases in debt financing.

Equity risk premium: A rate of return in addition to a risk-free rate to compensate for investing in equity instruments because they have a higher degree of probable risk than risk-free instruments (a component of the cost of equity capital or equity discount rate).

Excess earnings: That amount of anticipated benefits that exceeds a fair rate of return on the value of a selected asset base (often net tangible assets) used to generate those anticipated benefits.

Excess earnings method: A specific way of determining a value indication of a business, business ownership interest, or security determined as the sum of (a) the value of the assets obtained by capitalizing excess earnings and (b) the value of the selected asset base. Also frequently used to value intangible assets. See *excess earnings*.

Fair market value: The price, expressed in terms of cash equivalents, at which property would change hands between a hypothetical willing and able buyer and a hypothetical willing and able seller, acting at arm's length in an open and unrestricted market, when neither is under compulsion to buy or sell and when both have reasonable knowledge of the relevant facts. (*Note:* In Canada, the term "price" should be replaced with the term "highest price.")

Forced liquidation value: Liquidation value at which the asset or assets are sold as quickly as possible, such as at an auction.

Going concern: An ongoing operating business enterprise.

Going concern value: The value of a business enterprise that is expected to continue to operate into the future. The intangible elements of going concern value result from factors such as having a trained workforce, an operational plant, and the necessary licenses, systems, and procedures in place.

Goodwill: That intangible asset arising as a result of name, reputation, customer loyalty, location, products, and similar factors not separately identified.

Goodwill value: The value attributable to goodwill.

Income (income-based) approach: A general way of determining a value indication of a business, business ownership interest, security, or intangible asset using one or more methods that convert anticipated benefits into a present single amount.

Intangible assets: Nonphysical assets (such as franchises, trademarks, patents, copyrights, goodwill, equities, mineral rights, securities and contracts as distinguished from physical assets) that grant rights, privileges, and have economic benefits for the owner.

Invested capital: The sum of equity and debt in a business enterprise. Debt is typically (a) long-term liabilities or (b) the sum of short-term interest-bearing debt and long-term liabilities. When the term is used, it should be supplemented by a definition of exactly what it means in the given valuation context

Invested capital net cash flows: Those cash flows available to pay out to equity holders (in the form of dividends) and debt investors (in the form of principal and interest) after funding operations of the business enterprise and making necessary capital investments.

Investment risk: The degree of uncertainty as to the realization of expected returns.

Investment value: The value to a particular investor based on individual investment requirements and expectations. (*Note:* In Canada, the term used is "value to the owner.")

Key person discount: An amount or percentage deducted from the value of an ownership interest to reflect the reduction in value resulting from the actual or potential loss of a key person in a business enterprise.

Levered beta: The beta reflecting a capital structure that includes debt.

Liquidity: The ability to quickly convert property to cash or pay a liability.

Liquidation value: The net amount that can be realized if the business is terminated and the assets are sold piecemeal. Liquidation can be either "orderly" or "forced."

Majority control: The degree of control provided by a majority position.

Majority interest: An ownership interest greater than fifty percent (50%) of the voting interest in a business enterprise.

Market (market-based) approach: A general way of determining a value indication of a business, business ownership interest, security, or intangible asset by using one or more methods that compare the subject to similar businesses, business ownership interests, securities, or intangible assets that have been sold.

Marketability: The ability to quickly convert property to cash at minimal cost.

Marketability discount: See *Discount for Lack of Marketability.*

Minority discount: A discount for lack of control applicable to a minority interest.

Minority interest: An ownership interest less than fifty percent (50%) of the voting interest in a business enterprise.

Net book value: With respect to a business enterprise, the difference between total assets (net of accumulated depreciation, depletion, and amortization) and total liabilities of a business enterprise as they appear on the balance sheet (synonymous with Shareholder's Equity); with respect to an intangible asset, the capitalized cost of an intangible asset less accumulated amortization as it appears on the books of account of the business enterprise.

Net cash flow: A form of cash flow. When the term is used, it should be supplemented by a qualifier (i.e., "Equity" or "Invested Capital") and a definition of exactly what it means in the given valuation context.

Net tangible asset value: The value of the business enterprise's tangible assets (excluding excess assets and non-operating assets) minus the value of its liabilities, (*Note:* In Canada, tangible assets also include identifiable intangible assets.)

Non-operating assets: Assets not necessary to ongoing operations of the business enterprise. (*Note:* In Canada, the term used is "Redundant Assets.")

Orderly liquidation value: Liquidation value at which the asset or assets are sold over a reasonable period of time to maximize proceeds received.

Premise of value: An assumption regarding the most likely set of transactional circumstances that may be applicable to the subject valuation; e.g., going concern, liquidation.

Portfolio discount: An amount or percentage that may be deducted from the value of a business enterprise to reflect the fact that it owns dissimilar operations or assets that may not fit well together.

Rate of return: An amount of income (loss) and/or change in value realized or anticipated on an investment, expressed as a percentage of that investment.

Redundant assets: See *non-operating assets*

Report date: The date conclusions are transmitted to the client.

Replacement cost new: The current cost of a similar new property having the nearest equivalent utility to the property being valued.

Reproduction cost new: The current cost of an identical new property.

Residual value: The prospective value as of the end of the discrete projection period in a discounted benefit streams model.

Risk-free rate: The rate of return available in the market on an investment free of default risk.

Risk premium: A rate of return in addition to a risk-free rate to compensate the investor for accepting risk.

Rule of thumb: A mathematical relationship between or among variables based on experience, observation, hearsay, or a combination of these, usually applicable to a specific industry.

Special interest purchasers: Acquirers who believe they can enjoy post-acquisition economies of scale, synergies, or strategic advantages by combining the acquired business interest with their own.

Standard of value: The identification of the type of value being utilized in a specific engagement; e.g., fair market value, fair value, investment value.

Sustaining capital reinvestment: The periodic capital outlay required to maintain operations at existing levels, net of the tax shield available from such outlays.

Systematic risk: The risk that is common to all risky securities and cannot be eliminated through diversification. When using the capital asset pricing model, systematic risk is measured by beta.

Terminal value: See *residual value.*

Unlevered beta: The beta reflecting a capital structure without debt.

Unsystematic risk: The portion of total risk specific to an individual security that can be avoided through diversification.

Valuation: The act or process of determining the value of a business, business ownership interest, security, or intangible asset.

Valuation approach: A general way of determining a value indication of a business, business ownership interest, security, or intangible asset using one or more valuation methods.

Valuation date: The specific point in time as of which the valuator's opinion of value applies (also referred to as *effective date* or *appraisal date*).

Valuation method: Within approaches, a specific way to determine value.

Valuation procedure: The act, manner, and technique of performing the steps of an appraisal method.

Valuation ratio: A fraction in which a value or price serves as the numerator and financial, operating, or physical data serve as the denominator.

Value to the owner: See *investment value.*

Weighted average cost of capital (WACC):   The cost of capital (discount rate) determined by the weighted average, at market value, of the cost of all financing sources in the business enterprise's capital structure.

THE INSTITUTE OF BUSINESS APPRAISERS, BUSINESS APPRAISAL STANDARDS[6]

Publication P-311b

This publication supersedes and replaces the following IBA publications:

P-243 Standards of Business Appraisal Practice
P-244 Standards for Business Appraisal Reports
P-311a Business Appraisal Standards

    Foreword
    Preamble
    Format

Standard One

1.0 Professional Conduct and Ethics

    1.1   Competence
    1.2   Confidentiality
    1.3   Disinterestedness
    1.4   Nonadvocacy v. Advocacy
    1.5   Engagement
    1.6   Coherence and Production
    1.7   Supportable Opinion
    1.8   Replicability
    1.9   Appropriateness
    1.10 Jurisdictional Exception
    1.11 Fiduciary Duty to Clients and Other Duties
    1.12 Duty to Profession
    1.13 Substance v. Form
    1.14 Professional Fees

---

[6] Copies of these standards are available from The Institute of Business Appraisers, P.O. Box 17410, Plantation, Florida 33318; Phone: (954) 584-1144; Ask for publication P-311b.

Standard Two

2.0 Oral Appraisal Reports

Standard Three

3.0 Expert Testimony

Standard Four

4.0 Letter Form Written Appraisal Reports

Foreword

Only a small percentage of individuals representing themselves as business appraisers have been tested and certified by a professional business appraisal institute or society.

Those considering employing a business appraiser are undoubtedly doing so in relation to a matter that can have far reaching financial or legal ramifications. Beyond the obvious caution that a proper valuation cannot be done without adequate preparation, competency, and documentation, we suggest verification that the individual is certified as a business appraiser and intends to prepare the appraisal in compliance with these standards.

The Institute of Business Appraisers would like to thank those individuals whose efforts toward developing business appraisal standards and ethics have contributed greatly to the product of this committee.

Founding Standards Committee

David M. Bishop,
CBA, ASA, FIBA Chairman

Larry R. Cook, CBA, CPA

Steven F. Schroeder,
CBA, ASA, JD, FIBA,

Raymond C. Miles,
FIBA, CBA, ASA, Ex-Officio

Preamble

1. Certain professions, by their nature, and by the way they are perceived by the public, are capable of exerting substantial influence on the public welfare. It is our firm conviction that the practice of business appraisal falls in a similar category.

2. The performance of business appraisal/valuation requires a high degree of skill, imposes upon the appraiser a duty of non-advocacy to the client and an obligation to the general public as a third party beneficiary of the work. It is our purpose here to articulate standards by which those who aspire to participation, and those already established in business appraisal practice may be guided in the ethical and skillful execution of their tasks, and report the results and conclusions of their work in the most effective manner.

3. It is also our purpose to state these standards in such a clear and unequivocal way that the world at large, and especially those who may engage the services of a business appraiser, will know the parameters by which professional competence is to be measured, and by which its professional practitioners wish to be judged.

4. Each standard is qualified as: (i) should, (ii) must or (iii) shall.

Should and *must* standards are guidelines. While an appraiser may depart from a *should* standard without a statement of departure, such departure should be made knowingly. In those instances where the appraiser feels a departure from a *must* standard is warranted, the report *shall* include a statement of departure. It is the position of the IBA that standards designated *shall* are those from which departure is not justified.

5. These standards have been developed to provide guidance to appraisers who are members of the Institute of Business Appraisers (IBA) and others performing appraisals of closely held businesses, business ownership interests or securities. They have also been developed to assist in the evaluation and regulation of members of the IBA through creating uniform practices and procedures. Departures from the standards are not intended to provide a basis for civil liability, and should not be presumed to create evidence that any legal duty has been breached, or to imply the creation of any additional relationships or duties other than those specified herein.

Format

These standards are presented in a naturally progressive format beginning with overall professional conduct and ethics, followed by specific standards applicable to oral reports, expert testimony, letter reports, formal reports, and preliminary reports.

No attempt is made to anticipate every possible scenario or unique circumstance and create standards specific thereto. Conversely, these standards were developed under the premise that the professional business appraiser practicing within the proper standard of care can, on a case-by-case basis, adequately apply these standards in such a manner to result in a competent report while still permitting the flexibility necessary to meet the reasonable requests of the client and the vicissitudes of the assignment.

Within this publication, reference to all individuals has been in the masculine. This is done in the interest of simplicity and is not intended as a gender bias. Terms should be assumed to be in the singular or plural as appropriate to the context in which they are used.

Standard One

1.0 Professional Conduct and Ethics

1.1 Competence

The achievement of certification as a business appraiser (CBA) is a result of specialized training, study, practice, the successful completion of a proctored examination, and a favorable review of the candidate's actual appraisal reports by The Institute of Business Appraisers' Qualifications Review Committee. To maintain certification, a CBA will adhere to continuing education requirements and periodic recertification as required by IBA.

Prior to accepting an engagement to perform a business appraisal, the appraiser must judge his competence to complete the assignment. Should the appraiser have a meaningful lack of knowledge and experience, the appraiser *must* immediately disclose that fact to the client. If the client desires the appraiser to continue with the assignment, the appraiser *shall* take those steps necessary to perform the appraisal in a competent manner, or take those steps necessary to complete the assignment under the supervision of an appraiser who has the requisite skill, or with the permission of the client, refer the engagement to a qualified business appraiser.

It is essential that a business appraiser communicate the research and thought processes which led to his opinions and conclusions in a manner that is clear, meaningful and not misleading. Said communication, whether oral or written, shall not be rendered in a careless or negligent manner.

The appraiser as an individual must be competent. Software valuation programs and/or excessive reliance on rules of thumb are not surrogates for individual competence.

The professional business appraiser recognizes and understands that compliance with these standards and ethics is an essential part of competence.

1.2 Confidentiality

The very fact an appraiser has been retained to value all or a portion of a business enterprise, or its securities, is in itself confidential. Consequently, it is considered unethical for a business appraiser to disclose either the assignment itself or any of the reasonably identifiable contents of an appraisal report without the client's express permission.

1.3 Disinterestedness

It is unethical for a business appraiser to accept any assignment when the appraiser has a present or contemplated interest in the property being appraised, or a bias for or against any person associated therewith, either directly or indirectly. Such interests include, but are not limited to, present, contemplated or prospective activity with the business enterprise, its officers, directors, or owners, including possible acquirers or investors.

However, if a prospective client, after full disclosure by the appraiser of said interest or bias, still elects to engage the appraiser, the appraiser may accept the assignment. When accepting such an assignment, the business appraiser *shall* include a Statement of Departure as required by Standard 1.21(b). The Statement of Departure *shall* include a complete disclosure of the interest or bias.

1.4 Nonadvocacy v. Advocacy

Nonadvocacy is considered to be a mandatory standard of appraisal.

The appraiser's obligation to serve the public interest assures that the integrity of valuations will be preserved. Hence, the appraiser may only be an advocate for his unbiased process and conclusions. The appraiser *must* be guided by nothing other than his informed judgment, the dictates of the client (as permitted under these standards), applicable administrative rulings, and the law.

In the event the appraiser is engaged to function not as an appraiser but as an advisor or consultant, he may serve as an advocate. In such instances the appraiser *shall* include a statement of departure which states, that any positions taken were taken as an advocate for the client.

1.5 Engagement

Prior to performing an appraisal assignment, a business appraiser *should* obtain a written agreement signed by the client or his agent. At the very least, the engagement agreement *should* specify what the appraiser is being engaged to appraise, the function (use) of the appraisal, the purpose (standard of value) including the definition thereof, the effective date of the appraisal, the scope of the appraisal, that the appraisal will be performed on a nonadvocacy basis (see Standard 1.4), the amount of or method for calculating the appraiser's fee, together with the method for payment of same, and an indication of when the client may expect the report.

1.6 Coherence and Production

Appraisal reports must have logical organization. Readers' questions that can reasonably be anticipated should be answered. Data in one part of the report should not contradict other portions without reconciliation.

The appraiser should develop contributing conclusions from the various components of the appraisal process drawing them together in a cross-supporting manner that logically brings the reader to the appraiser's conclusion.

The report should be produced in a manner and style which brings credit to the appraiser and the profession. Typographical errors and the like shall be eliminated. In formal reports, page and exhibit numbers *should* be used together with a table of contents or index to enhance readability.

1.7 Supportable Opinion

The essence of business appraisal is a supportable opinion.

While it is intuitively logical that on a case-by-case basis certain opinions will be based on the informed, but subjective, judgment of the appraiser to a greater degree than others, the appraiser's goal is to have a supportable opinion. The reader should not be expected to accept critical elements such as adjustments to financial statements, the selected capitalization or discount rates or weightings, without support—even in those instances where the vicissitudes of the assignment dictate that support be primarily based on the informed judgment of the appraiser.

1.8 Replicability

The appraiser's procedures and conclusions in the formal report *must* be presented in sufficient detail to permit the reader to replicate the appraisal process.

1.9 Appropriateness

The standard of value, the type of report and the valuation approaches/methods utilized should be appropriate to the assignment. The material included in the report should be relevant, clear and cogent.

1.10 Jurisdictional Exception

If any part of these standards is contrary to the law or public policy of any jurisdiction, only that part shall be void and of no force and effect in that jurisdiction.

1.11 Fiduciary Duty to Clients, and Other Duties

Client. The one employing the business appraiser.

Third parties. Others who could be expected to review the report, e.g., attorneys, accountants, lenders, buyers, investors, regulatory agencies, courts, etc.

Public. Society at large.

(a) *Specialized character of business appraisal.* Seldom are others intimately familiar with the process of business appraisal. Therefore, it is anticipated the business appraiser will use his professional abilities properly, as more fully described throughout these standards.

(b) *Loyalty, obedience, and reasonable skill and care.* Agents have such duties to clients. While no fiduciary or other affirmative duty is owed to others, services provided in accordance with these standards should be clear as to meaning and not be misleading to others.

1.12 Duty to Profession

(a) *Professional cooperation and courtesy.* It is unethical to damage or attempt to damage the professional reputations or interfere with the performance of other business appraisers practicing within the scope of these standards through false or malicious statement or innuendo.

(b) *Conduct.* Every member is reminded that his demeanor and general conduct represents his profession and fellow practitioners, and unprofessional conduct damages more than his individual reputation.

(c) *Cooperation.* Each member *shall* cooperate fully with the efforts of the Institute and/or its Ethics and Discipline Committee when investigating possible activities which are contrary to these standards.

1.13 Substance v. Form

The form of an appraisal report can be oral or written with variations of each. However, it is only the form of the report that varies. The appraiser's responsibilities to gather data, analyze the data, and draw supportable conclusions as applicable to the type of assignment undertaken does not change. Regardless of whether the final valuation is reported orally, in a summarizing letter report or a formal report, the appraiser *must* have first completed an appropriate valuation determination process.

A preliminary report is an exception to the above requirement for a thorough, complete work process. By its nature, a preliminary report results from a more cursory evaluation. (See Standard Six, Preliminary Reports.)

1.14 Professional Fees

The fees charged for the services of an appraiser are a product of the marketplace; however, a business appraiser is ethically denied the selection of a fee that could in itself call to question the objectivity of the appraiser.

(a) *Finder's fees.* No appraiser will pay fees, or offer gain in any form, to others to promote the appraiser's work in such a way, or under any circumstances, that will diminish the dignity of, or reflect discredit or disrepute upon, the appraisal profession.

(b) *Referral fees.* It is the right of an appraiser and, therefore, not unethical to pay a referral fee to another professional for the referral of appraisal assignments.

(c) *Percentage fees.* To accept any engagement for which the compensation is based on a percentage of the valuation conclusion impairs independence and is thus unethical.

1.15 Access to Requisite Data

The business appraiser, *must* decide what documents and/or information are requisite to a competent appraisal.

(a) *Reliability of data.* An appraiser may rely upon documents and/or information provided by the client and/or his agents without further corroboration; provided, the report clearly states he has done so. This right, however, does not abrogate the appraiser's duty to ask or otherwise inquire regarding information that on its surface clearly appears to be incomplete or otherwise inaccurate.

(b) *Pertinent data.* In situations where access to "pertinent" data is denied to the appraiser, the appraiser may, at his option, withdraw from completing the assignment. However, should the appraiser elect to complete the assignment, the report *must* include a Statement of Departure as required under Standard 1.21(b). Such Statement of Departure *must* describe the limitation and/or restriction and its potential effect on the appraiser's conclusion.

(c) *Essential data.* When the business appraiser is denied access to data considered essential to a proper appraisal, the business appraiser *should* not proceed with the assignment.

1.16 Valuation Approaches/Methods

The approaches/methods used within a given assignment are a matter that must be determined by the business appraiser's professional judgment. The task is generally decided through consideration of the approaches/methods that are conceptually most appropriate and those for which the most reliable data is available.

1.17 Definitions

(a) *Terms.* The appraiser should be careful in the use of ambiguous or esoteric terms. Such terms require definition to prevent the reader from applying a different definition.

(b) *Computations.* All computations, particularly those used to compute ratios and weightings, should be clearly defined.

1.18 Principal Sources and References

(a) *Formal report.* A formal report *must* include a list of the principal sources of non-confidential information and references whenever their inclusion will materially contribute to the clarity and understanding of the report.

(b) *Oral and informal reports.* The appraiser's workpapers *must* include a general description of the principal sources of information and references.

1.19 Site Tours and Interviews

(a) *Tour.* Familiarity with an appraisal subject is a compelling necessity to a credible valuation. For this reason, it is desirable that a business appraiser make personal inspections or tours of appraisal subject sites whenever possible. When such activities are not performed, the appraiser's report *shall* disclose that the appraisal process did not include a site tour.

(b) *Interview.* An appraiser *should* not perform an appraisal without interviewing the management and other parties considered appropriate in the circumstances.

1.20 Eligibility of Data

An appraisal shall be based on what a reasonably informed person would have knowledge of as of a certain date. This shall be known as the appraisal's "date of valuation" or "effective date" and accordingly reflect the appraiser's supportable conclusion as of that date. Information unavailable or unknown on the date of valuation *must* not influence the appraiser or contribute to the concluding opinion of value.

(a) *Imminent change.* The appraiser is sometimes faced with the knowledge of a material imminent change in the business; a change not known of on the "date of valuation", but known as of the appraisal's "report" date. In such an event, the imminent change (positive or negative) *should* not affect the valuation conclusion, unless a reasonably informed person could have anticipated the imminent change. However, it is not uncommon for an appraiser to disclose such a change within the narrative portion of the report.

(b) *Data on guideline companies.* When an appraiser selects guideline companies, the data on the companies judged sufficiently similar *should* be information knowable, although perhaps not yet compiled, on or before the appraisal's date of valuation. Additionally, the data on the guideline companies should be for the same accounting period; however, if it is as of a different period, said different period *must* be on or before the appraisal's date of valuation.

This restriction should apply whether the guideline companies are specific companies or aggregate industry statistics or ratios.

1.21 Departure

A business appraiser may be engaged to perform an appraisal assignment that calls for something different from the work that would routinely result from the appraiser's compliance with all *must* standards; provided, that prior to entering into an agreement to perform such an assignment:

(a) The appraiser is of the opinion that the assignment is not so limited in scope that the resulting report would tend to mislead or confuse the client or other anticipated readers; and

(b) The appraiser has advised the client that the assignment calls for something different than that which would normally result from compliance with applicable standards and, therefore, the report *shall* include a statement of departure.

1.22 Hypothetical Reports

An analysis or appraisal may be prepared under a hypothetical assumption, or series thereof even though they may appear improbable. However, such a report *must* clearly state (i) the hypothetical assumption and (ii) the purpose of the analysis or appraisal, and any opinion of value *must* clearly be identified as resulting from a hypothetical assumption.

1.23 Dissenting Opinion

(a) *Dissenting opinion with other appraisers.* Collaborating appraisers, and review appraisers *must* sign the report. When a signing appraiser disagrees in whole or in part with any or all of the findings of other appraisers, said dissenting opinion *must* be included in the report, signed by the dissenting appraiser.

(b) *Dissenting opinon with case law and/or administrative regulation.* As any other member of society, appraisers are required to comply with statutory law and statutory definitions as they may exist from time to time and from jurisdiction to jurisdiction. However, case law and/or administrative regulations do not have the same force as statutory law. Therefore, the business appraiser may, when he believes it is warranted, express within the appraisal report a dissenting opinion to case law and/or an administrative regulation.

1.24 Membership Designations

It is considered unethical conduct for any individual to explicitly or implicitly indicate he is a Certified Business Appraiser (CBA) when he has not been awarded the designation.

(a) *Certified Business Appraisal Reports.* An appraisal report may be considered a "Certified Report" when it is signed by a Certified Business Appraiser who is taking technical responsibility for its content

(b) *Certification of firms.* The designation Certified Business Appraiser (CBA) is awarded to individuals, not business enterprises; therefore, it is unethical for an appraiser to explicitly or implicitly indicate that the firm is certified.

(c) *Misuse of certification.* Each Certified Business Appraiser is honor-bound to retain from any use of his professional designation in connection with any form of activity that may reflect discredit upon his designation, or the organization that conferred it, or deceive his client, or the public. As with actual appraisal conclusions, this has been left as a matter of individual judgment and conscience; those who abuse this privilege could be subject to disciplinary action by IBA's Ethics and Discipline Committee.

1.25 Certification

Each written report *must* contain a certification signed by the appraiser. Additional appraisers signing the report *must* accept responsibility for the full contents of the report. (In the event of a dissent-ing opinion, see Standard 1.23(a).) The certificate must be similar in content to the following:

(a) That to the best of the appraiser's knowledge, the statements of fact contained in the report are true and correct.

(b) That the reported analyses, opinions, and conclusions are lim-ited only by the reported assumptions and limiting conditions, and are the appraiser's personal, unbiased professional analy-ses, opinions and conclusions.

(c) That the appraisal was performed on a basis of nonadvocacy, including a statement that the appraiser has no present or contemplated interest in the property appraised and has no personal bias with respect to the parties involved, or a com-plete disclosure of any such interest or bias.

(d) That the appraiser's compensation is not contingent on an action or event resulting from the analyses, opinions, or con-clusions in, or the use of, the report.

(e) That the appraiser's analyses, opinions, and conclusions were developed and that the report has been prepared in confor-mity with the Business Appraisal Standards of The Institute of Business Appraisers.

(f) That no one provided significant professional assistance to the person signing the report. However, if there are excep-tions to this, then the name of each individual providing sig-nificant professional assistance must be disclosed.

1.26 Qualifications of the Appraiser

The reader cannot fully judge the quality of the appraisal report with-out being given the opportunity to judge the appraiser's qualifica-tions. Therefore, each appraisal report *must* include the appraiser's qualifications in a manner the appraiser believes accurately presents his appraisal experience, certification, professional activities, and other qualifications.

1.27 Force and Effect

These standards shall be in full force and effect on the date of their issuance. (Earlier compliance is encouraged.) Any and all prior stan-dards regarding business appraisal practices, reports, conduct, or ethics are superseded. Future amendments, to be effective, *shall* be initiated and passed in accordance with Standard 1.29.

1.28 Enforcement

The enforcement of these standards, including amendments or modifications as may occur in accordance with Standard 1.29, *shall* be the responsibility and duty of all members as to their own performance, and otherwise by the standing Ethics and Discipline Committee of The Institute of Business Appraisers and/or such other individuals or committees as are designated from time to time by the governing body of The Institute of Business Appraisers.

1.29 Amendments to Standards

The Standards Committee of The Institute of Business Appraisers is a standing committee. Certified members desiring to propose amendments, additions, or deletions to these standards should submit a clear expression of the proposed change to The Institute of Business Appraisers, Attention: Chairperson, Standards Committee. The chairperson reserves the right to return any submitted change for further clarification as to the precise change proposed. The chairperson shall distribute copies of the proposed change to the members of the Standards Committee for their opinions on the proposed change. Should two-thirds or more of the Committee support the change, it shall be endorsed by the Committee and an exposure draft will be provided to all CBAs. The exposure draft shall provide for a 30-day period for the vote of all CBAs. In the event that those certified members who vote "No" exceeds 50 percent of all CBAs (those voting plus those not voting), the Committee's vote will be overruled and the proposed change will die for lack of support. Otherwise, the change will be adopted as of the first day of the month following the date copies of the amendments are provided to all members.

1.30 Signing Reports

Each written report must be signed by the appraiser and any other appraisers, including those signing as a "Review-Appraiser" or "Collaborating Appraiser", *shall* accept responsibility for the full content of the report (In the event of a dissenting opinion, see Standard 1.23(a).)

(a) *Exception.* Should the policy of a given firm be that all reports are to be signed by a person authorized to sign reports on behalf of the firm, an exception to Standards 1.30 and 1.25 is permitted. However, in this event:

(i)   The designated signer *shall* take technical responsibility for the full content of the report; and

(ii) The report may not be considered a "Certified Appraisal Report" unless a Certified Business Appraiser taking technical responsibility signs the report.

(iii) The fact that a given appraisal report is signed under 1.30(a) is not intended in any way to justify or excuse deviation from any standard that would otherwise apply.

Standard Two

2.0 Oral Appraisal Reports

2.1 Usage

In general written reports are preferred; however, oral appraisal reports are permitted when ordered by the client.

2.2 Mandatory Content

When presenting an oral report; the business appraiser *shall* in a manner that is clear and not misleading communicate the following:

(a) *Introduction.* Identify the client, and set forth the property being appraised, the purpose and function of the appraisal, the definition of the standard of value, and the effective date of the appraisal.

(b) *Assumptions and limiting conditions.* Disclose any extraordinary assumptions or limiting conditions that in the appraiser's judgment affected the value.

(c) *Disinterestedness.* That the appraisal was performed on a basis of nonadvocacy, including a statement that the appraiser has no present or contemplated interest in the property appraised and has no personal bias with respect to the parties involved, or a complete disclosure of any such interest or bias. (See Standard 1.3.)

(d) *Valuation conclusion.* Represents a concluding opinion of value expressed as:

    (i)   a statement of a specific opinion of value; or

    (ii)   a range of values; or

    (iii) a preliminary estimate that *must* include a statement that an opinion of value resulting from a formal report might be different and that difference might be material. (See also Standard Six, Preliminary Reports.)

2.3 Conformity

Oral appraisal reports should comply with all applicable sections of Standard One, Professional Conduct and Ethics.

2.4 Written Follow-Up

By its nature, the oral report is less detailed than the written report. Therefore, whenever feasible, it is suggested that oral reports be followed by a written presentation of the salient features of the oral report. In general, the written follow-up *should* include:

(a) *Assumptions and limiting conditions.* All applicable assumptions and limiting conditions.

(b) *Support.* In general, a brief presentation of the information considered, the appraisal approaches used and the research and thought processes that support the appraiser's analyses, opinions and conclusions.

(c) *Appraiser's certification* as specified in Section 1.25.

2.5 Recordkeeping

An appraiser *should* retain written records of appraisal reports for a period of at least five (5) years after preparation or at least two (2) years after final disposition of any judicial proceeding in which the appraiser gave testimony, whichever period expires last.

Standard Three

3.0 Expert Testimony

3.1 Definition

Expert testimony is an oral report given in the form of testimony in a deposition and/or on the witness stand before a court of proper jurisdiction or other trier of fact.

3.2 Mandatory Content

The appraiser shall answer all questions put to him in a manner that is clear and not misleading. When giving testimony, the appraiser shall not advocate any position that is incompatible with the appraiser's obligation of nonadvocacy; i.e., it is unethical for the appraiser to suppress any facts, data, or opinions which are adverse to the case his client is trying to establish, or to over-emphasize any facts, data, or opinions which are favorable to his client's case, or in any other particulars become an advocate. The expert witness *must* at least comply in a manner that is clear and not misleading with the following:

(a) *Introduction.* Identify the client, and set forth the property being appraised, the purpose and function of the appraisal, the definition of the standard of value, and the effective date of the appraisal.

(b) *Assumptions and limiting conditions.* Disclose any extraordinary assumptions or limiting conditions that in the appraiser's judgment affected the value.

(c) *Disinterestedness.* That the appraisal was performed on a basis of nonadvocacy, including a statement that the appraiser has no present or contemplated interest in the property appraised and has no personal bias with respect to the parties involved, or a complete disclosure of any such interest or bias. (See Standard 1.3)

(d) *Valuation conclusion.* Any concluding opinion of value may be expressed as:
  (i)   a statement of a specific opinion of value; or
  (ii)   a range of values; or
  (iii) a preliminary estimate which *must* include a statement

that an opinion of value resulting from a formal report may be different and that difference may be material (See also Standard Six, Preliminary Reports.)

3.3 Conformity

Expert testimony reports *should* comply with all applicable sections of Standard One, Professional Conduct and Ethics.

3.4 Recordkeeping

An appraiser *should* retain written records of appraisal reports for a period of at least five (5) years after preparation or at least two (2) years after final disposition of any judicial proceeding in which the appraiser gave testimony, whichever period expires last.

Standard Four

4.0 Letter-Form Written Appraisal Reports

4.1 Definition

An appraiser's written report can be in the form of a letter report or a formal report. The letter report, which is shorter than the formal report, presents conclusions together with brief generalized comments. This type of report is often referred to as a short-form report, letter opinion, or an informal report.

By its nature, the letter-form report is an instrument of brevity. It should contain at least a summary of the material factors that led to its conclusions, but it is usually intended by the parties to reduce the normal appraisal burden of writing a comprehensive report, and thereby allow the client to realize some economic benefit. However, the appraiser is still required to perform materially the same investigation and analysis as would be required for a comprehensive formal report and maintain in his file the workpapers necessary to support the conclusions stated in the letter report.

4.2 Conformity

The letter-form written report *must* comply with all applicable provisions of Business Appraisal Standards, Standard One, Professional Conduct and Ethics.

4.3 Mandatory Content

All letter-form written appraisal reports *shall* minimally set forth in a manner that is clear and not misleading:

(a) Identity of the client, and a description of the business enterprise, security or other tangible and/or intangible property being appraised.

(b) Form of the organization and if incorporated, the state of incorporation, together with a description, adequate to the assignment, of all classes of securities outstanding and a list of shareholders whose interest should, in the appraiser's judgment, be specified. If the organization is a partnership, the type and the state of filing, together with a list of those partners, whether general or limited, whose interest should, in the appraiser's judgment, be specified.

(c) The purpose (standard of value) of the appraisal.

(d) The function (use) of the appraisal.

(e) The definition of the standard of value that is the purpose of the appraisal.

(f) The effective ("as of") date of the appraisal.

(g) The date the appraisal report was prepared.

(h) The report's assumptions and limiting conditions.

(i) Any special factors that affected the opinion of value. Such factors include, but are not limited to, buy–sell agreements, restrictive stock agreements, corporate articles, bylaws and resolutions, partnership agreements, litigation, regulatory compliance, or environmental hazards.

(j) Applicable discounts and premiums such as minority interest, control, marketability, or lack thereof.

(k) A certification consistent with the intent of section 1.25.

4.4 Distribution of Report.

The letter report *should* include a clear statement of the expected distribution of the report.

4.5 Valuation Conclusion

The letter report *must* include a clear statement of the appraiser's concluding opinion of value expressed as appropriate to the assignment:

(a) a statement of a specific opinion of value; or

(b) a range of values; or

(c) a preliminary estimate which *must* include a statement that an opinion of value resulting from a formal report might be different and that difference might be material (See also Standard Six, Preliminary Reports.)

4.6 Transmittal Letter

If a transmittal letter is used, it *should* include a summary of the engagement. It may be structured in the form of a letter, an executive summary, or a similar rendering. However, regardless of the structure used, if a transmittal is used, it *shall* refer to the report in a manner sufficient to discourage any attempt to remove and use the transmittal without the report.

4.7 Recordkeeping

An appraiser *should* retain written records of appraisal reports for a period of at least five (5) years after preparation or at least two (2) years after final disposition of any judicial proceeding in which the appraiser gave testimony, whichever period expires last.

Standard Five

5.0 Formal Written Appraisal Reports

5.1 Definition

The formal appraisal report is a comprehensive business appraisal report prepared to contain, at a minimum, the requirements described within this standard. It is sometimes called the long form, narrative, or comprehensive report.

5.2 Conformity

The formal written report *must* comply with all applicable provisions of Business Appraisal Standards, Standard One, Professional Conduct and Ethics.

5.3 Mandatory Content

All formal appraisal reports *shall* minimally set forth the following items in a manner that is clear and not misleading, including detail sufficient to permit the reader to reasonably replicate the appraiser's procedures:

(a) Identity of the client, and a description of the business enterprise, security, or other tangible and/or intangible property being appraised.

(b) Form of the organization and if incorporated, the state of incorporation, together with a description, adequate to the assignment, of all classes of securities outstanding and a list of shareholders whose interest should, in the appraiser's judgment be specified. If a partnership, the type and the state of filing, together with a list of those partners, whether general or limited, whose interest should, in the appraiser's judgment, be specified.

(c) The purpose (standard of value) of the appraisal.

(d) The function (use) of the appraisal.

(e) The definition of the standard of value that is the purpose of the appraisal.

(f) The effective ("as of") date of the appraisal.

(g) The date the appraisal report was prepared.

(h) The report's assumptions and limiting conditions.

(i) The principal sources and references used by the appraiser.

(j) The consideration of relevant data regarding:

　　(i)　The nature and history of the business.

　　(ii)　The present economic conditions and the outlook affecting the business, its industry, and the general economy.

(iii)   Past results, current operations, and future prospects of the business.

(iv)   Past sales of interests in the business enterprise being appraised.

(v)   Sales of similar businesses or interests therein, whether closely held or publicly held.

(vi)   The valuation approaches/methods considered and rejected, the approaches/methods utilized, and the research, sources, computations, and reasoning that supports the appraiser's analyses, opinions, and conclusions.

(vii)   Any special factors that affected the opinion of value. Such factors include, but are not limited to, buy–sell agreements, restrictive stock agreements, corporate articles, bylaws and resolutions, partnership agreements, litigation, regulatory compliance, or environmental hazards.

(viii) Applicable discounts and premiums such as minority interest control, marketability or lack thereof.

(ix)   When valuing a majority interest in a business on a "going concern" basis, consider whether the business's highest value may be achieved on a liquidation basis.

(k) A certification consistent with the intent of section 1.25.

5.4 Distribution of Report

The formal report *should* include a clear statement of the expected distribution of the report.

5.5 Valuation Conclusion

The formal report *must* include a clear statement of the appraiser's concluding opinion of value expressed as appropriate to the assignment:

(a) a statement of a specific opinion of value; or

(b) a range of values.

5.6 Transmittal Letter

If a transmittal letter is used, it *should* include a summary of the engagement. It may be structured in the form of a letter, an executive

---

summary, or a similar rendering. However, regardless of the structure, if used, the transmittal *shall* refer to the report in a manner sufficient to discourage any attempt to remove and use the transmittal without the report.

5.7 Recordkeeping

An appraiser *should* retain written records of appraisal reports for a period of at least five (5) years after preparation or at least two (2) years after final disposition of any judicial proceeding in which the appraiser gave testimony, whichever period expires last.

Standard Six

6.0 Preliminary Reports

6.1 Definition

A brief oral or written report reflecting the appraiser's limited opinion.

A preliminary report *must* clearly identify any valuation as a "limited" opinion of value as the appraiser has not performed the detailed investigation and analysis essential to a cogent appraisal. (See Standard 6.5.)

6.2 Conformity

The preliminary report *must* comply with all applicable provisions of Business Appraisal Standards, Standard One, Professional Conduct and Ethics.

6.3 Usage

The preliminary report has use when a client desires the appraiser's limited opinion.

6.4 Disclosure

The presentation of a preliminary opinion without disclosing its limitations is unethical.

6.5 Departure

If an appraiser makes a preliminary report without including a clear statement that it is preliminary, there is the possibility a user of the report could accord the report and its limited opinion of value a greater degree of accuracy and reliability than is inherent in the preliminary report process. Therefore, all preliminary reports *shall* include a Statement of Departure in accordance with Standard 1.21(b). The Statement of Departure *shall* include a statement that the report is preliminary and the conclusion subject to change following a proper appraisal and that said change could be material.

6.6 Oral v. Written

All preliminary reports whether oral or written are subject to Standard Six.

6.7 Recordkeeping

An appraiser *should* retain written records of appraisal reports for a period of at least five (5) years after preparation or at least two (2) years after final disposition of any judicial proceeding in which the appraiser gave testimony, whichever period expires last.

NACVA PROFESSIONAL STANDARDS[7]

Introduction

All members of the National Association of Certified Valuation Analysts, an association of Certified Public Accountants and other business valuation professionals who perform valuation services, are bound by the standards and definitions of the AICPA's Code of Professional Conduct and Statement on Standards for Consulting Services (SSCS). Under the statement on Standards for Consulting Ser-

---

[7] Reprinted with the permission of the National Association of Certified Valuation Analysts.

vices, litigation support and valuation services are considered "trans-action" consulting services when the practitioner's function is to pro-vide services related to a specific client transaction, generally in con-junction with a third party. NACVA members will be bound by the business valuation standards as promulgated by the AICPA and NACVA. NACVA will adopt changes and interpretations of the stan-dards when necessary to avoid conflicts and ambiguities between the Standards of Practice issued by the AICPA and NACVA.

General Standards

The following general standards are extracted from the AICPA's Code of Professional Conduct as minimum general standards governing a NACVA member's performance of either litigation support or valua-tion services. They are:

- *Professional competence.* A member of NACVA shall: "undertake only those professional services that the member or the member's firm can reasonably expect to be completed with professional compe-tence";
- *Due professional care.* A member of NACVA shall: "exercise due professional care in the performance of professional services";
- *Planning and supervision.* A member of NACVA shall: "adequately plan and supervise the performance of professional services";
- *Sufficient relevant data.* A member of NACVA shall: "obtain suffi-cient relevant data to afford a reasonable basis for conclusions or recommendations in relation to any professional services per-formed";
- *Independence.* A member of NACVA shall not express an opinion on value unless the member and the member's firm are inde-pendent with respect to such valuation.

Report Writing Standards

Overview

The final stage in the valuation process is the communication of the results of the valuation to the client or other user of the report Reports may differ in nature, but in all cases they must inform the parties of the degree of correspondence between quantifiable information and established criteria. Reports may also differ in form and can vary from highly technical, fully documented extensive reports to less technical, less extensive oral reports. The form and content of any particular report will depend on the nature of the engagement, its purpose, its findings, and the needs of the decision-makers that receive and rely upon it.

The business valuation profession has categorized the communication of the results into four modes or formats of reporting. They are:

- Full written reports
- Short-form written reports
- Oral (verbal) reports
- Limited scope reports

NACVA has adopted the following standards for each method of reporting. The purpose of these standards is to establish minimum reporting criteria pertaining to each form of communication. The objective of these standards is to ensure consistency and quality of valuation reports issued by members of the Association. The following standards will not only benefit the member by giving him or her direction on issuing reports, but they will also benefit the client and those individuals or institutions that use and rely upon valuation reports in various decision-making situations.

The intent of these standards is not to establish or attempt to define valuation engagement procedures. For purposes of these standards, the valuation analyst is the individual ultimately responsible for the valuation engagement.

Standards for Full Written Reports

General

NACVA has established the following minimum reporting requirements pertaining specifically to full written reports.

A full written report must be organized, well written, communicate the results, and identify the information relied upon in the valuation process. The wording used in the report should not be overly technical and complicated, but should effectively communicate important thoughts, methods, and reasoning and identify the supporting documentation in a simple and concise manner.

Often, circumstances arise where the analyst is confronted with issues requiring him/her to depart from certain criteria established by this standard. If this is the case, the analyst must fully document and explain the effect the departure may have on the estimate of value conclusion.

Content

The general content of full written reports is:

- Identification/cover page
- Table of contents
- Opinion letter
- Statement of limiting conditions
- Body of report
- Appendix

Identification/Cover Page. The identification/cover page must indicate the following:

- Identification or name of the enterprise that is the subject of the report
- Effective date of the valuation conclusion
- Identification of the analyst and/or his or her firm
- Date the report is issued

Table of Contents. Due to the extensive amount of material typically included in a full written report, a table of contents must be included. Any item having a material effect on the valuation report must be included in the table of contents.

Opinion Letter. For the purposes of this standard, an opinion letter must be presented setting forth minimum information concerning the valuation engagement and its results. The opinion letter must include the following:

- Identification of the entity being valued
- Effective date of the valuation and date of issuance
- Purpose of the valuation
- Identification of the standard and premise of value
- Description of the interest being valued
- Conclusion as to valuation results
- Limitation on use of report
- Signature of the valuation analyst

Statement of Limiting Conditions.   Each valuation engagement will require the valuation analyst to identify any material qualifying matters regarding the analyst's estimate of value. Since all valuation cases will vary as to their specific limiting conditions, the following examples are provided to assist the analyst's recognition of limiting conditions that are often encountered:

- We have no present or contemplated financial interest in the (subject company). Our fees for this valuation are based upon our normal hourly billing rates, and in no way are contingent upon the results of our findings. We have no responsibility to update this report for events and circumstances occurring subsequent to the date of this report.
- This report has been prepared for the specific purpose of valuing the (subject company's) (describe interest) as of (effective date of valuation) for (describe purpose of the valuation) and is intended for no other purpose. This report is not to be copied or made available to any persons without the express written consent of (your company).
- Our report is based on historical and prospective financial information provided us by management and other third parties. Had we audited or reviewed the underlying data, matters may have come to our attention which would have resulted our using amounts different from those provided; accordingly, we take no responsibility for the underlying data presented or relied upon in this report. (Alternative language would be appropriate where the analyst or the analyst's firm performed an audit or review of the financial statements.)
- We have relied upon the representations of the owners, management and other third parties concerning the value and useful

condition of all equipment, real estate, investments used in the business and any other assets or liabilities, except as specifically stated to the contrary in this report. We have not attempted to confirm if all assets of the business are free and clear of liens and encumbrances, or that the company has good title to all assets.

- The estimate of value included in this report assumes the existing company will maintain the character and integrity of the company through any sale, reorganization or reduction of any owner's/manager's participation in the existing activities of the company.

- (Your company) does not purport to be a guarantor of value. Valuation of closely held companies is an imprecise science, with value being a question of fact, and reasonable people can differ in their estimates of value. (Your company) has, however, used conceptually sound and commonly accepted methods and procedures of valuation in determining the estimate of value included in this report.

- The valuation analyst, by reason of performing this valuation and preparing this report, is not to be required to give expert testimony nor to be in attendance in court or at any government hearing with reference to the matters contained herein, unless prior arrangements have been made with (your company) regarding such additional engagement

Body of Report.   In addition to the opinion letter's minimum reporting requirements, a full written report must also include sufficient information clearly communicating the thoughts, reasoning, methods and information or data used and relied upon to reach the estimate of value conclusion. The following items of information are necessary to clearly communicate the determination of value reached and the description of information used and relied upon to support the value conclusion:

- *Purpose of valuation.* The purpose of the valuation is a critical aspect of the engagement. Although the purpose is stated in the opinion letter of the report, it must be restated in the body of the report. The purpose of the valuation must be clearly communicated in a manner that will not lead to any confusion on the part of the user of the report.

- *Discussion of valuation process.* A discussion describing the valuator's general or overall process in performing the valuation must be included. For example:

  "The standard of value used in arriving at our valuation conclusion is fair market value (or investment value, intrinsic value, etc.). Fair market value is defined as the amount at which property would change hands between a hypothetical willing seller and a hypothetical willing buyer when neither is acting under compulsion and when both have reasonable knowledge of the relevant facts. In arriving at our valuation conclusion, we considered the three commonly accepted approaches to value: the Cost Approach, the Market Approach, and the Income Approach.

  "Under the Cost Approach, we considered the adjusted book value method. Under the Market Approach we considered the comparable sales method and the guideline companies method. Under the Income Approach, we considered the capitalized earnings method and the discounted future cash flows method. (Other appropriate methods could be considered under each approach.) Descriptions of the methods considered are included within our report.

  "Both internal and external factors influencing the value of (subject company) have been reviewed, analyzed, and interpreted. Internal factors include the Company's financial position, results of operations, and the size and marketability of the interest being valued. External factors include, among other things, the status of the industry and the position of the Company relative to the industry. The condition of the economy, international, national, and local, can also have an impact on the value of the Company."

  (Note: Identification of information used and the degree of reliance on such information should be disclosed.)

- *Enterprise background and description.* Individuals and institutions relying on valuation reports are often not intimately or even generally informed about the business organization or its structure, background, products and markets. Therefore, it is necessary to adequately describe the enterprise in order to assist user(s) of the report. Users of the report are those users stated in the purpose of the report.

The following are examples of items that should be included, if applicable, to adequately describe the enterprise:

- Nature of the enterprise
- Type of enterprise (i.e., wholesaler, distribution, retailer, etc.)
- History of the enterprise
- Organization form (i.e., corporation, partnership, etc.)
- Description of service or products
- Competition
- Location of operations
- Markets
- Discussion of management's ability and depth, when appropriate
- Identification of sources of information utilized and degree of reliance such information
- Other items of information the analyst believes necessary to adequately describe the enterprise, the industry and the economic climate in which enterprise operates

- *Ownership size, nature, restrictions and agreements.* The size and nature of ownership interests and binding agreements between the owners of the entity being valued can impact the estimate of value conclusion, and should, if relevant, be described in the report. Any restrictions on the transferability of the subject interest should, if relevant, be fully described. Issues involving control, marketability, minority interest and restrictions (if any) should, if relevant, also be adequately communicated.
- *Financial analysis.* A financial analysis of the subject company's financial history is an essential procedure in the valuation process. Therefore, results of the financial analysis must be included in the report. The financial analysis must include an adequate description of the financial data included in the analysis, the period it covers, and the degree to which the analyst has relied on such data. The financial analysis must also include discussion of key factors that led the analyst to his or her conclusions regarding management performance, financial position and results

of operations. The source of the financial data must be disclosed along with discussion as to whether or not the data was adjusted by the analyst. If the analyst has made adjustments to the data, the adjustment and reasoning for the adjustment must be adequately disclosed.

- If the analyst has performed a comparative analysis between the subject company's data and data of comparative public or private companies, or if he or she has based the comparison on industry averages, the source of the data and the results of the comparative analysis must be adequately communicated.
- *Valuation methodology.* A discussion of the valuation methodology must be included in the report. The method(s) of valuation must be identified and adequately explained. The reasoning for selecting certain methods must be provided. The source, method and/ or basis for determining key variables utilized in the valuation method must be clearly described.
- The progression of the valuation methodology should flow in a logical manner and should result in the valuation conclusion. If third party appraisers of tangible assets were involved, their identity and conclusions should be incorporated in the report.
- All methods or sources of determining tangible asset values, estimated projected earnings, capitalization/discount rates, discounts or premiums or any other material factors utilized in the valuation methodology must be fully described.

Appendix.   Certain items of financial or other information should be included in the appendix, if not in the body of the report.

The following items must be included, if not included elsewhere in report:

- Historical financial statement summaries
- Adjustments to historical financial statements
- Adjusted financial statement summaries
- Projected and/or forecasted financial statements, if utilized, including the underlying assumptions

The following items (but not limited thereto) may be included:

- Common size analysis summaries
- Ratio analysis summaries
- Comparative analysis data
- Independent appraisals on tangible assets

Standards for Short-Form Reports

Overview

NACVA has established the following reporting requirements that pertain specifically to short-form written reports. A valuation analyst may be engaged to perform a valuation and issue a short-form report where the analyst has performed the necessary valuation procedures enabling him or her to issue a full written report.

A Short-Form Report Shall Include:

- An opinion letter with a report limitation statement, and
- The body of a short-form report.

Opinion Letter. The opinion letter of a short-form report should contain, at a minimum, the following information:

- Identification of the entity being valued
- Effective date of the valuation and date of report
- Purpose of the valuation
- Identification of the standard and premise of value
- Description of the interest being valued
- Report limitation statement
- Conclusion as to valuation results
- Limitation on use of report
- Signature of the valuation analyst

Report Limitation Statement. An example of a report limitation statement would be: "The valuation report is limited in its discussion regarding information utilized in the valuation process. We were engaged to perform a valuation of (subject company) where the scope of the valuation procedures was not limited. However, we were limited in the amount of discussion made in this report. The discussion omitted includes (identify discussions omitted). If the omitted discussions were included in this report, they might influence the user's level of understanding regarding the estimate of value contained in this report. Accordingly, this report is not designed for those who are not informed about such matters."

Body of Short-Form Report/Appendix. In addition to the stated requirements of the opinion letter of the short-form written report, other minimum information must also be included in the body of the short-form written report. These items must be included in the body of a short-form written report, if not included elsewhere:

- Purpose of the valuation
- Description of valuation process
- Statement of limiting conditions (in addition to scope or report limitations)
- Business description (including form of organization, brief history of subject company, products or services described, description of sources of information used and level of reliance on such information)
- Ownership size, nature, restrictions, and/or agreements
- Valuation methodology.

Standards for Oral Reports

Overview

Valuation analysts are often requested to report their valuation conclusion or estimate of value on a particular business by means of an oral presentation. For such purposes, the analyst must have performed the necessary valuation procedures enabling him or her to issue a full written report.

An oral report must be carefully worded, particularly as it leaves no written documentation and may result in insufficient comprehension of the estimate of value being communicated.

A written outline of the analyst's oral presentation is required. This will help ensure adequate communication occurs.

Adequate Communication

It is recommended that an oral report adequately communicate the following:

- Identification of entity being valued
- Effective date of the valuation
- Purpose of the valuation
- Identification of the standard and premise of value
- Description of the interest being valued
- Conclusion as to estimate of value results
- Limitation on use of the oral report
- Description of any limiting conditions, including any scope limitations

Standards for Limited Scope Reports

Overview

NACVA has established the following reporting requirements pertaining specifically to limited scope reports. A valuation analyst may be engaged to perform a valuation and issue a limited scope report where the scope of his or her procedures has been limited, and where limited procedures and consequently a limited report is adequate for the purpose of the valuation.

A limited scope report must follow the format for either a full written report, a short-form report, or an oral report, and include a scope limitation statement.

Scope Limitation Statement

"The scope of this valuation engagement and valuation report was limited. We were engaged to perform a valuation for (subject company) with the intent of ascertaining an approximate estimate of value. If (your company) was engaged to perform a more detailed analysis, matters may have come to our attention that could have a material impact on the estimate of value contained in this report."

Other Guidelines

Besides NACVA professional standards, valuation analysts may also find it necessary to consider guidelines and standards established by others, such as:

- Department of Labor (DOL)
- Internal Revenue Service (IRS)
- State laws
- USPAP

DOL.   DOL regulations apply to business valuations for ESOPs. In 1988, the DOL proposed a regulation prescribing procedures and reporting rules for valuations relating to ESOPs. Although the proposed regulation is not yet final, many valuation analysts have conformed their reports to the proposed new rules.

IRS.   The IRS has guidelines regarding business valuations. Revenue Ruling 59-60 identifies certain factors that should be considered in valuing a business for gift and estate tax purposes. Accordingly, a report for a tax-related valuation should discuss how it meets applicable IRS guidelines. If the report relates to a valuation of donated stock, the valuation analyst may also need to consult Revenue Procedure 6649, which provides general report guidelines for those types of valuations.

State Laws.   The analyst must be aware of state and other local legal requirements.

Uniform Standards of Professional Appraisal Practice (USPAP).   The Appraisal Foundation, a quasi-governmental organization, has issued standards (USPAP) for appraisals. These standards are required for certain "federal related transactions" such as appraisals supporting mortgage loans granted by banks. Certain of the USPAP standards relate to performance of business valuations.

UNIFORM STANDARDS OF PROFESSIONAL APPRAISAL PRACTICE[8]

As Promulgated by the Appraisal Standards Board
of The Appraisal Foundation

Table of Contents

Standards and Standards Rules

---

[8] We have included selected portions of the Uniform Standards of Professional Appraisal Practice; for a complete version of USPAP, you can access the standards on the internet at *www.appraisalfoundation.org*.

Standard 9
    Business Appraisal, Development
Standard 10
    Business Appraisal, Reporting

Statements on Appraisal Standards

SMT-1 Standards Rule 3-1(g) (Appraisal Review)
SMT-2 Discounted Cash Flow Analysis
SMT-3 Retrospective Value Opinions
SMT-4 Prospective Value Opinions
SMT-5 Confidentiality Section of the Ethics Rule
SMT-6 Reasonable Exposure Time in Real Property and Personal Property Market Value Opinions
SMT-7 Permitted Departure from Specific Requirements for Real Property and Personal Property Appraisal Assignments
SMT-8 Electronic Transmission of Reports
SMT-9 Identification of the Client's Intended Use in Developing and Reporting Appraisal, Appraisal Review, or Consulting Assignment Opinions and Conclusions

Addenda Reference Material
(for guidance only)

Advisory Opinions

AO-1 Sales History
AO-2 Inspection of Subject Property Real Estate
AO-3 Update of an Appraisal
AO-4 Standards Rule 1-5(b)
AO-5 Assistance in the Preparation of an Appraisal
AO-6 The Appraisal Review Function
AO-7 Marketing Time Opinions
AO-8 Market Value vs. Fair Value in Real Property Appraisals
AO-9 Responsibility of Appraisers Concerning Toxic or Hazardous Substance Contamination
AO-10 The Appraiser-Client Relationship
AO-11 Content of the Appraisal Report Options of Standards Rules 2-2 and 8-2

Preamble

The purpose of these standards is to establish requirements for professional appraisal practice, which includes appraisal, appraisal review, and consulting, as defined. The intent of these Standards is to promote and maintain a high level of public trust in professional appraisal practice.

These standards are for appraisers and users of appraisal services. To maintain a high level of professional practice, appraisers observe these standards. However; these standards do not in themselves establish which individuals or assignments must comply; neither The Appraisal Foundation nor its Appraisal Standards Board is a government entity with the power to make, judge, or enforce law. Individuals comply with these Standards either by choice or by requirement placed upon them, or upon the service they provide, by law, regulation, or agreement with the client or intended users to comply.

It is essential that professional appraisers develop and communicate their analyses, opinions, and conclusions to intended users of their services in a manner that is meaningful and not misleading. These *Uniform Standards of Professional Appraisal Practice* (USPAP) reflect the current standards of the appraisal profession.

The importance of the role of the appraiser places ethical obligations on those who serve in this capacity. These Standards include explanatory comments and begin with an *Ethics Rule* setting forth the requirements for integrity, impartiality, objectivity, independent judgment, and ethical conduct. In addition, these Standards include a *Competency Rule* that places an immediate responsibility on the appraiser prior to acceptance of an assignment as well as during the performance of an assignment. *Definitions* applicable to these Standards are also included. The standards contain binding requirements, as well as specific requirements to which the *Departure Rule* may apply under certain conditions. The *Departure Rule* does not apply to the *Preamble, Ethics Rule, Competency Rule, Jurisdictional Exception Rule, Supplemental Standards Rule,* or *Definitions* sections.

These standards deal with the procedures to be followed in performing an appraisal, appraisal review, or consulting service and the manner in which an appraisal, appraisal review, or consulting service is communicated. Standards 1 and 2 establish requirements for the development and communication of a real property appraisal. Standard 3 establishes requirements for reviewing a real property appraisal and reporting on that review. Standards 4 and 5 establish requirements for the development and communication of various real estate or real property consulting functions by an appraiser. Standard 6 establishes requirements for the development and reporting of mass appraisals for ad valorem tax purposes or any other universe of properties. Standards 7 and 8 establish requirements for developing and communicating personal property appraisals. Standards 9 and 10 establish requirements for developing and communicating business appraisals.

These Standards include Statements on Appraisal Standards issued by the Appraisal Standards Board for the purpose of clarification, interpretation, explanation, or elaboration of a standard or a standards rule.

> **Comment.** Comments are an integral part of the Uniform Standards and are extensions of the Rules, Definitions, and Standards Rules. Comments provide interpretation from the Appraisal Standards Board concerning the background or

application of certain Rules, Definitions, or Standards Rules. Comments also establish the context of certain requirements and the conditions that apply only in specific situations or type of assignments.

Endnotes referring to Advisory Opinions do not incorporate the Advisory Opinions into the *Uniform Standards of Professional Appraisal Practice.*

Ethics Rule

To promote and preserve the public trust inherent in professional appraisal practice, an appraiser must observe the highest standards of professional ethics. This Ethics Rule is divided into four sections: conduct, management, confidentiality, and recordkeeping.

Comment. This rule specifies the personal obligations and responsibilities of the individual appraiser. However, it should also be noted that groups and organizations engaged in appraisal practice share the same ethical obligations.

Compliance with these standards is required when either the service or the appraiser is obligated by law or regulation, or by an agreement with the client or intended users, to comply.

Conduct

An appraiser must perform assignments ethically and competently in accordance with these standards, and must not engage in criminal conduct. An appraiser must perform assignments with impartiality, objectivity, and independence, and without accommodation of personal interests.

An appraiser must not accept an assignment that includes the reporting of predetermined opinions and conclusions.

An appraiser must not communicate assignment results in a misleading or fraudulent manner. An appraiser must not use or communicate a misleading or fraudulent report or knowingly permit an employee or other person to communicate a misleading or fraudulent report.[9]

An appraiser must not use or rely on unsupported conclusions relating to characteristics such as race, color, religion, national origin, gender, marital status, familial status, age, receipt of public assistance income, handicap, or an unsupported conclusion that homogeneity of such characteristics is necessary to maximize value.

> **Comment.** An individual appraiser employed by a group or organization that conducts itself in a manner that does not conform to these standards should take steps that are appropriate under the circumstances to ensure compliance with the standards.

Management

The payment of undisclosed fees, commissions, or things of value in connection with the procurement of appraisal, appraisal review, or consulting assignments is unethical.

> **Comment.** Disclosure of fees, commissions, or things of value connected to the procurement of an assignment must appear in the certification of a written report and in any transmittal letter in which conclusions are stated. In groups or organizations engaged in appraisal practice, intra-company payments to employees for business development are not considered to be unethical. Competency, rather than financial incentives, should be the primary basis for awarding an assignment.

Whenever an appraiser develops an opinion of value, it is unethical for the appraiser to accept compensation in developing that opinion when it is contingent upon the following:

1. The reporting of a predetermined value, or
2. A direction in value that favors the cause of the client, or
3. The amount of the value opinion, or

---

[9] See Advisory Opinion AO-5. References to Advisory Opinions are for guidance only and do not incorporate Advisory Opinions into the Standards Rules.

4. The attainment of a stipulated result, or
5. The occurrence of a subsequent event directly related to the value opinion.

Whenever an opinion of real property value is a necessary part of developing a real property consulting assignment performed by an appraiser with contingent compensation, the consulting appraiser must do the following:

1. Make arrangements with the client such that the consulting appraiser's compensation for developing the real property appraisal is on a basis that complies with this ETHICS RULE; or
2. Retain (or suggest that the client retain) another appraiser to perform the real property appraisal under compensation arrangements that do not violate this ETHICS RULE; and
3. Properly certify the real property consulting report, including therein a clear disclosure of the separate compensation arrangements for the appraisal portion and the real property consulting portion of the assignment.

> **Comment.** The purpose of this rule is to ensure that appraisers properly understand how they may comply with USPAP when performing a real property consulting assignment in which a real property appraisal is necessary and compensation for performing the assignment is contingent on the attainment of a stipulated result or the occurrence of a subsequent event (such as in connection with a real property tax appeal).

Advertising for or soliciting appraisal assignments in a manner that is false, misleading, or exaggerated is unethical.

> **Comment.** In groups or organizations engaged in appraisal practice, decisions concerning finder or referral fees, contingent compensation, and advertising may not be the responsibility of an individual appraiser, but for a particular assignment, it is the responsibility of the individual appraiser to ascertain that there has been no breach of ethics, that the appraisal is prepared in accordance with these Standards, and that the report can be properly certified as required by Standards Rules 2-3, 3-2, 5-3, 6-8, 8-3, or 10-3.

Confidentiality[10]

An appraiser must protect the confidential nature of the appraiser–
client relationship. An appraiser must act in good faith with regard
to the legitimate interests of the client in the use of confidential information and in the communication of assignment results. In addition, an appraiser must not disclose confidential information or assignment results prepared for a client to anyone other than (1) the
client and persons specifically authorized by the client; (2) state enforcement agencies and such third parties as may be authorized by
due process of law; and (3) a duly authorized professional peer review committee. It is unethical for a member of a duly authorized
professional peer review committee to disclose confidential information presented to the committee.

> **Comment.** When all confidential elements of confidential in-
> formation are removed through redaction or the process of ag-
> gregation, client authorization is not required for the disclosure
> of the remaining information, as modified.

Recordkeeping

An appraiser must prepare a workfile for each assignment The
workfile must include the name of the client and the identity, by name
or type, of any other intended users; true copies of any written reports, documented on any type of media; summaries of any oral
reports or testimony, or a transcript of testimony, including the
appraiser's signed and dated certification; all other data, information, and documentation necessary to support the appraiser's opinions and conclusions and to show compliance with this rule and all
other applicable Standards, or references to the location(s) of such
other documentation.

An appraiser must retain the workfile for a period of at least
five (5) years after preparation or at least two (2) years after final

---

[10] See Statement on Appraisal Standards No. 5.

disposition of any judicial proceeding in which testimony was given, whichever period expires last, and have custody of his or her workfile, or make appropriate workfile retention, access, and retrieval arrangements with the party having custody of the workfile.

> **Comment.** A workfile preserves evidence of the appraiser's consideration of all applicable data and statements required by USPAP and other information as may be required to support the findings and conclusions of the appraiser. For example, the content of a workfile for a Complete Appraisal must reflect consideration of all USPAP requirements applicable to the specific Complete Appraisal assignment. However, the content of a workfile for a Limited Appraisal need only reflect consideration of the USPAP requirements from which there has been no departure and that are required by the specific Limited Appraisal assignment.
>
> A photocopy or an electronic copy of the entire actual written appraisal, appraisal review, or consulting report sent or delivered to a client satisfies the requirement of a true copy. As an example, a photocopy or electronic copy of the Self-Contained Appraisal Report, Summary Appraisal Report, or Restricted Use Appraisal Report actually issued by an appraiser for a real property Complete Appraisal or Limited Appraisal assignment satisfies the true copy requirement for that assignment.
>
> Care should be exercised in the selection of the form, style, and type of medium for written records, which may be handwritten and informal, to ensure they are retrievable by the appraiser throughout the prescribed record retention period.
>
> A workfile must be in existence prior to and contemporaneous with the issuance of a written or oral report. A written summary of an oral report must be added to the workfile within a reasonable time after the issuance of the oral report.
>
> A workfile must be made available by the appraiser when required by state enforcement agencies or due process of law. In addition, a workfile in support of a Restricted Use Appraisal Report must be available for inspection by the client in accordance with the *Comment* to Standards Rule 2-2(c)(ix), 8-2(c)(ix) and 10-2(b)(ix).

Competency Rule

Prior to accepting an assignment or entering into an agreement to perform any assignment, an appraiser must properly identify the problem to be addressed and have the knowledge and experience to complete the assignment competently; or alternatively:

1. Disclose the lack of knowledge and/or experience to the client before accepting the assignment; and
2. Take all steps necessary or appropriate to complete the assignment competently; and
3. Describe the lack of knowledge and or experience and the steps taken to complete the assignment competently in the report.

> **Comment.** Competency applies to factors such as, but not limited to, an appraiser's familiarity with a specific type of property, a market, a geographic area, or an analytical method. If such a factor is necessary for an appraiser to develop credible appraisal assignment results, the appraiser is responsible for having the competency to address that factor, or for following the steps outlined above to satisfy this Competency Rule.
>
> The background and experience of appraisers varies widely, and a lack of knowledge or experience can lead to inaccurate or inappropriate appraisal practice. The *Competency Rule* requires an appraiser to have both the knowledge and the experience required to perform a specific appraisal service competently.
>
> If an appraiser is offered the opportunity to perform an appraisal service but lacks the necessary knowledge or experience to complete it competently, the appraiser must disclose his or her lack of knowledge or experience to the client before accepting the assignment and then take the necessary or appropriate steps to complete the appraisal service competently. This may be accomplished in various ways including, but not limited to, personal study by the appraiser; association with an appraiser reasonably believed to have the necessary knowledge or experience; or retention of others who possess the required knowledge or experience.
>
> In an assignment where geographic competency is necessary,

an appraiser preparing an appraisal in an unfamiliar location must spend sufficient time to understand the nuances of the local market and the supply and demand factors relating to the specific property type and the location involved. Such understanding will not be imparted solely from a consideration of specific data such as demographics, costs, sales, and rentals. The necessary understanding of local market conditions provides the bridge between a sale and a comparable sale or a rental and a comparable rental. If an appraiser is not in a position to spend the necessary amount of time in a market area to obtain this understanding, affiliation with a qualified local appraiser may be the appropriate response to ensure development of credible assignment results.

Although this rule requires an appraiser to identify the problem and disclose any deficiency in competence prior to accepting an assignment, facts or conditions uncovered during the course of an assignment could cause an appraiser to discover that he or she lacks the required knowledge or experience to complete the assignment competently. At the point of such discovery, the appraiser is obligated to notify the client and comply with items 2 and 3 of the rule.

Departure Rule[11]

This rule permits exceptions from sections of the Uniform Standards that are classified as specific requirements rather than binding requirements. The burden of proof is on the appraiser to decide before accepting an assignment and invoking this rule that the scope of work applied will result in opinions or conclusions that are credible. The burden of disclosure is also on the appraiser to report any departures from specific requirements.

An appraiser may enter into an agreement to perform an assignment in which the scope of work is less than, or different from,

---

[11] See Statement on Appraisal Standards No. 7. See also Advisory Opinion AO-15 on page 132. References to Advisory Opinions are for guidance only and do not incorporate Advisory Opinions into the Standards Rules.

the work that would otherwise be required by the specific requirements, provided that prior to entering into such an agreement:

1. The appraiser has determined that the appraisal or consulting
    process to be performed is not so limited that the results of the
    assignment are no longer credible;
2. The appraiser has advised the client that the assignment calls for
    something less than, or different from, the work required by the
    specific requirements and that the report will clearly identify and
    explain the departure(s); and
3. The client has agreed that the performance of a limited appraisal
    or consulting service would be appropriate, given the intended
    use.

> **Comment.** Not all specific requirements are *applicable* to every
> assignment. When a specific requirement is *not applicable* to a
> given assignment, the specific requirement is irrelevant, and
> therefore no departure is needed.
>
> A specific requirement is *applicable* under these conditions:
>
> - It addresses factors or conditions that are present in the given
>   assignment, or
> - It addresses analysis that is typical practice in such an as-
>   signment.
>
> A specific requirement is *not applicable* under these conditions:
>
> - It addresses factors or conditions that are not present in the
>   given assignment, or
> - It addresses analysis that is not typical practice in such an
>   assignment, or
> - It addresses analysis that would not provide meaningful re-
>   sults in the given assignment.
>
> Of those specific requirements that are *applicable* to a given
> assignment, some may be *necessary* in order to result in opinions
> or conclusions that are credible. When a specific requirement is
> *necessary* to a given assignment, departure is not permitted.

Departure is permitted from those specific requirements that are *applicable* to a given assignment, but *not necessary* in order to result in opinions or conclusions that are credible.

A specific requirement is considered to be both *applicable* and *necessary* under these conditions:

- It addresses factors or conditions that are present in the given assignment, or
- It addresses analysis that is typical practice in such an assignment, and
- Lack of consideration for those factors, conditions, or analyses would significantly affect the credibility of the results.

Typical practice for a given assignment is measured by the following:

- The expectations of the participants in the market for appraisal services, and
- What an appraiser's peers' actions would be in performing the same or a similar assignment.

If an appraiser enters into an agreement to perform an appraisal or consulting service that calls for something less than, or different from, the work that would otherwise be required by the specific requirements, Standards Rules 2-2(a)(xi), 2-2(b)(xi), 2-2(c)(xi), 5-2(i), 8-2(a)(xi), 8-2(b)(xi), 8-2(c)(xi), 10-2(a)(x) and 10-2(b)(x) require that the report clearly identify and explain departure(s) from the specific requirements.

Departure from the following development and reporting rules is not permitted: Standards Rules 1-1, 1-2, 1-5, 2-1, 2-2, 2-3, 2-5, 3-1, 3-2, 4-1, 5-1, 5-3, 6-1, 6-3, 6-6, 6-7, 6-8, 7-1, 7-2, 7-5, 8-1, 8-2, 8-3, 8-5, 9-1, 9-2, 9-3, 9-5, 10-1, 10-2, 10-3, and 10-5. This restriction on departure is reiterated throughout the document with the reminder: "This Standards Rule contains binding requirements from which departure is not permitted."

The Departure Rule does not apply to the Preamble, Ethics Rule, Competency Rule, Jurisdictional Exception Rule, Supplemental Standards Rule, or Definitions Section.

Jurisdictional Exception Rule

If any part of these standards is contrary to the law or public policy of any jurisdiction, only that part shall be void and of no force or effect in that jurisdiction.

> **Comment.** The purpose of the *Jurisdictional Exception Rule* is strictly limited to providing a saving or severability clause intended to preserve the balance of USPAP if one or more of its parts are determined to be contrary to law or public policy of a jurisdiction. By logical extension, there can be no violation of USPAP by an appraiser disregarding, with proper disclosure, only the part or parts of USPAP that are void and of no force and effect in a particular assignment by operation of legal authority. It is misleading for an appraiser to disregard a part or parts of USPAP as void and of no force and effect in a particular assignment without identifying in the appraiser's report the part or parts disregarded and the legal authority justifying this action.
>
> As used in the *Jurisdictional Exception Rule*, law means a body of rules with binding legal force established by controlling governmental authority. This broad meaning includes, without limitation, the federal and state constitutions, legislative and court-made law and administrative rules, regulations, and ordinances. Public policy refers to more or less well-defined moral and ethical standards of conduct, currently and generally accepted by the community as a whole, and recognized by the courts with the aid of statutes, judicial precedents, and other similar available evidence. Jurisdiction relates to the legal authority to legislate, apply, or interpret law in any form at the federal, state, and local levels of government.

Supplemental Standards Rule

These Uniform Standards provide the common basis for all appraisal practice. Supplemental standards applicable to assignments prepared for specific purposes or property types may be issued by public agencies and certain client groups—e.g., regulatory agencies, eminent domain authorities, asset managers, and financial institutions. An appraiser and client must ascertain whether any supplemental standards in addition to these Uniform Standards apply to the assignment being considered.[12]

> **Comment.** The purpose of the *Supplemental Standards Rule* is to provide a reasonable means to augment USPAP with additional requirements set by clients, employers, governmental entities, and/or professional appraisal organizations. Supplemental standards cannot diminish the purpose, intent, or content of the requirements of SPAP.
>
> By certifying conformity with USPAP for an assignment in which an appraiser satisfied a professional appraisal ethics or practice standard not in USPAP, the appraiser acknowledges that this supplemental standard adds to but does not diminish the purpose, intent, or content of USPAP.

Definitions

For the purpose of these Standards, the following definitions apply:

Appraisal: (noun) The act or process of developing an opinion of value; an opinion of value. (adjective) of or pertaining to appraising and related functions—e.g., appraisal practice, appraisal services.

> *Complete appraisal.* The act or process of developing an opinion of value or an opinion of value developed without invoking the *Departure Rule.*
>
> *Limited appraisal.* The act or process of developing an opinion of value or an opinion of value developed under and resulting from invoking the *Departure Rule.*
>
> **Comment.** An opinion of value may be expressed as a single point, as a range, or as a relationship (e.g., not more than, not less than) to a previous value opinion or established benchmark (e.g., assessed value, collateral value).

---

[12] See Advisory Opinions AO-7 on page 110 and AO-8. References to Advisory Opinions are for guidance only and do not incorporate Advisory Opinions into the Standards Rules.

Appraisal Practice: The work or services performed by appraisers, defined by three terms in these standards: appraisal, appraisal review, and consulting.

> **Comment.** These three terms are intentionally generic, and not mutually exclusive. For example, an opinion of value may be required as part of an appraisal, appraisal review, or consulting assignment. The use of other nomenclature by an appraiser (e.g., analysis, counseling, evaluation, study, submission, valuation) does not exempt an appraiser from adherence to these standards.

Appraisal Review: The act or process of developing and communicating an opinion about the quality of another appraiser's work.

> **Comment.** The subject of an appraisal review assignment may be all or part of an appraisal report, the work file, or a combination of these.

Assignment: An appraisal, appraisal review, or consulting service provided as a consequence of an agreement between an appraiser and a client.

Assignment Results: An appraiser's opinions and conclusions developed specific to an assignment.

> **Comment.** Assignment results are an appraiser's:
>
> * opinions or conclusions developed in an appraisal assignment, such as, value;
> * opinions of adequacy, relevancy or reasonableness developed in an appraisal review assignment;
>   or
> * opinions, conclusions or recommendations developed in a consulting assignment.

Assumption: That which is taken to be true.

Bias: A preference or inclination used in the development or communication of an appraisal, appraisal review, or consulting assignment that precludes an appraiser's impartiality.

Binding Requirements: All or part of a Standards Rule of USPAP from which departure is not permitted. (See *Departure Rule.*)

Business Enterprise: An entity pursuing an economic activity.

Business Equity: The interests, benefits, and rights inherent in the ownership of a business enterprise or a part thereof in any form (including, but not necessarily limited to, capital stock, partnership interests, cooperatives, sole proprietorships, options, and warrants).

Cash Flow Analysis: A study of the anticipated movement of cash into or out of an investment.

Client: The party or parties who engage an appraiser (by employment or contract) in a specific assignment.

> **Comment.** The client identified by the appraiser in an appraisal, appraisal review, or consulting assignment (or in the assignment workfile) is the party or parties with whom the appraiser has an appraiser-client relationship in the related assignment, and may be an individual, group, or entity.

Confidential information: Information received from a client, not available from any other source, which the client identifies as confidential when providing it to an appraiser.

> **Comment.** Information available to the appraiser from other sources does not become confidential when given to the appraiser by the client.

Consulting: The act or process of providing information, analysis of real estate data, and recommendations or conclusions on diversified problems in real estate, other than an opinion of value.

Extraordinary assumption: An assumption, directly related to a specific assignment, which, if found to be false, could alter the appraiser's opinions or conclusions.

> **Comment.** Extraordinary assumptions presume as fact otherwise uncertain information about physical, legal, or economic characteristics of the subject property or about conditions external to the property, such as market conditions or trends, or the integrity of data used in an analysis.

Feasibility analysis: A study of the cost-benefit relationship of an economic endeavor.

Hypothetical condition: That which is contrary to what exists, but is supposed for the purpose of analysis.

> **Comment.** Hypothetical conditions assume conditions contrary to known facts about physical, legal, or economic characteristics of the subject property or about conditions external to the property, such as market conditions or trends, or the integrity of data used in an analysis.

Intangible property (intangible assets):   Nonphysical assets, including but not limited to franchises, trademarks, patents, copyrights, goodwill, equities, mineral rights, securities, and contracts, as distinguished from physical assets such as facilities and equipment.

Intended use: The use or uses of an appraiser's reported appraisal, appraisal review, or consulting assignment opinions and conclusions, as identified by the appraiser based on communication with the client at the time of the assignment.

Intended user: The client and any other party as identified, by name or type, as users of the appraisal, appraisal review, or consulting report, by the appraiser based on communication with the client at the time of the assignment.

Investment analysis: A study that reflects the relationship between acquisition price and anticipated future benefits of a real estate investment.

Market analysis: A study of market conditions for a specific type of property.

Mass appraisal: The process of valuing a universe of properties as of a given date using standard methodology employing common data, and allowing for statistical testing.

Mass appraisal model: A mathematical expression of how supply and demand factors interact in a market.

Personal property: Identifiable tangible objects that are considered by the general public as being "personal"—e.g., furnishings, artwork, antiques, gems and jewelry, collectibles, machinery and equipment; all tangible property that is not classified as real estate.

Real estate: An identified parcel or tract of land, including improvements, if any.

Real property: The interests, benefits, and rights inherent in the ownership of real estate.

> **Comment.** In some jurisdictions, the terms *real estate* and *real property* have the same legal meaning. The separate definitions recognize the traditional distinction between the two concepts in appraisal theory.

Report: Any communication, written or oral, of an appraisal, appraisal review, or consulting service that is transmitted to the client upon completion of an assignment.

> **Comment.** Most reports are written and most clients mandate written reports. Oral report requirements (see the *Recordkeeping* section of the *Ethics Rule*) are included to cover court testimony and other oral communications of an appraisal, appraisal review, or consulting service.
>
> The types of written reports listed below apply to real property, personal property and business valuation appraisal assignments, as indicated.
>
> *Appraisal report:* A written report prepared under Standards Rule 10-2(a).
>
> *Self-contained appraisal report:* A written report prepared under Standards Rule 2-2(a) or 8-2(a).

Summary appraisal report: A written report prepared under Standards Rule 2-2(b) or 8-2(b).

Restricted use appraisal report: A written report prepared under Standards Rule 2-2(c), 8-2(c) or 10-2(b).

Scope of work: The amount and type of information researched and the analysis applied in an assignment. Scope of work includes, but is not limited to, the degree to which the property is inspected or identified; the extent of research into physical or economic factors that could affect the property; the extent of data research; and the type and extent of analysis applied to arrive at opinions or conclusions.

Signature: Personalized evidence indicating authentication of the work performed by the appraiser and acceptance of the responsibility for content, analyses, and the conclusions in the report.

> **Comment.** A signature can be represented by a handwritten mark, a digitized image controlled by a personalized identification number or other media, where the appraiser has sole personalized control of affixing the signature.

Specific requirements: All or part of a Standards Rule of USPAP from which departure is permitted under certain limited conditions. (See *Departure Rule.*)

Supplemental standards: An assignment performance requirement that adds to the requirements in USPAP.

Workfile: Documentation necessary to support an appraiser's analysis, opinions, and conclusions.

Standard 9 Business Appraisal, Development

In developing a business or intangible asset appraisal, an appraiser must identify the problem to be solved and the scope of work necessary to solve the problem, and correctly complete the research and analysis steps necessary to produce a credible appraisal.

Comment. Standard 9 is directed toward the substantive aspects of developing a competent business or intangible asset appraisal. The requirements of Standard 9 apply when the specific purpose of an assignment is to develop an appraisal of a business or intangible asset.

Standards Rule 9-1

(This Standards Rule contains binding requirements from which departure is not permitted.)

In developing a business or intangible asset appraisal, an appraiser must:

(a) be aware of, understand, and correctly employ those recognized methods and procedures that are necessary to produce a credible appraisal;

> **Comment.** Changes and developments in the economy and in investment theory have a substantial impact on the business appraisal profession. Important changes in the financial arena, securities regulation, tax law and major new court decisions may result in corresponding changes in business appraisal practice.

(b) not commit a substantial error of omission or commission that significantly affects an appraisal;

> **Comment.** In performing appraisal services an appraiser must be certain that the gathering of factual information is conducted in a manner that is sufficiently diligent, given the scope of work as identified according to Standards Rule 9-2(e), to reasonably ensure that the data that would have a material or significant effect on the resulting opinions or conclusions are identified and, where a material or significant effect on the resulting opinions or conclusions are identified and, where necessary, analyzed. Further, an appraiser must use sufficient care in analyzing such data to avoid errors that would significantly affect his or her opinions and conclusions.

(c) not render appraisal services in a careless or negligent manner, such as by making a series of errors that, although individually might not significantly affect the results of an appraisal, in the aggregate affect the credibility of those results.

Comment. Perfection is impossible to attain and competence does not require perfection. However, an appraiser must not render appraisal services in a careless or negligent manner. This rule requires an appraiser to use diligence and care.

Standards Rule 9-2

(This Standards Rule contains binding requirements from which departure is not permitted.)

In developing a business or intangible asset appraisal, an appraiser must identify:

(a) the client and any other intended users of the appraisal and the client's intended use of the appraiser opinions and conclusions;

    Comment. An appraiser must not allow a client's objectives or intended use of the appraisal to cause an analysis to be biased.

(b) the purpose of the assignment, including the standard of value (definition) to be developed;
(c) the effective date of the appraisal;
(d) the business enterprises, assets, or equity to be valued; and
    (i)   identify any buy-sell agreements, investment letter stock restrictions, restrictive corporate charter or partnership agreement clauses, and any similar features or factors that may have an influence on value.
    (ii) ascertain the extent to which the interests contain elements of ownership control.

    Comment. Special attention should be paid to the attributes of the interest being appraised including the rights and benefits of ownership. The elements of control in a given situation may be affected by law, distribution of ownership interests, contractual relationships, and many other factors. As a consequence, the degree of control or lack of it depends on a broad variety of facts and circumstances which must be evaluated in the specific situation.

Equity interests in a business enterprise are not necessarily worth the pro rata share of the business enterprise value as a whole. Conversely, the value of the business enterprise is not necessarily a direct mathematical extension of the value of the fractional interests.

(e)   the scope of work that will be necessary to complete the assignment:

Comment. The scope of work is acceptable when it is consistent with the following:

- The expectations of participants in the market for the same or similar appraisal services; and
- What the appraiser's peers' actions would be in performing the same or a similar business valuation assignment in compliance with USPAP[13]

An appraiser must have sound reasons in support of the scope of work decision, and be prepared to support the decision to exclude any information or procedure that would appear to be relevant to the client, an intended user, or the appraiser's peers' in the same or a similar assignment. (See the *Departure Rule.*)

An appraiser must not allow assignment conditions to limit the extent of research or analysis to such a degree that the resulting opinions and conclusions developed in an assignment are not credible in the context of the intended use of the appraisal.

(f)   any extraordinary assumptions necessary in the assignment; and

Comment. An extraordinary assumption may be used in an appraisal only if:

---

[13] See SMT-7 for an example of qualification criteria for an "appraiser's peers." (An "Appraiser's peers" are other competent, qualified appraisers who have expertise in similar types of assignments involving similar types of property.)

- It is required to properly develop credible opinions and con-clusions;
- The appraiser has a reasonable basis for the extraordinary assumption;
- Use of the extraordinary assumption results in a credible analysis; and
- The appraiser complies with the disclosure requirements set forth in USPAP for extraordinary assumptions.

(g) any hypothetical conditions necessary in the assignment.

> **Comment.** A hypothetical condition may be used in an appraisal only if:
>
> - Use of the hypothetical condition is clearly required for le-gal purposes, for purposes of reasonable analysis, or for purposes of comparison;
> - Use of the hypothetical condition results in a credible analy-sis; and
> - The appraiser complies with the disclosure requirements set forth in USPAP for hypothetical conditions.

Standards Rule 9-3

(This Standards Rule contains binding requirements from which departure is not permitted)

In developing a business or intangible asset appraisal relating to an equity interest with the ability to cause liquidation of the enter-prise, an appraiser must investigate the possibility that the business enterprise may have a higher value by liquidation of all or part of the enterprise than by continued operation as is. If liquidation of all or part of the enterprise is the indicated basis of valuation, an appraisal of any real estate or personal property to be liquidated may be ap-propriate.

> **Comment.** This rule requires the appraiser to recognize that continued operation of a business is not always the best premise of value as liquidation of all or part of the enterprise may result in a higher value. However, this typically applies only when the business equity being appraised is in a position to cause liquida-

tion. If liquidation of all or part of the enterprise is the appropriate premise of value, competency in the appraisal of assets such as real estate (Standard 1) and tangible personal property (Standard 7) may be required to complete the business valuation assignment.

Standards Rule 9-4

(This Standards Rule contains specific requirements from which departure is permitted. See the *Departure Rule*)

In developing a business or intangible asset appraisal, an appraiser must collect and analyze all information pertinent to the appraisal problem, given the scope of work identified in accordance with Standards Rule 9-2(e).

(a) An appraiser must develop value opinion(s) and conclusion(s) by use of one or more approaches that apply to the specific appraisal assignment.

   Comment. This rule requires the appraiser to use all relevant approaches for which sufficient reliable data are available. However, it does not mean that the appraiser must use all approaches in order to comply with the rule if certain approaches are not applicable.

(b) Include in the analyses, when relevant, data regarding:
   (i)   the nature and history of the business;
   (ii) financial and economic conditions affecting the business enterprise, its industry, and general economy;
   (iii) past results, current operations, and future prospects of the business enterprise;
   (iv) past sales of capital stock or other ownership interests in the business enterprise being appraised;
   (v)   sales of similar businesses or capital stock of publicly held similar businesses;
   (vi) prices, terms, and conditions affecting past sales of similar business equity;
   (vii) economic benefit of intangible assets.

Comment. This rule directs the appraiser to study the prospective and retrospective aspects of the business enterprise and to study it in terms of the economic and industry environment within which it operates. Further, sales of securities of the business itself or similar businesses for which sufficient information is available should also be considered.

Standards Rule 9-5

(This Standards Rule contains binding requirements from which departure is not permitted)

In developing a business or intangible asset appraisal, an appraiser must reconcile the indications of value resulting from the various approaches to arrive at the value conclusion.

Comment. The appraiser must evaluate the relative reliability of the various indications of value. The appraiser must consider the quality and quantity of data leading to each of the indications of value. The value conclusion is the result of the appraiser's judgment and not necessarily the result of a mathematical process.

Advisory Opinion 18 (AO-18)

This communication by the Appraisal Standards Board (ASB) does not establish new standards or interpret existing standards. Advisory opinions are issued to illustrate the applicability of appraisal standards in specific situations and to offer advice from the ASB for the resolution of appraisal issues and problems. They do not constitute a legal opinion of the ASB.

Subject: Use of an Automated Valuation Model (AVM)

The Issue. What steps should an appraiser take when using an AVM as a tool in the development of appraisal, appraisal review, or consulting opinions and conclusions concerning an individual property?

In addition, what steps should an appraiser take when he or she is using an AVM only to process information and communicate the AVM's output but is not performing an appraisal, appraisal review, or consulting assignment?

Background. This advisory opinion addresses how an appraiser may use an AVM. An AVM is a computer software program that analyzes data using an automated process. For example, AVMs may use regression, adaptive estimation, neural network, expert reasoning, and artificial intelligence programs.

The output of an AVM is not, by itself, an appraisal. An AVM's output may become a basis for appraisal, appraisal review, or consulting opinions and conclusions if the appraiser believes the output to be credible and reliable for use in a specific assignment. An appraiser can use an AVM as a tool in the development of appraisal, appraisal review, or consulting opinions and conclusions. However, the appropriate use of an AVM is, like any tool, dependent upon the skill of the user and the tool's suitability to the task at hand.

This advisory opinion applies when an appraiser uses an AVM in connection with an individual property. This Advisory Opinion does not apply to mass appraising. An appraiser needs to know, before using an AVM, whether it is to be used to perform an appraisal, appraisal review, or consulting service, or solely to provide the client with AVM output.

When an appraiser uses an AVM to develop his or her own opinions or conclusions in an appraisal, appraisal review, or consulting assignment, all of the USPAP rules governing that assignment apply, and all of this advisory opinion is relevant.

An appraiser is not performing an appraisal, appraisal review, or consulting assignment when he or she simply runs an AVM by using information provided by the client and (1) does not alter the input or affect the output of the AVM, and (2) does not communicate his or her own appraisal, appraisal review, or consulting opinions or conclusions regarding the AVM's output.

If the appraiser uses an AVM only to provide the client with the AVM output, only the references to the *Conduct* section of the *Ethics Rule* and the "Communicating the AVM Output" section in this advisory opinion are relevant.

Advice from the ASB on the Issue

Relevant USPAP References

Conduct section of the *Ethics Rule.* "An appraiser must perform assignments ethically and accordance with these standards, and must not engage in criminal conduct. An appraiser must perform assignments with impartiality, objectivity, and independence, and without accommodation of personal interests." Further, "An appraiser must not communicate assignment results in a misleading or fraudulent manner. An appraiser must not use or communicate a misleading or fraudulent report or knowingly permit an employee or other person to communicate a misleading or fraudulent report."

Competency Rule. "Prior to accepting an assignment or entering into an agreement to perform any assignment, an appraiser must properly identify the problem to be addressed and have the knowledge and experience to complete the assignment competently."

Departure Rule. "An appraiser may enter into an agreement to perform an assignment in which the scope of work is less than, or different from, the work that would otherwise be required by the specific requirements. . . ."

Standards Rule l-l(a). An appraiser must "be aware of, understand, and correctly employ those recognized methods and techniques that are necessary to produce a credible appraisal."

Standards Rule l-l(b). An appraiser must "not commit a substantial error of omission or commission that significantly affects an appraisal."

Standards Rule l-l(c). An appraiser must "not render appraisal services in a careless or negligent manner such as by making a series of errors that, although individually might not significantly affect the results of an appraisal, in the aggregate affect the credibility of those results."

Standards Rule l-5(c). An appraiser must "reconcile the quality and quantity of data available and analyzed within the approaches used and the applicability or suitability of the approaches used."

Standard 2. "In reporting the results of a real property appraisal, an appraiser must communicate each analysis, opinion, and conclusion in a manner that is not misleading."

Standard 3. "In performing an appraisal review assignment involving a real property or personal property appraisal, an appraiser acting as a reviewer must develop and report a credible opinion as to the quality of another appraiser's work and must clearly disclose the scope of work performed in the assignment."

Statement on Appraisal Standards No. 7 (SMT-7), quoting from the Departure Rule. "The burden of proof is on the appraiser to decide before accepting an assignment and invoking this rule that the scope of work applied will result in opinions or conclusions that are credible."

Statement on Appraisal Standards No. 9 (SMT-9). "Although an appraiser bound by the *Uniform Standards of Professional Appraisal Practice* must identify and consider the client's intended use of the appraiser's reported appraisal, appraisal review, or consulting opinions and conclusions, an appraiser must not allow a client's intended use or the requirements of any user of the report to affect the appraiser's independence and objectivity in performing an assignment. An appraiser must not allow a client's objectives to cause the analysis or report to be biased."

Competency

When an appraiser is asked to use an AVM in an assignment, the appraiser must ensure that he or she can comply with the requirements of the *Competency Rule* both prior to accepting the assignment and in the course of performing it.

In an appraisal assignment, an appraiser must have a basic understanding of how the AVM works in order to reasonably determine the following:

1. Use of the AVM is appropriate for the assignment;
2. The output of the AVM is credible for use in the assignment; and
3. The AVM does not exclude relevant market measures or factual information necessary for a credible calculation.

A client may suggest or request the use of an AVM in an appraisal, appraisal review, or consulting assignment, but ultimately the appraiser is responsible for the decision to use or not use the AVM and its output. The appraiser must be able to reasonably conclude that the AVM's output is credible before deciding to use the AVM or rely on its output. For example, in an appraisal assignment, the credibility of the AVM output may be established by comparison to the subject market. If the appraiser concludes that using the AVM output in an assignment would be misleading, the appraiser should either use other tools to perform the analysis or decline the assignment.

If use of the AVM involves invoking departure, the *Departure Rule* requires the appraiser to advise the client of the appraisal's limitations, and to disclose those limitations in the report, provided the client has agreed that the limited service is appropriate.

Under What Conditions May AVMs Be Used?

There are five critical questions to which the appraiser should answer "yes" before deciding to use an AVM in an appraisal, appraisal review, or consulting assignment:

1. Does the appraiser have a basic understanding of how the AVM works?
2. Can the appraiser use the AVM properly?
3. Are the AVM and the data it uses appropriate given the intended use of assignment results?
4. Is the AVM output credible?
5. Is the AVM output sufficiently reliable for use in the assignment?

The answers to these questions may be affected by the degree to which the appraiser can interact with the AVM. The decision to use an AVM may also be affected by support information supplied by the AVM's developer, the appraiser's previous experience in using the AVM, or other available information.

Database

Credibility of the AVM output depends on the quality of its database and how well the AVM is designed to analyze that database. When using an AVM in an appraisal, appraisal review, or consulting assignment, the appraiser must have reason to believe the AVM appropriately uses data that are relevant.

Understanding and Control of the AVM

When using an AVM in an appraisal, appraisal review, or consulting assignment, an appraiser should have a basic understanding of how the AVM analyzes data to determine whether the AVM measures and reflects market activity for the subject property. The appraiser does not need to know, or be able to explain, the AVM's algorithm intricacies of its statistical or mathematical formulae. However the appraiser should be able to describe the AVM overall process and verify that the AVM is consistent in producing results that accurately reflect prevailing market behavior for the subject property.

AVMs differ in the number and type of data characteristics as well as the volume of data analyzed. The appraiser should know which characteristics (e.g., size, location, quality) are analyzed and how the analysis is tested for accuracy and reasonableness. The appraiser should ascertain that the characteristics analyzed are those to which the market responds.

Some AVMs allow the appraiser to select the data analyzed, on the basis of, for example, distance from subject, size, or age of the improvements. An appraiser's ability to change the AVM's selection parameters may affect the appraiser's decision to use or rely on the AVM output.

The appraiser should be aware that the AVM may not perform consistently given the same input criteria. The appraiser should be confident of the AVM's credibility when applied to a specific property. The appraiser decides whether to rely on the AVM output, regardless of the AVM's overall test performance. In some cases, the appraiser may accept the AVM's output, while in other cases that same AVM's output would not be acceptable.

Communicating the AVM Output

An appraiser must ensure that his or her communication of an AVM's output is not misleading.

An AVM's output is not, by itself, an appraisal, and communication of an AVM's output is not, in itself, an appraisal report. When an AVM is used in an appraisal, appraisal review, or consulting assignment, information furnished about an AVM in the appraiser's report must satisfy the reporting requirements applicable to the type of report provided (e.g., in the case of a real property appraisal, a Self-Contained, Summary, or Restricted Use Appraisal Report). The appraiser should cite the name and version of the AVM software and provide a brief description of its methods, assumptions, and level of allowed user intervention. The report should, to the extent possible, identify the database (e.g., Multiple Listing Services) and the data analyzed.

An appraiser bound by USPAP may be asked to run an AVM and communicate its output without performing an appraisal, appraisal review, or consulting assignment. For example, an appraiser may be asked to simply enter property characteristics provided by the client, but not alter the input or affect the AVM's output. In this specific instance, the appraiser is not acting in the capacity of an appraiser but rather is functioning only as an AVM operator. In such a situation, an appraiser must carefully avoid any action that could be considered misleading or fraudulent in that communication. The appraiser should take steps to ensure that communication of the AVM's output is not misconstrued as an appraisal, appraisal review, or consulting report. For example, the appraiser should:

1. not communicate his or her opinions or conclusions as an appraiser regarding the credibility or reliability of the AVM's output;
2. not provide an appraiser's certification or statement of limiting conditions in connection with the AVM's output; and

3. ensure that his or her role as only an AVM operator is clearly indicated if his or her signature or other identification marks appear on document(s) used to communicate the AVM's output.

Analyzing an AVM's Effectiveness

An appraiser may be asked to analyze and comment on the effectiveness of an AVM for a stated intended use. This is a consulting assignment under USPAP. In order to accept such an assignment, an appraiser bound by USPAP must ensure compliance with the *Competency Rule* and Standards 4 and 5. To meet the *Competency Rule*, at a minimum, the appraiser should also have a basic understanding of how the AVM works.

Review of the Output of an AVM

An appraiser may be asked if the output of an AVM is reliable for a specific property, given the purpose and intended use of the AVM's output. Making this determination is a consulting assignment under USPAP. The appraiser must ensure compliance with the *Competency Rule* and Standards 4 and 5.

Review of an Appraisal Report Containing Output of an AVM

An appraiser may be asked to review an appraisal report that includes an opinion of value based on the output of an AVM. This kind of appraisal review assignment may be accepted if the appraiser performing the review (1) understands how the AVM works and (2) can form an opinion as to the adequacy and relevancy of the data and the appropriateness of the analysis, based on the information provided in the report under review.

Use of an AVM in an Appraisal Review Assignment

An AVM may be used in the process of reviewing a real property appraisal report. The appraisal reviewer may use the AVM to test the reasonableness of the value conclusion in the report under review if the appraisal reviewer (1) has a basic understanding of how the AVM works, (2) can use the AVM properly, (3) determines that use of the AVM is appropriate for the appraisal review assignment, and (4) believes the AVM output is credible and sufficiently reliable for the appraisal review assignment.

Illustrations

1A. Staff Appraiser D, who has access to market databases, is asked to use an AVM to process information. When Appraiser D runs the AVM, she has done no other appraisal research. Appraiser D does not apply any of her appraisal knowledge or judgment in operating the AVM. Appraiser D has entered only property characteristics provided by the client and does not know how the AVM analyzes the data. Is the AVM output an appraisal?

No. The AVM output by itself is not an appraisal. Appraiser D did not apply her appraisal knowledge, judgment, or expertise, nor did she represent that the output was her own opinion of value.

Appraiser D must be very careful in communicating the AVM output to ensure that there is no misunderstanding as to her role in operating the AVM or communicating its output. For example, Appraiser D should (1) not communicate her opinions or conclusions as an appraiser regarding the credibility or reliability of the AVM's output; (2) not provide an appraiser's certification or statement of limiting conditions in connection with the AVM's output; and (3) ensure that her role as only an AVM operator is clearly indicated if her signature or other identification mark appears on documents used to communicate the AVM's output.

1B. Staff Appraiser D receives AVM output from a co-worker who is not an appraiser. Appraiser D is requested to determine if the AVM output is reliable, given the intended use. What can Appraiser D do?

Appraiser D should not express an opinion regarding value. Appraiser D can indicate if the AVM output is reliable. However, this service is a consulting assignment because it considers the quality of the output relative to the client's intended use. Appraiser D must, therefore, ensure compliance with the Competency Rule and Standards 4 and 5.

1C. After staff Appraiser D has received the AVM output, can she incorporate the information into the appraisal process?

Yes. However, Appraiser D must be able to understand how the AVM works and determine that the information analyzed is credible and reliable.

2. Appraiser V provides residential appraisals to Client A, whose intended use is to document security for equity lines of credit. Appraiser V has determined that Orange Box AVM is sufficiently reliable to use as a tool in these appraisals. Orange Box AVM was recently used by Appraiser V on a house in a suburban single-family residential subdivision.

Client B requests Appraiser V to use Orange Box AVM, alone, for a relocation appraisal assignment on an identical house in the same subdivision. Can Appraiser V use Orange Box AVM alone, in this relocation appraisal assignment?

Not without further investigation, because assumptions made by Appraiser V in qualifying the AVM itself and the AVM output for Client A's needs may not be appropriate for Client B's needs.

Client A's intended use of the appraisal is to document security for an equity line of credit. Typically, Client A's lending decision is based primarily on the homeowner's capacity to pay the debt and only secondarily on the value of the house. The reliability expectation of the value opinion needed by Client A is relatively low.

The intended use of the relocation appraisal for Client B is to develop an opinion of a sale price of the house under very specific conditions. Typically, the reliability expectation of the opinion needed by Client B is relatively high because his or her intended use involves a near-term transfer of the house, with immediate financial implications. Appraiser V must determine if Orange Box AVM's output is sufficiently reliable to meet Client B's expectations.

3A. Appraiser A developed a regression analysis model that suggests a relationship between the size of residence and the price per square foot of similar residences in a specific market. This relationship has been confirmed by market behavior, and the database used is believed to be reliable. Can the appraiser use the regression analysis model in other appraisal assignments of similar properties in the same market?

Yes, because the appraiser knows how the regression analysis model works, has independently tested the conclusions it provides, and believes the database is reliable. However the appraiser must consider whether the AVM output is credible and reliable for each assignment on a case-by-case basis.

3B. Appraiser A's friend, Appraiser B, works in a different market area. Appraiser B is impressed with Appraiser A's model and wants to use the model in Appraiser B's market area. Can Appraiser B use Appraiser A's model?

Yes, if Appraiser B understands how Appraiser A's model works and verifies by independent testing that the model produces reliable results in Appraiser B's market area and that the database used by Appraiser B reflects behavior in Appraiser B's market area. However, the appraiser must consider whether the AVM output is credible and reliable for each assignment on a case-by-case basis.

4A. A client of Appraiser A requests that Appraiser A use Blue Box AVM. The client says, "Since we are only doing residential appraisals you can skip the cost and income approach. To lower the cost of the appraisal just use the Blue Box AVM results as the basis for your value conclusion." The client also says, "Blue AVM makes 13 adjustments, and that is all that the appraiser needs to be concerned with." The Blue AVM developer feels that appraisers cannot understand this new technology and that appraisers do not need to know how the 13 adjustments are made. What should Appraiser A do?

Appraiser A should learn how the Blue Box AVM works; determine if he can use the AVM properly; given the intended use, determine if the output of Blue Box AVM is credible and sufficiently reliable for use in the assignment; and review the Departure Rule to determine whether not performing the cost and income approaches would result in a Limited Appraisal assignment.

If Appraiser A cannot understand how the Blue Box AVM works or concludes that the results are unreliable, given the intended use, Appraiser A should discuss the issue with the client. This discussion may result in a modified assignment or in the appraiser's declining the assignment.

4B. Another client requests that Appraiser A consider Green Box AVM. The client indicates that Appraiser A can modify 6 of the 13 items analyzed in Green Box AVM, such as the distance within which the comparables are selected and the size range (square footage) of the comparables. The developer of Green Box AVM will also describe how the AVM works and provide the results of test data, which indicate that the model is reliable. What should Appraiser A do?

Appraiser A needs to follow the same steps as indicated in 4A.

5. Appraiser C's client has licensed the Red Box AVM. The client requests that Appraiser C use the Red Box AVM as a tool in a consulting assignment. The client knows that Appraiser C has a reliable internal residential database. The client also knows that Appraiser C has tested Red Box AVM and has found it to be reliable. Further, the software developer of Red Box AVM has given Appraiser C information about how Red Box AVM works and test data showing its results. Can Appraiser C apply the Red Box AVM in the consulting assignment?

Yes, if the Red Box AVM is used for that part of the process for which it has been determined to be credible and reliable. However, the appraiser must consider whether the AVM output is credible and reliable for each assignment.

This advisory opinion is based on presumed conditions without investigation or verification of actual circumstances. There is no assurance that this advisory opinion represents the only possible solution to the problems discussed or that it applies equally to seemingly similar situations.

Approved July 9, 1997
Revised September 16, 1998

American Arbitration Association Commercial Arbitration Rules*

INTRODUCTION

Each year, many millions of business transactions take place. Occasionally, disagreements develop over these business transactions. Many of these disputes are resolved by arbitration, the voluntary submission of a dispute to a disinterested person or persons for final and binding determination. Arbitration has proven to be an effective way to resolve these disputes privately, promptly, and economically.

The American Arbitration Association (AAA) is a public-service, not-for-profit organization offering a broad range of dispute-resolution services to business executives, attorneys, individuals, trade associations, unions, management, consumers, families, communities, and all levels of government. Services are available through AAA headquarters in New York City and through offices located in major cities throughout the United States. Hearings may be held at locations convenient for the parties and are not limited to cities with AAA offices. In addition, the AAA serves as a center for education and training, issues specialized publications, and conducts research on all forms of out-of-court dispute settlement.

The parties can provide for arbitration of future disputes by inserting the following standard arbitration clause into their contracts.

---

*As Amended and Effective on November 1, 1993.

Any controversy or claim arising out of or relating to this contract, or the breach thereof, shall be settled by arbitration administered by the American Arbitration Association under its Commercial Arbitration Rules, and judgment on the award rendered by the arbitrator(s) may be entered in any court having jurisdiction thereof.

Arbitration of existing disputes may be accomplished by use of the following.

We, the undersigned parties, hereby agree to submit to arbitration administered by the American Arbitration Association under its Commercial Arbitration Rules the following controversy: (cite briefly). We further agree that the above controversy be submitted to (one) (three) arbitrators). We further agree that we will faithfully observe this agreement and the rules, that we will abide by and perform any award rendered by the arbitrators), and that a judgment of the court having jurisdiction may be entered on the award.

The services of the AAA are generally concluded with the transmittal of the award. Although there is voluntary compliance with the majority of awards, judgment on the award can be entered in a court having appropriate jurisdiction if necessary.

ADMINISTRATIVE FEES

The AAA's administrative fees are based on service charges. There is a filing fee based on the amount of the claim or counterclaim, ranging from $500 on claims below $10,000 to a maximum of $5,000 for claims in excess of $1 million. In addition, there are service charges for hearings held and postponements and a processing fee for prolonged cases. This fee information allows the parties to exercise control over their administrative fees. The fees cover AAA administrative services; they do not cover arbitrator compensation or expenses, if any, reporting services, or any postaward charges incurred by the parties in enforcing the award.

MEDIATION

The parties might wish to submit their dispute to mediation prior to arbitration. In mediation, the neutral mediator assists the parties in reaching a settlement but does not have the authority to make a binding decision or award. Mediation is administered by the AAA in accordance with its Commercial Mediation Rules. There is no additional administrative fee where parties to a pending arbitration attempt to mediate their dispute under the AAA's auspices.

If the parties want to adopt mediation as a part of their contractual dispute settlement procedure, they can insert the following mediation clause into their contract in conjunction with a standard arbitration provision.

> If a dispute arises out of or relates to this contract, or the breach thereof, and if the dispute cannot be settled through negotiation, the parties agree first to try in good faith to settle the dispute by mediation administered by the American Arbitration Association under its Commercial Mediation Rules before resorting to arbitration, litigation, or some other dispute resolution procedure.

If the parties want to use a mediator to resolve an existing dispute, they can enter into the following submission.

> The parties hereby submit the following dispute to mediation administered by the American Arbitration Association under its Commercial Mediation Rules. (The clause may also provide for the qualifications of the mediator(s), method of payment, locale of meetings, and any other item of concern to the parties.)

COMMERCIAL ARBITRATION RULES

1.   Agreement of Parties

The parties shall be deemed to have made these rules a part of their arbitration agreement whenever they have provided for arbitration by the American Arbitration Association (hereinafter AAA) or under its Commercial Arbitration Rules. These rules and any amendment of them shall apply in the form obtaining at the time the demand for arbitration or submission agreement is received by the AAA. The parties, by written agreement, may vary the procedures set forth in these rules.

2.   Name of Tribunal

Any tribunal constituted by the parties for the settlement of their dispute under these rules shall be called the Commercial Arbitration Tribunal.

3.   Administrator and Delegation of Duties

When parties agree to arbitrate under these rules, or when they provide for arbitration by the AAA and an arbitration is initiated under these rules, they thereby authorize the AAA to administer the arbitration. The authority and duties of the AAA are prescribed in the agreement of the parties and in these rules, and may be carried out through such of the AAA's representatives as it may direct.

4.   National Panel of Arbitrators

The AAA shall establish and maintain a National Panel of Commercial Arbitrators and shall appoint arbitrators as provided in these rules.

5.   Regional Offices

The AAA may, in its discretion, assign the administration of an arbitration to any of its regional offices.

6.   Initiation under an Arbitration Provision in a Contract

Arbitration under an arbitration provision in a contract shall be initiated in the following manner:

(a) The initiating party (hereinafter claimant) shall, within the time period, if any, specified in the contract(s), give written notice to the other party (hereinafter respondent) of its intention to arbitrate (demand), which notice shall contain a statement setting forth the nature of the dispute, the amount involved, if any, the remedy sought, and the hearing locale requested, and

(b) shall file at any regional office of the AAA three copies of the notice and three copies of the arbitration provisions of the contract, together with the appropriate filing.

The AAA shall give notice of such filing to the respondent or respondents. A respondent may file an answering statement in duplicate with the AAA within 10 days after notice from the AAA, in which event the respondent shall at the same time send a copy of the answering statement to the claimant. If a counterclaim is asserted, it shall contain a statement setting forth the nature of the counterclaim, the amount involved, if any, and the remedy sought. If a counterclaim is made, the appropriate fee shall be forwarded to the AAA with the answering statement. If no answering statement is filed within the stated time, it will be treated as a denial of the claim. Failure to file an answering statement shall not operate to delay the arbitration.

7.   Initiation under a Submission

Parties to any existing dispute may commence an arbitration under these rules by filing at any regional office of the AAA three copies of a written submission to arbitrate under these rules, signed by the parties. It shall contain a statement of the matter in dispute, the amount involved, if any, the remedy sought, and the hearing locale requested, together with the appropriate filing.

8.   Changes of Claim

After filing of a claim, if either party desires to make any new or different claim or counterclaim, it shall be made in writing and filed with the AAA, and a copy shall be mailed to the other party, who shall have a period of 10 days from the date of such mailing within which to file an answer with the AAA. After the arbitrator is appointed, however, no new or different claim may be submitted except with the arbitrator's consent.

9.   Applicable Procedures

Unless the AAA in its discretion determines otherwise, the Expedited Procedures shall be applied in any case where no disclosed claim or counterclaim exceeds $50,000, exclusive of interest and arbitration costs. Parties may also agree to using the Expedited Procedures in cases involving claims in excess of $50,000. The Expedited Procedures shall be applied as described in Sections 53 through 57 of these rules, in addition to any other portion of these rules that is not in conflict with the Expedited Procedures.

All other cases shall be administered in accordance with Sections 1 through 52 of these rules.

10.   Administrative Conference, Preliminary Hearing, and Mediation Conference

At the request of any party or at the discretion of the AAA, an administrative conference with the AAA and the parties and/or their representatives will be scheduled in appropriate cases to expedite the arbitration proceedings. There is no administrative fee for this service.

In large or complex cases, at the request of any party or at the discretion of the arbitrator or the AAA, a preliminary hearing with the parties and/or their representatives and the arbitrator may be scheduled by the arbitrator to specify the issues to be resolved, to stipulate to uncontested facts, and to consider any other matters that will expedite the arbitration proceedings. Consistent with the expedited nature of arbitration, the arbitrator may, at the preliminary hearing, establish (i) the extent of and schedule for the production of relevant documents and other information, (ii) the identification of any witnesses to be called, and (iii) a schedule for further hearings to resolve the dispute. There is no administrative fee for the first preliminary hearing.

With the consent of the parties, the AAA at any stage of the proceeding may arrange a mediation conference under the Commercial Mediation Rules, in order to facilitate settlement. The mediator shall not be an arbitrator appointed to the case. Where the parties to a pending arbitration agree to mediate under the AAA's rules, no additional administrative fee is required to initiate the mediation.

11. Fixing of Locale

The parties may mutually agree on the locale where the arbitration is to be held. If any party requests that the hearing be held in a specific locale and the other party files no objection thereto within ten days after notice of the request has been sent to it by the AAA, the locale shall be the one requested. If a party objects to the locale requested by the other party, the AAA shall have the power to determine the locale and its decision shall be final and binding.

12. Qualifications of an Arbitrator

Any neutral arbitrator appointed pursuant to Section 13, 14, 15, or 54, or selected by mutual choice of the parties or their appointees, shall be subject to disqualification for the reasons specified in Section 19. If the parties specifically so agree in writing, the arbitrator shall not be subject to disqualification for those reasons.

Unless the parties agree otherwise, an arbitrator selected unilaterally by one party is a party-appointed arbitrator and is not subject to disqualification pursuant to Section 19.

The term *arbitrator* in these rules refers to the arbitration panel, whether composed of one or more arbitrators and whether the arbitrators are neutral or party appointed.

13. Appointment from Panel

If the parties have not appointed an arbitrator and have not provided any other method of appointment, the arbitrator shall be appointed in the following manner: immediately after the filing of the demand or submission, the AAA shall send simultaneously to each party to the dispute an identical list of names of persons chosen from the panel.

Each party to the dispute shall have ten days from the transmittal date in which to strike names objected to, number the remaining names in order of preference, and return the list to the AAA. In a single-arbitrator case, each party may strike three names on a peremptory basis. In a multiarbitrator case, each party may strike five names on a peremptory basis. If a party does not return the list within the time specified, all persons named therein shall be deemed acceptable. From among the persons who have been approved on both lists, and in accordance with the designated order of mutual preference, the AAA shall invite the acceptance of an arbitrator to serve. If the parties fail to agree on any of the persons named, or if acceptable arbitrators are unable to act, or if for any other reason the appointment cannot be made from the submitted lists, the AAA shall have the power to make the appointment from among other members of the panel without the submission of additional lists.

14. Direct Appointment by a Party

If the agreement of the parties names an arbitrator or specifies a method of appointing an arbitrator, that designation or method shall be followed. The notice of appointment, with the name and address of the arbitrator, shall be filed with the AAA by the appointing party. Upon the request of any appointing party, the AAA shall submit a list of members of the panel from which the party may, if it so desires, make the appointment.

If the agreement specifies a period of time within which an arbitrator shall be appointed and any party fails to make the appointment within that period, the AAA shall make the appointment.

If no period of time is specified in the agreement, the AAA shall notify the party to make the appointment. If within 10 days thereafter an arbitrator has not been appointed by a party, the AAA shall make the appointment.

15. Appointment of Neutral Arbitrator by Party-Appointed Arbitrators or Parties

If the parties have selected party-appointed arbitrators, or if such arbitrators have been appointed as provided in Section 14, and the parties have authorized them to appoint a neutral arbitrator within a specified time and no appointment is made within that time or any agreed extension, the AAA may appoint a neutral arbitrator, who shall act as chairperson.

If no period of time is specified for appointment of the neutral arbitrator and the party-appointed arbitrators or the parties do not make the appointment within 10 days from the date of the appointment of the last party-appointed arbitrator, the AAA may appoint the neutral arbitrator, who shall act as chairperson.

If the parties have agreed that their party-appointed arbitrators shall appoint the neutral arbitrator from the panel, the AAA shall furnish the party-appointed arbitrators, in the manner provided in Section 13, a list selected from the panel, and the appointment of the neutral arbitrator shall be made as provided in that section.

16. Nationality of Arbitrator in International Arbitration

Where the parties are nationals or residents of different countries, any neutral arbitrator shall, upon the request of either party, be appointed from among the nationals of a country other than that of any of the parties. The request must be made prior to the time set for the appointment of the arbitrator as agreed by the parties or set by these rules.

17. Number of Arbitrators

If the arbitration agreement does not specify the number of arbitrators, the dispute shall be heard and determined by one arbitrator, unless the AAA, in its discretion, directs that a greater number of arbitrators be appointed.

18. Notice to Arbitrator of Appointment

Notice of the appointment of the neutral arbitrator, whether appointed mutually by the parties or by the AAA, shall be sent to the
arbitrator by the AAA, together with a copy of these rules, and the
signed acceptance of the arbitrator shall be filed with the AAA prior
to the opening of the first hearing.

19. Disclosure and Challenge Procedure

Any person appointed as neutral arbitrator shall disclose to the AAA
any circumstance likely to affect impartiality, including any bias or
any financial or personal interest in the result of the arbitration or
any past or present relationship with the parties or their representatives. Upon receipt of such information from the arbitrator or another source, the AAA shall communicate the information to the
parties and, if it deems it appropriate to do so, to the arbitrator and
others. Upon objection of a party to the continued service of a neutral arbitrator, the AAA shall determine whether the arbitrator should
be disqualified and shall inform the parties of its decision, which shall
be conclusive.

20. Vacancies

If for any reason an arbitrator is unable to perform the duties of the
office, the AAA may, on proof satisfactory to it, declare the office
vacant. Vacancies shall be filled in accordance with the applicable
provisions of these rules.

 In the event of a vacancy in a panel of neutral arbitrators after
the hearings have commenced, the remaining arbitrator or arbitrators may continue with the hearing and determination of the controversy, unless the parties agree otherwise.

21. Date, Time, and Place of Hearing

The arbitrator shall set the date, time, and place for each hearing.
The AAA shall send a notice of hearing to the parties at least 10 days

in advance of the hearing date, unless otherwise agreed by the parties.

22. Representation

Any party may be represented by counsel or other authorized representative. A party intending to be so represented shall notify the other party and the AAA of the name and address of the representative at least three days prior to the date set for the hearing at which that person is first to appear. When such a representative initiates an arbitration or responds for a party, notice is deemed to have been given.

23. Stenographic Record

Any party desiring a stenographic record shall make arrangements directly with a stenographer and shall notify the other parties of these arrangements in advance of the hearing. The requesting party or parties shall pay the cost of the record. If the transcript is agreed by the parties to be, or determined by the arbitrator to be, the official record of the proceeding, it must be made available to the arbitrator and to the other parties for inspection, at a date, time, and place determined by the arbitrator.

24. Interpreters

Any party wishing an interpreter shall make all arrangements directly with the interpreter and shall assume the costs of the service.

25. Attendance at Hearings

The arbitrator shall maintain the privacy of the hearings unless the law provides to the contrary. Any person having a direct interest in the arbitration is entitled to attend hearings. The arbitrator shall otherwise have the power to require the exclusion of any witness, other than a party or other essential person, during the testimony of any other witness. It shall be discretionary with the arbitrator to determine the propriety of the attendance of any other person.

26. Postponements

The arbitrator for good cause shown may postpone any hearing upon the request of a party or upon the arbitrator's own initiative, and shall also grant such postponement when all of the parties agree.

27. Oaths

Before proceeding with the first hearing, each arbitrator may take an oath of office and, if required by law, shall do so. The arbitrator mat require witnesses to testify under oath administered by any duly qualified person and, if it is required by law or requested by any party, shall do so.

28. Majority Decision

All decisions of the arbitrators must be by a majority. The award must also be made by a majority unless the concurrence of all is expressly required by the arbitration agreement or by law.

29. Order of Proceedings and Communication with Arbitrator

A hearing shall be opened by the filing of the oath of the arbitrator, where required; by the recording of the date, time, and place of the hearing, and the presence of the arbitrator, the parties, and their representatives, if any; and by the receipt by the arbitrator of the statement of the claim and the answering statement, if any.

   The arbitrator may, at the beginning of the hearing, ask for statements clarifying the issues involved. In some cases, part or all of the above will have been accomplished at the preliminary hearing conducted by the arbitrator pursuant to Section 10.

The complaining party shall then present evidence to support its claim. The defending party shall then present evidence supporting its defense. Witnesses for each party shall submit to questions or other examination. The arbitrator has the discretion to vary this procedure but shall afford a full and equal opportunity to all parties for the presentation of any material and relevant evidence.

Exhibits, when offered by either party, may be received in evidence by the arbitrator.

The names and addresses of all witnesses and a description of the exhibits in the order received shall be made a part of the record.

There shall be no direct communication between the parties and a neutral arbitrator other than at oral hearing, unless the parties and the arbitrator agree otherwise. Any other oral or written communication from the parties to the neutral arbitrator shall be directed to the AAA for transmittal to the arbitrator.

30. Arbitration in the Absence of a Party or Representative

Unless the law provides to the contrary, the arbitration may proceed in the absence of any party or representative who, after due notice, fails to be present or fails to obtain a postponement. An award shall not be made solely on the default of a party. The arbitrator shall require the party who is present to submit such evidence as the arbitrator may require for the making of an award.

31. Evidence

The parties may offer such evidence as is relevant and material to the dispute and shall produce such evidence as the arbitrator may deem necessary to an understanding and determination of the dispute. An arbitrator or other person authorized by law to subpoena witnesses or documents may do so upon the request of any party or independently.

The arbitrator shall be the judge of the relevance and materiality of the evidence offered, and conformity to legal rules of evidence shall not be necessary. All evidence shall be taken in the presence of all of the arbitrators and all of the parties, except where any of the parties is absent in default or has waived the right to be present.

32. Evidence by Affidavit and Posthearing Filing of Documents or Other Evidence

The arbitrator may receive and consider the evidence of witnesses by affidavit, but shall give it only such weight as the arbitrator deems it entitled to after consideration of any objection made to its admission.

If the parties agree or the arbitrator directs that documents or other evidence be submitted to the arbitrator after the hearing, the documents or other evidence shall be filed with the AAA for transmission to the arbitrator. All parties shall be afforded an opportunity to examine such documents or other evidence.

33. Inspection or Investigation

An arbitrator finding it necessary to make an inspection or investigation in connection with the arbitration shall direct the AAA to so advise the parties. The arbitrator shall set the date and time and the AAA shall notify the parties. Any party who so desires may be present at such an inspection or investigation. In the event that one or all parties are not present at the inspection or investigation, the arbitrator shall make a verbal or written report to the parties and afford them an opportunity to comment.

34. Interim Measures

The arbitrator may issue such orders for interim relief as may be deemed necessary to safeguard the property that is the subject matter of the arbitration, without prejudice to the rights of the parties or to the final determination of the dispute.

35. Closing of Hearing

The arbitrator shall specifically inquire of all parties whether they have any further proofs to offer or witnesses to be heard. Upon receiving negative replies or if satisfied that the record is complete, the arbitrator shall declare the hearing closed.

If briefs are to be filed, the hearing shall be declared closed as of the final date set by the arbitrator for the receipt of briefs. If documents are to be filed as provided in Section 32 and the date set for their receipt is later than that set for the receipt of briefs, the later date shall be the date of closing the hearing. The time limit within which the arbitrator is required to make the award shall commence to run, in the absence of other agreements by the parties, upon the closing of the hearing.

36. Reopening of Hearing

The hearing may be reopened on the arbitrator's initiative, or upon application of a party, at any time before the award is made. If reopening the hearing would prevent the making of the award within the specific time agreed on by the parties in the contract(s) out of which the controversy has arisen, the matter may not be reopened unless the parties agree on an extension of time. When no specific date is fixed in the contract, the arbitrator may reopen the hearing and shall have 30 days from the closing of the reopened hearing within which to make an award.

37. Waiver of Oral Hearing

The parties may provide, by written agreement, for the waiver of oral hearings in any case. It the parties are unable to agree as to the procedure, the AAA shall specify a fair and equitable procedure.

38. Waiver of Rules

Any party who proceeds with the arbitration after knowledge that any provision or requirement of these rules has not complied with and who fails to state an objection in writing shall be deemed to have waived the right to object.

39. Extensions of Time

The parties may modify any period of time by mutual agreement. The AAA or the arbitrator may for good cause extend any period of time established by these rules, except the time for making the award. The AAA shall notify the parties of any extension.

40. Serving of Notice

Each party shall be deemed to have consented that any papers, notices, or process necessary or proper for the initiation or continuation of an arbitration under these rules; for any court action in connection therewith; or for the entry of judgment on any award made under these rules may be served on a party by mail addressed to the party or its representative at the last known address or by personal service, in or outside the state where the arbitration is to be held, provided that reasonable opportunity to be heard with regard thereto has been granted to the party.

    The AAA and the parties may also use facsimile transmission, telex, telegram, or other written forms of electronic communication to give the notices required by these rules.

41. Time of Award

The award shall be made promptly by the arbitrator and, unless otherwise agreed by the parties or specified by law, no later than 30 days from the date of closing the hearing, or, if oral hearings have been waived, from the date of the AAA's transmittal of the final statements and proofs to the arbitrator.

42. Form of Award

The award shall be in writing and shall be signed by a majority of the arbitrators. It shall be executed in the manner required by law.

43. Scope of Award

The arbitrator may grant any remedy or relief that the arbitrator deems just and equitable and within the scope of the agreement of the parties, including, but not limited to, specific performance of a contract. The arbitrator shall, in the award, assess arbitration fees, expenses, and compensation as provided in Sections 48, 49, and 50 in favor of any party and, in the event that any administrative fees or expenses are due the AAA, in favor of the AAA.

44. Award upon Settlement

If the parties settle their dispute during the course of the arbitration, the arbitrator may set forth the terms of the agreed settlement in an award. Such an award is referred to as a consent award.

45. Delivery of Award to Parties

Parties shall accept as legal delivery of the award the placing of the award or a true copy thereof in the mail addressed to a party or its representative at the last known address, personal service of the award, or the filing of the award in any other manner that is permitted by law.

46. Release of Documents for Judicial Proceedings

The AAA shall, upon the written request of a party, furnish to the party, at its expense, certified copies of any papers in the AAA's possession that may be required in judicial proceedings relating to the arbitration.

47. Applications to Court and Exclusion of Liability

(a) No judicial proceeding by a party relating to the subject matter of the arbitration shall be deemed a waiver of the party's right to arbitrate.
(b) Neither the AAA nor any arbitrator in a proceeding under these rules is a necessary party in judicial proceedings relating to the arbitration.

(c) Parties to these rules shall be deemed to have consented that judgment upon the arbitration award may be entered in any federal or state court having jurisdiction thereof.

(d) Neither the AAA nor any arbitrator shall be liable to any party for any act or omission in connection with any arbitration conducted under these rules.

48. Administrative Fees

As a not-for-profit organization, the AAA shall prescribe filing and other administrative fees and service charges to compensate it for the cost of providing administrative services. The fees in effect when the fee or charge is incurred shall be applicable.

The filing fee shall be advanced by the initiating party or parties, subject to final apportionment by the arbitrator in the award.

The AAA may, in the event of extreme hardship on the part of any party, defer or reduce the administrative fees.

49. Expenses

The expenses of witnesses for either side shall be paid by the party producing such witnesses. All other expenses of the arbitration, including required travel and other expenses of the arbitrator, AAA representatives, and any witness and the cost of any proof produced at the direct request of the arbitrator, shall be borne equally by the parties, unless they agree otherwise or unless the arbitrator in the award assesses such expenses or any part thereof against any specified party or parties.

50. Neutral Arbitrator's Compensation

Unless the parties agree otherwise, members of the National Panel of Commercial Arbitrators appointed as neutrals will serve without compensation for the first day of service.

Thereafter, compensation shall be based on the amount of service involved and the number of hearings. An appropriate daily rate and other arrangements will be discussed by the administrator with the parties and the arbitrator. If the parties fail to agree to the terms of compensation, an appropriate rate shall be established by the AAA and communicated in writing to the parties.

Any arrangement for the compensation of a neutral arbitrator shall be made through the AAA and not directly between the parties and the arbitrator.

51. Deposits

The AAA may require the parties to deposit in advance of any hearings such sums of money as it deems necessary to cover the expense of the arbitration, including the arbitrator's fee, if any, and shall render an accounting to the parties and return any unexpended balance at the conclusion of the case.

52. Interpretation and Application of Rules

The arbitrator shall interpret and apply these rules insofar as they relate to the arbitrator's powers and duties. When there is more than one arbitrator and a difference arises among them concerning the meaning or application of these rules, it shall be decided by a majority vote. If that is not possible, either an arbitrator or a party may refer the question to the AAA for final decision. All other rules shall be interpreted and applied by the AAA.

Expedited Procedures

53. Notice by Telephone

The parties shall accept all notices from the AAA by telephone. Such notices by the AAA shall subsequently be confirmed in writing to the parties. Should there be a failure to confirm in writing any notice hereunder, the proceeding shall nonetheless be valid if notice has, in fact, been given by telephone.

54. Appointment and Qualifications or Arbitrator

(a) Where no disclosed claim or counterclaim exceeds $50,000, exclusive of interest and arbitration costs, the AAA shall appoint a single arbitrator, from the National Panel of Commercial Arbitrators, without submission of lists of proposed arbitrators.

(b) Where all parties request that a list of proposed arbitrators be sent, the AAA upon payment of the service charge as provided in the Administrative Fees shall submit simultaneously to each party an identical list of five proposed arbitrators, drawn from the National Panel of Commercial Arbitrators, from which one arbitrator shall be appointed. Each party may strike two names from the list on a peremptory basis. The list is returnable to the AAA within seven days from the date of the AAA's mailing to the parties.

   If for any reason the appointment of an arbitrator cannot be made from the list, the AAA may make the appointment from among other members of the panel without the submission of additional lists.

(c) The parties will be given notice by telephone by the AAA appointment of the arbitrator, who shall be subject to disqualification for the reasons specified in Section 19. The parties shall notify the AAA, by telephone, within seven days of any objection to the arbitrator appointed. Any objection by a party to the arbitrator shall be confirmed in writing to the AAA with a copy to the other party or parties.

55. Date, Time, and Place of Hearing

The arbitrator shall set the date, time, and place of the hearing. The AAA will notify the parties by telephone, at least seven days in advance of the hearing date. A formal notice of hearing will also be sent by the AAA to the parties.

56. The Hearing

Generally, the hearing shall be completed within one day, unless the dispute is resolved by submission of documents under Section 37.

The arbitrator, for good cause shown, may schedule an additional hearing to be held within seven days.

57. Time of Award

Unless otherwise agreed by the parties, the award shall be rendered not later than 14 days from the date of the closing of the hearing.

Administrative Fees

The AAA's administrative charges are based on filing and service fees. Arbitrator compensation, if any, is not included in the schedule. Unless the parties agree otherwise, arbitrator compensation and administrative fees are subject to allocation by the arbitrator in the award.

Filing Fees

A nonrefundable filing fee is payable in full by a filing party when a claim, counterclaim or additional claim is filed, as provided below.

Amount of Claim	Filing Fee
Up to $10,000	$500
Above $10,000 to $50,000	$750
Above $50,000 to $250,000	$1,500
Above $250,000 to $500,000	$3,000
Above $500,000 to $1,000,000	$4,000
Above $1 million	$5,000

When no amount can be stated at the time of filing, the minimum filing fee is $1,500, subject to increase when the claim or counterclaim is disclosed.

When a claim or counterclaim is not for a monetary amount, an appropriate filing fee will be determined by the AAA.

The minimum filing fee for any case having three or more arbitrators is $1,500.

Expedited Procedures, outlined in sections 53-57 of the rules, are applied in any case where no disclosed claim or counterclaim exceeds $50,000, exclusive of interest and arbitration costs. Under those procedures, arbitrators are directly appointed by the AAA. Where the parties request a list of proposed arbitrators under those procedures, a service charge of $150 will be payable by each party.

Hearing Fees

For each day of hearing held before a single arbitrator, an administrative fee of $150 is payable by each party.

For each day of hearing held before a multiarbitrator panel, an administrative fee of $200 is payable by each party.

There is no hearing fee for the initial hearing in cases administered under the Expedited Procedures.

Index

Supreme courts (state), 86
Surrebuttal, 15

Tables of contents (for reports), 145–
    149, 153 n.44, 153 n.45
*Target Market Publishing, Inc. v. ADVO,
    Inc.,* 127–128, 150 n.7
Tax court opinions, 89 n.1, 89 n.3
Tax returns, 101–102
Teaching attorneys about business
    appraisal, 155–162
    adjustments to financial statements,
        157–158
    and appraiser's limits of
        competence, 162
    different-sized companies,
        application of data to, 160–161
    discount vs. capitalization rates,
        158–159
    last year's/next year's earnings, use
        of, 159
    minority and marketability,
        discounts/premiums for, 159
    reliability of financial documents,
        156–157
    and risks affecting businesses, 158
Technical journals, 66–67
Temporary injunctions, 32
Terms:
    explaining, 188
    matching, to jury instructions, 16,
        17
Testifying appraiser, *see* Expert
    witness(es)
Testimony:
    appraisal, by defendant, 123 n.1
    cross-examination, 189–190
    direct, 185–188
    expert, 15–16, 79, 99–100
    fee for, 77
    hearsay, 93–94
    by lay witnesses (Rules of Evidence),
        98–99
    opinion, 100–101
    preparation for, 184

    redirect, 190–191
    restricting, in depositions, 166–167
Third-party claims, 9
Third-party plaintiff, 9
*Tokio Marine & Fire Insurance Co., Ltd. v.
    Norfolk & Western Railway Co.,* 140,
    153 n.40
Tort claims, 29–30
Tortfeasor, 29
Training, *see* Qualifications of
    appraisers
Trending (in reports), 179
Trial(s):
    bench, 17
    cross-examination in, 189–190
    direct testimony in, 185–188
    expert witness in, 183–190
    preparation for, 183–185
    redirect testimony in, 190–191
Trial courts, 85–86, 88
Trial Techniques (Mauet), 23 n.11
Trugman, Gary, 156
*Trustees of the University of Pennsylvania
    v. Lexington Insurance Co.,* 61, 63
    n.11

Unclean hands, 32
Understanding Business Valuation (Gary
    Trugman), 156
Uniform Standards of Professional
    Appraisal Practice (USPAP), 67–
    68, 75, 83–84 n.3, 118, 133, 140,
    287–323
U.S. Supreme Court, xix, 86

Valuation(s):
    business (glossary of terms), 240–
        248
    replicability of, 135
Value(s):
    range of, 143–144
    selection of, 141–142
    standard of, *see* Standard of value
Venire, 13
Venue, 6